The Jesus Quotient

The Jesus Quotient

IQ to EQ to AQ

JENNIE A. HARROP

Foreword by Ken Vanden Hoek

 CASCADE *Books* • Eugene, Oregon

THE JESUS QUOTIENT
IQ to EQ to AQ

Cascade Books
An Imprint of Wipf and Stock Publishers
199 W. 8th Ave., Suite 3
Eugene, OR 97401

www.wipfandstock.com

PAPERBACK ISBN: 978-1-5326-6176-1
HARDCOVER ISBN: 978-1-5326-6177-8
EBOOK ISBN: 978-1-5326-6178-5

Cataloguing-in-Publication data:

Names: Harrop, Jennie A.

Title: The Jesus quotient : IQ to EQ to AQ / Jennie A. Harrop.

Description: Eugene, OR: Pickwick Publications, 2018 | Includes bibliographical references.

Identifiers: ISBN 978-1-5326-6176-1 (paperback) | ISBN 978-1-5326-6177-8 (hardcover) | ISBN 978-1-5326-6178-5 (ebook)

Subjects: LCSH: Christianity—Psychology. | Emotional intelligence. | Interpersonal relations—religious aspects—Christianity.

Classification: BR110 .H325 2019 (paperback) | BR110 2019 (ebook)

In some instances, names, dates, locations, and other details have been purposefully changed to protect the identities and privacy of those discussed in this book.

Manufactured in the U.S.A. 06/20/19

To Miles, Piper, Mattie, Josie, & Carson:

May you lead with remarkable faith, compassion, wisdom, intentionality, and joy.

How monotonously alike all the great tyrants and conquerors have been:

how gloriously different are the saints.

C. S. Lewis

Contents

Foreword

Why are some pastors and leaders able to cultivate consistent spiritual and numerical church growth in their churches while other pastors and churches struggle to survive? Why do some church staffs function as a healthy integrated team while others act more like a dysfunctional family? Why are we seemingly losing the ability to engage people with the gospel? WHY? I've asked myself these questions and many more over my fifty years of pastoral ministry.

Five years ago, I was introduced to Jennie Harrop. During this time, I've to come to appreciate her sensitivity to ministry and desire to make the Gospel of Jesus Christ applicable to all. In her book, *The Jesus Quotient: IQ to EQ to AQ*, Dr. Jennie Harrop does a brilliant job of helping us understand the need for pastors and church leaders to develop mentoring resources that draw from the life and ministry of Jesus as their guide. I can only wish now that Jennie's book had been available at the beginning of my ministry.

My own story reflects the widespread pastoral changes of the past fifty years. Serving the church today is far different than my experience in the 1960s. Following five years of working with delinquent youth and twenty years of youth and children's ministry, I accepted a call to become the pastor of a medium-sized urban church in Sherwood, Oregon. The community was poised for exponential growth. So I moved into this new role with a lot of fear, trepidation, and excitement. However, before moving to Oregon, a mentor and friend gave me this bit of advice: "Always remember, the Lord has called you to serve his church, so go with confidence, preach the Word, love your people, and you will do fine." Still I wondered, could I relate to an adult world? Could I keep pace with the added responsibility of preaching, visitation, weddings, funerals, hospital calls, special events, and more? Could I work with a staff and other church leaders? With the passing of time and many lessons learned, I retired from this same church twenty-two years later.

Throughout those years, I sought to adjust our methodology of ministry without compromising the gospel message. With this goal in mind, our church remained stable and outwardly focused. In the later years, my church denomination began to struggle through doctrinal and theological shifts. This created an even greater need to assess who we were as a church, speaking Jesus into our ever-changing culture. Mentoring staff and elders throughout this intellectual and emotional upheaval ultimately confirmed our message "to be all things to all people" without compromising the message of Jesus.

The words of the Apostle Paul in Colossians 2:8 helped solidify my thinking process about change, message, and audience. Paul cautioned the people of Colossae "not to be taken captive through the hollow and deceptive philosophies of man," or as the Living Bible says "high sounding nonsense!" Could I, in good conscience, have mentored my staff and church leaders to disrespect sound biblical doctrine and theological thought in order to remain relevant in today's culture? NO! Therefore, the challenge was to remain intellectually true to God's word while emotionally connecting the message of love, mercy, grace, and forgiveness to my friends, community, and world.

Some of my most regrettable experiences as a pastor were the result of miscommunication. Could I have benefited from a better awareness as to how my words and/or actions were perceived and how they negatively impacted the members of my leadership team and ultimately people in my congregation? Absolutely! Had I a more fully developed understanding of the importance of EQ and AQ, some of these painful situations could have been avoided. Suffice it to say, a more Jesus-like clarity of heart and mind would have saved me and my congregation from misunderstanding one another.

The most agonizing of these experiences for me, my staff, and our congregation, culminated in my terminating a staff member. My relationship with this person and their eventual dismissal was largely due to a lack of effective mentoring on my part. Had I been able to identify from the very beginning of the interview process the challenges we eventually would encounter, this situation could have been avoided. I soon learned terminations, especially in a church family, are hard to manage, and the ripple effect is oftentimes damaging not only for the one terminated but also fellow staff and church members.

My faltering steps to connect intellect with the heart and audience are not unique. For the last two years, my wife and I were charged with the role of encouraging pastors/spouses within our denomination. We quickly learned that all churches had a variety of needs. Some were scarcely hanging on while seeking ways to maintain a presence in their community. Some churches had a vision for reaching into the community but were stymied in knowing how to implement that vision. Still others were excited about their ministry opportunities and thriving. These thriving churches had a contagious liveliness wrapped around visionary leadership that connected with their target audience of nonbelievers. All the churches we visited were concerned about sharing the Gospel. However, a high percentage of our churches struggled to effectively master the emotional and audience quotient needed to connect with people outside the church building. Many had plateaued and appeared to be aging out. It was obvious to us that our churches today desperately need leaders who are self-aware and healthy in their understanding of *The Jesus Quotient: IQ to EQ to AQ* of ministry.

Ken Vanden Hoek
Retired Pastor

Preface

When I walked into the classroom at a few minutes before six on a Thursday evening in May, the students slumped in their seats, thumbing through social media on their phones and clearly wary of whatever might come next. I plugged in my laptop, clicked on the hum of the overhead projector, stacked my books neatly beside my computer, and sat on the front table to face them. I rested my palms on the table, my legs swinging freely from my tabletop perch. My hearty "welcome" was met with smiles and nods, but the tension in the room was palpable. Two students bent over their phones, either hurrying to close out a genuine crisis at home or—more likely—feigning busyness in hopes of foiling whatever truths I might be about to declare.

"Just so you know, we are all atheists," one student said firmly, her eyes locked on mine. Her bleached hair was cropped short, and the dark ink of a tattoo twirled across her right arm. Despite her defiance, she had a slight tremor in both hands. "We really don't know why we have to take this course," she continued.

Titled "Christian Faith & Thought," the class is required for degree completion for undergraduate students at the university where I teach, and I had been warned by fellow professors that this particular cohort wanted nothing to do with faith, religion, Scripture, or God. Knowing of their skepticism, I had been looking forward to this evening for months.

I have taught this course for many years, and each time I teach it, we wrestle through the course content in a startlingly new way depending on the students in attendance. I have had courses crowded with confident Christians; courses speckled with believers, nonbelievers, Mormons, Catholics, and Jews; and courses filled with a lively mix of conservative Jesus-followers and ardent atheists. As a lifelong skeptic, postmodernist, and academician, I love the naysayers the most: They bring a curiosity and newness to the classroom that the comfortable Christian does not.

Much like prodigal children, when we wrestle and then arrive, we are far more likely to anchor ourselves deeply than if we accept without the battle. As a former crime reporter, I have witnessed the pulse of anger and skepticism. As an elder in the Presbyterian church for nearly two decades, I have experienced the sting of insults and abuse pronounced in Jesus' name. And it pains me to see the number of adult students who enter my classrooms openly reeling from hurts wrought under the guile of "Christianity." The hurt far outweigh the healed, and I find myself as exhausted as they are. The script has to shift.

My greatest hope in my classroom is that students feel heard, seen, understood, challenged, and safe after our first evening together—safe enough to begin to articulate and then press against their own belief systems, whatever those might be, and emboldened enough to ponder new concepts that abrade the comfort of the intellectual homes they have built for themselves. When I introduce the concept of *worldview*, most students nod approvingly, prepping themselves to define and dissect the worldviews of those around them while ardently declaring themselves worldview-free. What a gift it would be to hold a god-like perspective that stands outside of cultural swings, societal pressures, linguistic boxes, and personal doubt, I tell them, and usually we laugh. But the emotional and intellectual limitations of our human brains simply won't allow such a stretch.

While some of us are better able to identify the lenses that color our world than others, every one of us has a worldview. And the sooner we learn to articulate and own the components of that worldview, the better we will be able to engage effectively with the world around us. The students who sat before me that evening were prepared to hear about a worldview that presumably would clash violently with their own: a Christian outpouring of rules, obligations, judgments, guilt, anger, impatience, authority, and hypocritical promises. Their shoulders slumped because they had heard this monologue before; their phones were on because they really, really did not want to hear what I had to say. But instead of a one-way lashing, we talked.

I began with my story—a tale of searching, belief, doubt, pain, skepticism, anger, postmodern quandary, and, at long last, resolve—and I could feel the tension begin to dissipate. The students were surprised that I, too, had doubted, questioned, and rejected, and that my journey had brought me to a place of deep peace, appreciation, and joy. They were surprised that I was not there to proclaim commandments or unearth their sin. They were surprised that I wanted to hear from them. We spent the bulk of the four-hour class listening to their stories: their experiences with the church, with religion, with pastors, with hypocrisy, with shame, with broken promises, with skepticism, and with hurt so deep that several of them could not yet see how it defined their worldviews and, ultimately, their lives.

The student who first pronounced her atheism told us that the last time she tried to attend a church service with a friend, she passed out in the church atrium when the trauma of past hurts engulfed her: One moment she was chatting with a church usher as she watched the lights embedded in the ceiling above flex and descend, and the next moment she was splayed flat on the thin carpet, faces silhouetted above her as she struggled to remember where she was. Her hands shook notably as she told the story. The church service had not even begun.

Another student revealed that a male pastor she had known in her teen years had told her and her family repeatedly that if she did not change her assertive ways, she would never be allowed into heaven. She had listened to his words and subsequently crushed into distortion her natural ability to engage others, her delightfully inquisitive tendencies, her fast humor, and her confidence. She pressed the truth of who she was so deep that she could no longer recognize herself or her place in the world; alcohol and recreational drugs became her only respite from a soul turned against itself.

Other students recounted memories of angry sermons and shaming conversations with self-described Christians. We realized together that the nonbelief of atheism did not accurately define these students' experiences. Every student in that course had been wounded by the church or by someone claiming to represent the church, and the only way they knew to absorb their pain was to reject the God who condoned such evil. They were angry and hurt, but they wanted desperately for "God" to be real—just not in the way religion and the culture had presented him to them.

In our six weeks together, the students covered the classroom's white boards with unfiltered questions; role-played varying worldviews to learn to better articulate their own; listened through one another's tears about the past, and joys and fears about the future; quarreled, laughed, and wondered; and acknowledged their own desire for something broader, more meaningful, and more steadfast than they. While these students opened themselves to consider Christianity anew, many never have that opportunity, instead remaining mired in anger and hurt caused by an unseeing church. In my more than two decades of university teaching and church leadership, I have witnessed again and again the ramifications of Pharisaical Christianity. While the deliverers may be well-intended, their inattention to the ripples of damage reverberating from their teaching is destroying lives. Those who might seek the peace and joy of Christianity are repelled by the judgment, anger, and hypocrisy they see. In a twenty-first-century era of fractured identities when the gospel should be the greatest, most centering story told, words like *faith, Christian, Bible,* and *Jesus* are dismissed as irrelevant and simplistic. So what has gone awry?

God came to earth in human form more than two millennia ago to warn us about our hypocritical allegiance to empty laws, and yet we continue to repeat the very patterns that he spoke against. Without integrity, intentionality, and love for both our neighbor and our enemy, we cannot expect more than dismissive disdain from those outside the church. But if our first response is defensiveness or blame, the essence of Christianity will continue to slide further and further afield from the gospel. If we hope to be heard, we have to begin with ourselves. "Woe to you, teachers of the law and Pharisees, you hypocrites!" Jesus warns in Matthew 23. "You shut the door of the kingdom of heaven in people's faces. You yourselves do not enter, nor will you let those enter who are trying to."[1] How will we open the door and hold it open, ensuring as we do that our faces reflect the joy and love that Jesus promises?

While leaders in the church have discussed home churches and missional community involvement in recent decades, we have done little to acknowledge that the vernacular Tim Keller calls us to[2] is nearly impossible to achieve in a culture that is deeply entrenched with biblical mythologies. How do we speak without raising walls of assumption, judgment, defensiveness, or anger? How do we assess the criticisms or hurt of others if we cannot identify our own? Jesus did not ponder his own Intelligence Quotient (IQ) or Emotional Quotient (EQ). He knew his God-given purpose and emotional character so deeply that he was able to operate out of those foundations without pausing to ponder his next best step. Jesus' example presses us to step into a third quotient that is best referred to as "Audience Quotient." AQ is our ability to focus fully on another: to love as we have been loved, to see as we are seen, and to teach and disciple as Jesus taught.

How different might the world be if we trained leaders to transcend from IQ to EQ to AQ, aspiring to a Jesus Quotient that aligns with the Great Commission in ways that will help us to (re)sign the church[3] as a safe place for renewal, energy, peace, and joy, rather than the hypocrisy and judgmentalism that has maligned its name for generations? *The Jesus Quotient* argues for a new kind of leader and a new kind of Christian: one who loves easily, embodies joy, and inspires others with a contextual sensibility that surpasses individual insecurities or burdens. The growth is progressive: First, one acknowledges and accepts IQ; next, one encounters and engages

1. Matt 23:13 (NIV).
2. Keller, "The Missional Church."
3. Downing, *Changing Signs*, 83.

EQ; and, finally, one recognizes and embraces AQ. The fullness of the trio is what Jesus embodied in the Gospel stories, an example that is defined more broadly as the "Jesus Quotient."

Chapter 1, "A Twenty-First-Century Problem," introduces the misfire of the twenty-first-century church, offering examples of Pharisaical hypocrisy, simple-mindedness, and judgmentalism as seen through the eyes of a postmodern, primarily nonbelieving American culture.

Chapter 2, "The Twentieth-Century Answer," defines and discusses the missional church movement: its intentions, foundations, and misappropriations.

Chapter 3, "The Jesus Problem," looks to Jesus' incarnational example, examining stories from the Gospels as Jesus encounters individuals, small groups, and large crowds, exhibiting his perfect IQ, EQ, and AQ in every instance.

Chapter 4, "Intelligence Quotient (IQ)," summarizes a brief history of the IQ assessment, including its benefits, limitations, and psychological ramifications.

Chapter 5, "Emotional Quotient (EQ)," looks at the origins and rise of emotional intelligence, examining its popularity in the secular workplace and considering its application among leaders in the church and in Christian universities.

Chapter 6, "Audience Quotient (AQ)," defines and discusses the new phrase "Audience Quotient," relying on Jesus' example as its foundation and moving forward into a look at how twenty-first-century Christian leaders might benefit from an AQ self-analysis.

Chapter 7, "The Future Church," looks to future directions of the church in an era of social media, an increasingly global economy, and unprecedented demands of high efficiency. What role can EQ and AQ play in the Christian church as leaders enter more fully into a wounded, unchurched society?

Chapter 8, "AQ Assessment Tools," offers initial assessments for denominational, church, and university use. It is my hope that others will build on these concepts, embracing the Jesus Quotient as a helpful means of speaking truth, love, peace, and hope into a broken church and, ultimately, a broken culture.

Acknowledgements

When we lay before Yahweh a well-defined plan and ask for a blessing, he may bless. But when we lay *ourselves* before Yahweh with unreachable dreams and an exhale of humility, he begins to make the impossible possible. When we find his lens, the world becomes a tapestry of *no's* morphed into *yes*. *The Jesus Quotient* is just one of many.

Introduction

It was January and the classroom was cold when I dialed my pastor, hoping that the letter he had drafted was an error. I walked between the desks as I waited for him to pick up, sweeping bits of paper with my fingers and straightening the chairs. When he answered, I was relieved to hear his Southern drawl.

"Marcus," I said in a rush. "How are you? How's Tara?" I wanted to step inside the phone, out of this chilly classroom and back into the warm familiarity of their Wyoming kitchen.

"We're fine," Marcus answered, his voice iron-cool. "You needed help with something?"

"I do," I said, sitting on the desk at the front of the room, facing my students' chairs as if they were still there. I had dismissed my class only thirty minutes earlier, and I could see their faces before me as if time had rolled back an hour: Leslie in the back corner with her sandals kicked to one side and her kids' photos taped to her binder; Arturo in the front to my left, his pen scratching diligently across the page each time I spoke; Marlys on the right with her three pads of sticky notes and six highlighter pens lined across the desk.

Marcus's voice was strained, but it was the middle of a workday and I knew he likely had back-to-back meetings. Marcus, Tara, and I had been close friends for more than eight years, and I missed knowing that they were a coffee invitation away. My move a month prior to exit an abusive marriage and return to family several states away had been difficult on all fronts, and I was thankful for their friendship. "The reference letter surprised me," I said. "Did you intend the changes you made? The paragraph about my contributions these past few years was deleted."

"I sent the correct letter," Marcus said coolly, and for a moment the line was quiet. I had returned to work that month as a full-time college professor after ten years at home with babies and preschoolers, and I was shuffling as many courses as I could manage as a newly single mother of five. Marcus's first reference letter for me, the one he wrote before I told him I was moving, was supportive, affirming, even boastful. Because of it, I was now teaching five English and composition courses at a college in my former home state, and hoping to take on more at a university across the country that was seeking an online PhD-level professor—hence, the second reference letter.

"You know I can't use this letter," I protested, still believing there had been a mistake. "You question my ethics, and you left out everything you said in your first letter about leadership skills, loyalty, longevity at the church."

"I'm sorry it's not what you wanted," Marcus replied, his words careful.

"What's going on?" I asked. "Are you angry about something?"

"I'm not pleased with your choices," Marcus said.

"You knew the marriage was unsafe. You offered the church as a safe haven if things got worse. And you knew my family was coming to get us."

"Those were your perceptions," Marcus said.

"Perceptions? Two months ago, you agreed and urged me to get help."

"That was a different situation."

"It was the same marriage," I said. "I'm the same person, and I have the same five kids who deserve to feel safe in their own home."

The line was silent. "Marcus, are you there?" I pressed. "Where is my friend, my pastor?"

"I am *not* your pastor," Marcus said angrily, his careful composure lost. "You left us. You chose to move. And when you did, I stopped being your pastor."

"Is that how it works?" I was incredulous. "Because I moved, I'm out?"

"You moved, and you will find a new pastor," Marcus replied.

I waited, wondering how I could nudge my friend of nearly a decade, hoping desperately that one of us would have something else to say. I had not wanted to leave the church that had been my home for so many years, the place where I had baptized my children, taught countless Bible studies, and served on the elder board. I had not wanted to leave a life that I had once seen as God-ordained and idyllic. I had not wanted to leave a comfortable friendship with my pastor and his wife. And I had not expected this. "Then I guess this is it—?" I said.

"I guess so," Marcus answered.

I said goodbye, and I felt a wall begin to rise.

~

Angela pushed the deep red, velvety curtain back with her fingertips and stepped nervously inside, wondering whether she should perch on the front of the tiny bench or force herself to lean back. She thought she could see a shadow behind the iron grid on the left side of the confessional, but she wasn't sure. "Hello?" she said gently, her voice lilting through the air like a petal caught on an upturned breeze.

"Bienvenido, señorita," the priest said. "Que puedo hacer por ti, mi hija?"

Angela took a breath, allowing her brain a moment to shift from English to Spanish. She filtered through the images in her brain, wondering what was appropriate to share and what was permissible to leave out: a scuffling evening on the couch with Brian, a lung-searing inhale from a friend's unfiltered cigarette, four bottles of Syrah from La Mancha. She pulled the curtain closed and knelt on the dusty floor. "Perdoname, padre," she said. "Han pasado dos semanas desde mi última confesión . . ."

She had arrived in Madrid four months prior, and life was good. Her courses at the university were easy, she loved the dance clubs that opened at 11 p.m. and pulsed with energy until five or six each morning, she adored the Spanish men who complimented her blue eyes and American accent, and she appreciated this little church where she could always find a priest to assuage her sins.

The priest listened silently, his face turned to the side so all Angela could see was a faint silhouette, and Angela told him about her nights in the clubs along the Plaza Mayor, her skipped assignments in art history at the University of Madrid, and her envy of the friends back home who had reminded her that her time abroad would negate her chances to ever sit on a high school homecoming court. Angela left out the more intimate details of her dates with Brian, and she declined to speak of her growing doubt about God, the church, and her own salvation. If God were real, wouldn't he know already?

Angela spoke for ten, fifteen, twenty minutes, and then waited silently. She stared at the wall of the confessional and watched for the dim shadows to shift, wondering if the priest was young or old. She longed for the priest to step through the confessional curtain, imploring her to stand for a proper hug as he assured her that she is loved, she is valued, and she can do better. Instead she listened to the shuffle of shoes in the sanctuary beyond and inhaled the sweet, musky incense smells that made her feel like she was eight again. When the priest suggested three Hail Marys, four Our Fathers, and a deeper commitment to her studies, Angela agreed with a mixture of relief and consternation.

Later that night, as Angela repeated her assigned prayers on her knees in her fifth-floor flat, the heaviness of repetition was suffocating. Angela inhaled softly and exhaled quickly, longing for something more. And she felt a wall begin to rise.

~

Tom shifted in his seat, straining to see the teenagers three rows to his left. He was surprised to find so many gathered in one place on a Sunday morning, and he wondered why they were there. Had their parents made them come? Was it an excuse to be together? Did they really believe this stuff?

"The Word of the Lord," the pastor said as he finished reading and closed his book. A low murmur echoed through the room as people recited something back to him; Tom couldn't make out the words, but it solidified the oddity of the club. He leaned into Lisa, wanting to read her mind as she took this all in. Were these just pleasant reminders of a childhood past? Was there something more she needed here? She leaned back into him but did not respond otherwise, her eyes locked on the man up front.

The pastor was a decent speaker. He clearly was enjoying himself as he paced back and forth, occasionally raising a hand in emphasis or pausing dramatically, sweeping his eyes across the room as if expecting an answer. He wore a beige button-down Oxford tucked into dark jeans, which was curious to Tom. Was he appealing to the teenaged crowd, a Silicon Valley culture, a new era of come-as-you-are? Tom's dad would have been appalled, had he been alive. He was never a church person, but Tom's dad would have expected any speaker to have the dignity to dress nicely—certainly more than jeans and a shirt. For Tom's dad, the casual dress would have solidified his disdain for religious types.

Tom pressed his index finger into his knee: one, two, three, four. He was counting the number of times the pastor repeated his question, "What did Jesus come to save us from?" The repetitions were rhythmic and attention-getting, Tom could see that as he surveyed those around him, but the pastor did not seem to have any idea how rife with undefined terms his repetitions were—let alone the annoyance of a dangling preposition, another glitch that would have irritated his father. Did Jesus come at all? Did he have intent? Was he capable of saving? Why did people need to be saved? Was all of this past or present tense? Was the pastor suggesting that Tom needed to be saved from something? And yes, what did Jesus intend to save people *from*?

"What do you think?" the pastor implored loudly, gesturing at the audience with his right hand. "What does Jesus save us from?"

"Satan," one woman answered.

"The culture," said a man to Tom's right.

"Ourselves," another woman said.

"All true," the pastor nodded, clearly not hearing the word he hoped to hear. "Do you want to hear a secret?" he asked, looking straight at Tom and Lisa. Tom stared back, willing the guy to look away. In a moment, he did, walking left to the other end of the stage. "The answer is not what you think," he said to the people in the front rows. He walked back to the middle and stood with his arms outstretched, an expectant look on his face as he waited for all eyes to land on him. "Jesus came to save us from God," he said, his voice loud and sure.

Ouch, Tom thought. Tom felt Lisa pull back a little, and he sensed a general stirring around him. Were they agreeing, disagreeing, or just shifting? *From God?* Really?

"Jesus came to save us from the righteous wrath of God," the man continued, walking and waving his hands again. "Because our hearts are dark and our will is weak, the truth of who we are is actually shameful to God. Jesus came to take that shame and anger on himself so that God can look at us with new eyes."

And so admission to the cult begins, Tom thought. Why would anyone want to believe in an angry, vengeful creator? Were these people here because of fear? Were the afraid of their God, themselves, or each other? And how was this weekly reminder relevant or helpful in a twenty-first-century era that moved at lightning speed and demanded the fullness of who you were? Tom surveyed the room methodically: his wife, the pastor, other congregants, the teenagers. Why were they here? Why was this necessary? The pastor gestured in Tom's direction again, his voice rising as he read verses that spoke of despair, agony, pits, and longing. Each time the pastor looked up, his eyes met Tom's. The fourth time that happened, Tom could have sworn the man winked knowingly. Tom shifted uncomfortably in his seat.

What depraved, ridiculous, and ill-defined assumptions, Tom concluded. Did anyone here realize that speeches like this are grounded in logical fallacies? Did anyone here really believe this bunk? Tom looked at his watch, willing the minutes to tick by more quickly so they could move on to lunch. And he felt a wall begin to rise.

~

The last time Gretchen tried to attend church with a friend, she passed out cold. She had arrived early that Sunday and parked on the far end of the parking lot, texting her friend from her car to see if she had arrived yet. As Gretchen waited in the safety of her car, the heat humming and the stereo thumping a low backbeat, she watched the people as they parked and filed into the church. She was watching for something, she knew, but she wasn't exactly sure what: friends from high school? her grandmother? conservative types she could easily dismiss? liberal types ready to tell her what to eat, wear, and think? The senior pastor who had told her for years that her rebellious streak would one day be her demise?

"In the mezzanine with COFFEE!" her friend texted. "Come NOW!"

Gretchen took a breath and tucked her phone into her pocket. A blue Ford Escort backed into the space to her left, and she watched for the elderly couple to emerge. Gretchen assumed the woman was waiting for the man to walk around the car and open his wife's door, but instead the woman walked over to take her husband's arm, supporting his unsteady steps as they strolled together toward the open front doors. Another family three cars to the right unloaded from a gray Honda Odyssey, with three or four preteens dashing ahead of their parents.

"You will never be a Proverbs 31 woman," the pastor had told her some twenty years prior, and Gretchen sometimes wondered if the echo of his voice was God's voice, a steady reminder in her brain of the deficiencies she needed to correct if she wanted to go to church. But these days she hardly wanted to ponder Christianity, let alone claim it. What right did people have to tell others how to live their lives? What motivated them to want to meddle in everyone else's business, telling them that it was their way or no way at all? And what was a Proverbs 31 woman besides an outdated misogynistic construct anyway?

Gretchen stepped out of her car and inhaled deeply, steadying herself to walk through the open doors and find her friend. Coffee will help, she reminded herself. Just walk to the coffee. As she entered the mezzanine, the lights dazzled her eyes and the voices gathered into a wave of sound, beckoning enticingly at the same time as it threatened to crash down upon her. Gretchen's friend waved from the edge of what looked like a coffee bar, and Gretchen walked toward her, measuring her steps and breathing carefully. "You can't continue this way," she heard him say again, a tiresome monotone chant that sometimes thrummed along as the throbbing bass line of her most tedious days: "You can't continue."

One moment she was walking, and the next moment she was squinting up into the lights, her shoulders blades pressed into the hard, clean floor, and her friend gently shaking her shoulders. "Gretchen?" her friend pleaded. "What happened? Are you all right?"

What an astute question, Gretchen thought: "Am I all right?" Mostly yes, she concluded as she smiled up at her friend, but not in this place. Never in this place. And she felt a wall begin to rise.

~

When Anthony's college department downsized and the position he had drawn up eighteen years prior was eliminated from the budget, he felt like his world had tilted in a dangerously unfamiliar way. The projects that been his greatest accomplishments were nearly meaningless, and the skills that had garnered praise and propelled him forward now carried little weight. Where was the meaning? Where would he find purpose? What did he have to hope in?

Anthony had grown up and then raised his own children in a church with beautiful accoutrements and traditions: a pipe organ that filled the entire choir loft, Easter and Christmas Eve services that boasted multiple choirs and musical ensembles, frequent dramatic monologues and skits, children's and youth classes that attracted dozens, and impeccably landscaped grounds. The sermons were standard and the people were kind, and Anthony attended every Sunday that he was in town and available. He knew the church offered other activities that met mid-week—community groups, seasonal activities, and social gatherings—but he preferred to confine his church attendance to Sunday mornings, just as his parents had.

When Anthony lost his job and sought help from an associate pastor, the man's words were kind, but something rang hollow: "Wait on God," he told Anthony.

"Your good works will bear fruit."

"Remember to practice listening prayer."

"God's timing is the best timing."

"God has a plan."

"Lean on him."

Anthony nodded and agreed, wanting to encourage the man that he was pastoring well, but the words meant little to him. How would waiting, listening, or leaning pay his mortgage? What if God chose not to answer? What if God wasn't there at all?

Anthony was surprised to find the church services increasingly devoid as well. How long had he been accepting as truth words that ultimately held very little meaning for him? Most everyone smiled, encouraging him to be encouraged, and offered hugs, but where was a job? Where was his next step? Where was God?

When the congregation stood to sing the doxology, Anthony felt an irritation rising that surprised and scared him. "Praise God, from whom all blessings flow." All blessings? And by whose timing?

"Praise Him, all creatures here below." All creatures? Really?

"Praise Him above, ye heavenly hosts." Heavenly hosts? What were they, and what did they have to do with him?

"Praise Father, Son, and Holy Ghost." These three never made sense. A father? A ghost?

Anthony surveyed the room around him, considering the smiling faces and the family-like camaraderie, and he realized something: As kind as people can be, most do not want to enter in too fully. Even when Anthony met with the associate pastor, his comments were careful and measured, almost scripted; he did not ask Anthony too many questions.

"Wait on God," Anthony remembered as he made his way to the door, and he shook his head in frustration, relieved to be walking out of that place. What he was seeking was not inside these walls of careful plentitude, measured levity, and quiet judgment. What he was seeking was an enormity that outmeasured the carefully defined mathematics of this childhood habit. Why had he not seen this before? As Anthony walked to his car, he said a silent farewell to the familiar building behind him. And he felt a wall begin to rise.

~

In the years that I have taught courses in Christian apologetics and leadership, my classes have consistently been comprised of atheists, agnostics, skeptics, and—above all—men and women who have been deeply wounded by the church. This latter population is what concerns me the most and what has inspired *The Jesus Quotient*. When people have not yet heard Jesus' message of joy and peace, we can approach them with a certain boldness that the gift we bring is life-giving, life-saving, and eternal. But when people have been wounded by that very gift in the past, the inroad is far more difficult. If we are not sensitive to the language we use, the assumptions we make, the emotions that may arise on any side, and the baggage we ourselves shoulder, we will not communicate well.

Matthew 28 calls us to share the gospel far and wide, boldly and well, but how can we do that when the words we use communicate pain and the gestures we make are demeaning? How can we expect to communicate well when we are not sensitive to the reverberations of our own souls? Why is it that we teach pastors and other Christian leaders to exegete Scripture, and yet we don't press them to articulate their own fears?

How can we send missionaries into our neighborhoods and neighboring countries without teaching them about the limitations and expansive horizons of their own intelligence and emotions? How can we ask our appointed leaders to speak to both individuals and massive crowds with a Jesus sensibility but no training about how to read a room? Once the wall begins to rise, it can be difficult to lower; a chief goal, therefore, should be to produce leaders who have an astute awareness of the wall—what causes it, what lowers it, what prevents it.

In a course I taught recently, one young man shook visibly at the mention of Jesus, another averted her eyes any time we spoke of God in the paternal sense, and still another failed the course because she could not bring herself to attend a church of her own choosing for a final assignment. None of these students were lazy or flippant. All were hard-working professionals, mothers, fathers, wives, husbands, and students. And all carried wounds from decades prior when a pastor or other church authority shamed, criticized, berated, or scolded them. If we are concerned about our unchurched culture, perhaps it is time we look beyond the culture, the church, and the systems that inform our religion; perhaps it is time we look at ourselves, acknowledging the logs and helping one another to replace the splinters with the glint of Jesus.

~

A current trend in both secular business leadership and in behavioral studies is the concept of "Emotional Intelligence" or "Emotional Quotient" (EQ) popularized in Daniel Goleman's 1995 book *Emotional Intelligence*. Goleman acknowledges that his work draws into a single forum more than a decade of scientific study that preceded his book, demonstrating an increasing interest in the role our emotions play in who we are and how we behave. In *Emotional Intelligence,* Goleman walks his readers through the neurobiological data and brain-imaging technologies of the 1980s and 1990s that introduced scientific credence to the flood of self-help books wallowing in the perplexities of love, anger, and sorrow, for example. As Goleman writes in his opening pages, the question is whether IQ is stagnant and one's life path is genetically fixed: "What can we change that will help our children fare better in life?" he asks. "What factors are at play, for example, when people of high IQ flounder and those of modest IQ do surprisingly well? The difference quite often lies in the abilities called here *emotional intelligence,* which includes self-control, zeal and persistence, and the ability to motivate oneself."[1] Where are theologians and Christian leaders in this exploration of EQ? Where are the New Testament scholars ready to draw parallels between the tenets of EQ and the characteristics of Jesus Christ?

The larger question I see at play is this: If we are called to be teachers for Christ, telling others of the wisdom and hope of the gospel as we create safe places for them to listen and receive well, how can we ensure that (1) our purpose is clear and current, and (2) our self-awareness is thorough enough to bely our need to waste emotional energy pondering our own path and effect on the world, and instead focus on those around us who need this kind of encouragement in order to live kingdom lives? How do we take "EQ" and draw it in to the ecclesiastical realm, and how do we take "missional" and fit it into the secular realm? Is it possible that the path we need to explore leads us from IQ to EQ to AQ, a new quotient that points us directly to our Audience Quotient, just as Jesus' natural, all-consuming empathy for others defined the way that he presented himself in nearly every instance in the gospels?

While the build-it-and-they-will-come approach of the 1970s and 1980s is clearly considered passé, the missional focus on God's sent people does not seem to be bringing nonbelievers to faith as we had hope it might. What more is needed? How do we encourage, train, and gather disciples in a postmodern culture that eschews Christianity? How do we move beyond an ordination-required Bible Content Exam that focuses on old-school rote memorization and instead seek to train, mentor, and assess the Emotional Quotient and Audience Quotient of pastors and other church leaders who will be daily engaging with people who need to be heard clearly and well? *The Jesus Quotient* attempts to answer these questions in a way that is mindful of current dialogue but also cognizant of the cultural trends that are

1. Goleman, *Emotional Intelligence,* xii.

carrying us full-tilt into a Google-influenced twenty-first-century future. As Leonard Sweet writes in *Aqua Church 2.0*,

> In a world where change is permanent, one has to be prepared to unlearn everything and begin all over again in the course of a lifetime. . . . Leaders must settle for nothing but the latest intelligence, the best information. But leaders must also realize that information is perishable. If learning is at base "making sense of things," then we may need to unlearn some things so that we can make sense of things like never before.[2]

The Jesus Quotient encourages us to unlearn and learn again.

2. Sweet, *Aqua Church 2.0*, 307.

Chapter 1

A Twenty-First-Century Problem

When Texas Pastor David Grisham of Last Frontier Evangelism shouted anti-Santa sentiments at Westgate Mall in Amarillo in December 2016, parents waiting in line with their children to see Santa Claus were not amused. "'Kids, I want to tell you today that there is no such thing as Santa Claus,' [Grisham] yelled at the crowd waiting in line. 'The Christmas season is about Jesus. . . . The man you're going to see today is just a man in a suit, dressed up like Santa, but Santa does not exist. Santa's not real.'"[1] Parents attempted to confront Grisham to get him to stop, but Grisham was nonplussed as he continued his tirade, filming himself with a cell phone as he evangelized in a video that has since gone viral. "It's the spirit of Jesus that moved the pas-

1. Chasmar, "Texas pastor."

tor of Last Frontier Evangelism to rail against Santa," CNN correspondent Jeanne Moos quipped, equating Grisham's comments with an absent spirit of Christmas.[2] Unfortunately, the reporter's sentiment is far from isolated.

Consider philosopher Bertrand Russell's words in *Why I Am Not a Christian*: "The more intense has been the religion of any period and the more profound has been the dogmatic belief, the greater has been the cruelty and the worse has been the state of affairs."[3] Russell later argues that Christian religion, "as organized in its churches," is the "principal enemy of moral progress in the world": "In the so-called ages of faith, when men really did believe the Christian religion in all its completeness, there was the Inquisition, with its tortures; there were millions of unfortunate women burned as witches; and there was every kind of cruelty practiced upon all sorts of people in the name of religion."[4] In a phrase, Christians have a horrible reputation—and the sooner we acknowledge the depth of the pain, distrust, and anger, the better equipped we will be to humble ourselves to a new way of loving others well.

MYOPIA

It is difficult to right a wrong when we have no awareness of the wrong that occurred in the first place. A pastor confessed recently his great surprise when a friend expressed wariness about the church. Church people are hypocritical, this man told the pastor, and the risk of rejection and betrayal is just too great. The pastor expressed surprise and sorrow at his words, since this was not his experience with the church and he was unsure why this friend would have such an impression. As a professor and bivocational church leader, I can see where a pastor dutifully trained in seminary and mentored in how best to shepherd his flock might inadvertently sidestep the cultural wave that says *no* to church hypocrisy and *yes* to relativism and self-help. But our lens has to be wider, our worldview a little broader.

Another pastor friend has mourned aloud that his time and circles are so narrow that he does not have nonbelieving friends and therefore feels out of touch with the anger and assumptions of his neighbors who are outside of the church. Jesus came in part to clarify that the *us versus them* dichotomy we so easily slide into is not only erroneous but dangerous; two millennia later, the challenge has intensified. Rather than embracing individuals more wholly, listening to their stories and questions with a deep sense of love,

2. Moos, "Pastor to kids."

3. Russell, *Why I Am Not a Christian*, 20.

4. Russell, *Why I Am Not a Christian*, 20–21.

grace, and respect for humanity, we use terms like post-church and post-Christianity to further alienate ourselves from a culture that we are—like it or not—intrinsically a part of. Yes, we may rely on 1 John 2 as a reminder to not hold too tightly to worldly things, but verses like these are not a pass to extricate ourselves from life and elevate ourselves above those who most need love and affirmation. God created a world with connections so intricate that even our highest levels of mathematics cannot yet define potential leaps across time and space, matter and spirit. The Christian church is a part of his vast plan, and every decision we make casts ripples reverberating outward in ways that we prefer to deny or excuse or ignore. When will we acknowledge our errors and step boldly into a new future with Holy Spirit-confidence, optimism, and joy, rather than back-pedaling, anxiety, and fear?

Jody Wiley Fernando argues that our fear of conflict is often the reason why do not fully engage—whether in situations of religion or race. When whites portray themselves as "colorblind," for example, they are not listening to the realities around them: "When white people 'participate' in the conversation by smugly crossing our arms, silently observing from a distance, assuming we know better, or arrogantly refusing to consider other perspectives, we only perpetuate the system we've inherited."[5] For Debby Irving, the myopia of whiteness is unintentional and personally frustrating: "If you can't see a problem for what it is, how can you step in and be a part of its solution no matter how good a person you are?"[6] As she began to explore her own cultural presumptions in adulthood, Irving realized that her myopic outlook on life had been created for her at an early age: "Over time I internalized what I'd been taught as right, so that it didn't just feel right—it felt normal, like the only legitimate way to think and act. Anyone who followed a different code of behavior was not only different but weird, or perhaps even rude."[7] In the church, our cultural short-sightedness mirrors the myopia Wiley Fernando and Irving describe, drastically limiting our ability to have any kind of notable impact on the very people we hope to share the gospel with.

In his book *The Social Animal*, David Brooks blames our myopia on human overconfidence:

> The human mind is an overconfidence machine. The conscious level gives itself credit for things it really didn't do and confabulates tales to create the illusion it controls things it really doesn't determine. Ninety percent of drivers believe they are above

5. Wiley Fernando, *Pondering Privilege*, 42.
6. Irving, *Waking Up White*, 98.
7. Irving, *Waking Up White*, 65.

> average behind the wheel. Ninety-four percent of college professors think they are above-average teachers. Ninety percent of entrepreneurs think that their new business will be a success. Ninety-eight percent of students who take the SAT say they have average or above-average leadership skills.[8]

When we assume our own righteousness, it is difficult to be humble. Daniel Migliore equates this over-confidence with a dangerously incomplete understanding of who God is. "Apart from hope in God, every Christian doctrine becomes distorted," Migliore argues, and a flawed doctrine is precisely what can lead to the hurt the church has inflicted.[9] A Holy Spirit-inspired biblical witness does not confabulate or distort, and any human short-sightedness is repeatedly broadened by hope and faith. Dan Merchant suggests that our tendency to slide into a false us-versus-them dichotomy is the culprit: "There are people who feel the division in America is justified and inevitable because they are right and the others are wrong," Merchant writes. "Some of these people write books explaining how uninformed or dishonest the other side is. I wonder sometimes if their books would sell as many if they chose a theme other than 'us versus them.'"[10] The problem, Merchant continues, is that we typically ignore information that does not adequately contextualize or affirm our agenda, a realization that aligns with both Brooks's and Migliore's assertions.

PRISON-HOUSE

But our myopia may not be entirely our own doing. As literary critic and political theorist Fredric Jameson posits in his 1972 book *The Prison-House of Language,* the symbolic nature of the words we use to express our reality are problematic in themselves: "My guiding thread and permanent preoccupation in these pages has been to clarify the relationships possible between the synchronic methods of Saussurean linguistics and the realities of time and history itself."[11] In Jameson's view, we need not stand in moralistic opposition to cultural phenomenon when they are indicative of linguistic limitations and unique modes of experience. Instead it behooves us to analyze cultural swings with a sensitivity toward the markers that limit: labor conditions that lead to inadequate basic needs, for example, or distinct social classes that

8. Brooks, *The Social Animal,* 218.

9. Migliore, *Faith Seeking Understanding,* 347.

10. Merchant, *Lord Save Us,* 20.

11. Jameson, *The Prison-House,* x.

muddy a normative grounding. Jameson continues in *The Political Unconscious:* "It would seem therefore more useful to ask ourselves, in conclusion, how History as a ground and as an absent cause can be conceived in such a way as to resist such thematization or reification, such transformation back into one optional code among others."[12] As church leaders, what responsibility do we hold in differentiating between signs and history, symbols and meaning? How do we help the culture to resist reification of codes that suggest the myopic limitations of us-versus-them and other non-biblical moral entrapments?

For Marshall McLuhan, the prison-house shackles came in the form of a new kind of twentieth-century media finding itself at odds with the restrictive assumptions of nineteenth-century perceptions. Consider his words in *Understanding Media:*

> The power of the arts to anticipate future social and technological developments, by a generation and more, has long been recognized. In this century Ezra Pound called the artist "the antennae of the race." Art as radar acts as "an early alarm system," as it were, enabling us to discover social and psychic targets in lots of time to prepare to cope with them. This concept of the arts as prophetic, contrasts with the popular idea of theme as mere self-expression. If art is an "early warning system," to use the phrase from World War II, when radar was new, art has the utmost relevance not only to media study but to the development of media controls.[13]

In his recent book *Bounce*, Matthew Syed complicates the matter by suggesting that our faith in itself is the placebo that misleads, not our encounter with the culture that surrounds us. This argument is not a moral one, Syed insists, but a practical one that acknowledges that religion, much like packaging or a medium, communicates emotional assurances that can have a placebo effect:

> The key point in all this is that the power of the mind is exercised through the medium of belief, and it doesn't matter whether the belief is true or false or how the delusion is created—so long as it is created successfully. It doesn't matter if it is created by a reassuring doctor, slick packaging, price, advertising, color, invasiveness, ritual, or any of countless other possibilities. It

12. Jameson, *The Political Unconscious,* 1187.

13. McLuhan, *Understanding Media,* 16.

> does not matter if it is supported by fabricated evidence or no evidence at all. All that matters is that the patient *believes*.[14]

Syed makes a point here that should not be overlooked. As Christians, in our effort to be good people—as Irving suggests—we may choose to confront our own myopic worldview and the prison-house of our language with an intentional reliance on God, faith, and belief. And while this may appear at the outset like an admirable and biblical move, we need to take care not to affirm Syed's pithy statement that Christians are "understandably quick to trumpet this phenomenon, proclaiming that God is actively involved in dishing out health benefits to his chosen few."[15] The danger arises when the belief that has become our placebo is grounded in myopic assumptions rather than Holy Spirit love; therein lies the prison-house of the twenty-first-century church.

(RE)SIGNING

When signifiers become intrinsically embedded within signifieds, it can be nearly impossible to speak to one another without offending or at least imparting meanings that we never intended or may never realize were received. Crystal Downing acknowledges the complexity of semiotic context in her book *Changing Signs of Truth:* "Separating the signifier from the signified within a particular synchronic system is like trying to detach one side of a sheet of paper from another," Downing writes. "Like it or not, we must be sensitive to how changes in *langue* alter the signified meaning of the signifiers we use."[16] The problem, Downing continues, is when the words we use function as "stop-signs to communication."[17] When the signifiers no longer point to the appropriate signifieds, it is time for us to (re)sign the language we use.[18]

According to John Piper, we need to be bold enough to find new ways to impart the enormity of the gospel: "Most of us are virtually impervious to the radical implications of familiar language," Piper writes in defense of his decision to rely on the word *hedonism* in *Desiring God*. "My heart has been arrested and my life has been deeply jolted by the teachings of Christian Hedonism. It is not an easy or comfortable philosophy. It is extremely

14. Syed, *Bounce*, 158.
15. Syed, *Bounce*, 159.
16. Downing, *Changing Signs*, 109.
17. Downing, *Changing Signs*, 63.
18. Downing, *Changing Signs*, 22.

threatening to nominal Christians."[19] And yet that is precisely why Piper chooses to (re)sign language as he does: "The chief effect of the term is not that it creates a stumbling block to the truth," Piper continues, "but that it wakens people to the fact that the truth itself is a stumbling block—and often a very different one than they expected."[20] We see Jesus doing this throughout the New Testament—when he compares his coming to that of a thief in Matthew 24:42–44, for example, or when he praises a dishonest and shrewd manager in Luke 16:1–15.

Another challenge we face is that the human brain operates by pattern recognition rather than logic, which means that it naturally seeks existing patterns in order to make meaning out of new information. As Kathleen Taylor and Catherina Marienau discuss in *Facilitating Learning with the Adult Brain in Mind*, a new idea is typically described by another name that most closely parallels the new; consider *horseless carriage*, for example. "In essence, the brain cannot recognize (*re-cognize*: literally, know again) that which it does not already know, at least by analogy," Taylor and Marienau write.[21] As patterns are repeatedly reactivated in the adult brain, the pathways begin to entrench themselves, easing difficult neural networks but complicating the process of introducing new ideas: "Although the brain is plastic and constantly changing, deeply rooted patterns become not just the Broadways but the Grand Canyons of neural networks, where the rivers of experience have cut deeply into the bedrock. Anthropologists and sociologists call these patterns *culture*."[22] How curiously concerning it is, therefore, when church leaders lay blame on "the media" or "the culture," when both are essentially offshoots of who we are and how we think. Rather than placing blame or otherwise enforcing a dangerous us-versus-them mentality, how can we instead focus our energy on (re)signing the myopic signifiers that define our unfortunate reputation in a culture that is thirsting for greater meaning?

N. T. Wright is a bishop and scholar who seeks to redefine the church's message in ways that may begin to open the right pathways. *Simply Christian*, Wright's twenty-first-century rewriting of C. S. Lewis's twentieth-century *Mere Christianity*, is Wright's attempt to make relevant the brilliant apologetics that Lewis employed in the 1930s and 1940s. In *Surprised By Hope*, Wright seeks to define the hope of the gospel in twenty-first-century terms, as well as articulate practical ways for people to foster hope in their

19. Piper, *Desiring God*, 311.

20. Piper, *Desiring God*, 311.

21. Taylor and Marienau, *Facilitating Learning*, 42.

22. Taylor and Marienau, *Facilitating Learning*, 44.

communities. And in *The Day the Revolution Began,* Wright argues that we Christians have lost the meaning behind the cross as signifier for something far greater than mere good works:

> The Western church . . . has been so concerned with getting to heaven, with sin as the problem blocking the way, and therefore with how to remove sin and its punishment, that it has jumped straight to passages in Paul that can be made to serve that purpose. It has forgotten that the gospels are replete with atonement theology, through and through—only they give it to us not as a neat little system, but as a powerful, sprawling, many-sided, richly revelatory narrative in which we are invited to find ourselves, or rather to lose ourselves and to be found again on the other side.[23]

While I admire Wright's work and I appreciate his passion to move things forward, the language in all three of his books mentioned here is mired in the same signifier-signified prison-house that Donald Miller eschews. As Wright presents Christianity as a viable answer in *Simply Christian,* for example, he slides into the Christianese that too often slams stop signs into the faces of secular skeptics: "Christianity is all about the belief that the living God, in fulfillment of his promises and as the climax of the story of Israel, has accomplished all this—the finding, the saving, the giving of new life—in Jesus."[24] Nearly every word in Wright's sentence here rings with misappropriated signifiers and myopic Christian assumptions of how and what will be received: *Christianity, belief, living God, fulfillment of promises, story of Israel, finding, saving, new life, Jesus.* If the word *Jesus* is the ultimate signified that calls forth the most erroneous signifiers, how can we expect to embark on the Great Commission[25] with any degree of success?

FEAR IN THE NAME OF JESUS

Doomsayers rarely bring anything productive to a conversation, and yet Christians have consistently stood at the forefront, decrying the culture and pining for the better years of yesterday. That kind of whining sounds ridiculous to an educated nonbeliever, curious to a seeker, and indescribably painful to those who feel accused or alienated. If I bemoan change or proclaim an anxiety about the future, is the crux of my fear biblical? Am I longing

23. Wright, *The Day the Revolution Began,* 415–16.

24. Wright, *Simply Christian,* 92.

25. Matt 28:16–20.

for peace and comfort for all Christians, as if that is something promised in Paul's letters? Am I clinging to verses like 1 John 2:15–17 in exclusion of Jesus command to "Love your neighbor as yourself"? Jesus calls us to enter fully in a way that is mindful and intentional, loving and grace-filled, and yet we so often define ourselves versus the other with language that divides and isolates.

When I ask a roomful of adult students about the cultural shifts they have witnessed in their lifetimes, the non-Christian students are more likely to speak with acuity and foresight of conversations that are uncomfortable but necessary, or new means of communication that are surprising but helpful. The Christian students are typically the ones who speak of fear, decline, degradation, collapse, and even panic. We are called as Christians to walk in the culture with Holy Spirit confidence, not direct or critique it from afar. If we want to proclaim the peace and joy of the gospel to an audience that is able to hear us, we must learn to acknowledge and measure the words that we use and the intent with which we speak them.

The twenty-first century has exploded forward with a complexity of human communication that we never anticipated nor metered. Our ability to communicate with one another instantly and from nearly any corner of the world is staggering, and the ultimate outflow of this capability should be relief that we are finally engaging in conversations we were once too fearful to broach. But because we are in the midst of the cultural anomaly—because the voices are in multitude, cacophonous, and, for the first time, unregulated—we are afraid. And fear can be a dangerous emotion in both humans and animals. Any domesticated animal that is afraid, whether a dog, cat, or hamster, is far more likely to respond aggressively as a means of self-protection; humans do the same. When we play the aggressor from a linchpin of fear, we hold on to a power that falsely assures us of our own safety and further marginalizes those who are not part of our inner circle. When we pair fear with power and aggression with reactionary behaviors, we do not have a recipe for love, grace, or an ability to hear deeply and well. Nonbelievers know this. Why don't we?

Four key concepts that have arisen in my classrooms with increasing ferocity over the years, always demanding space for debate, are as follows: (1) the Google Age, (2) Social Media, (3) Worldview, and (4) Postmodernism. When the secular world enters boldly into conversations like these, we are compelled to listen and consider as well, rather than retreating and holding tightly to what is familiar. How will Christians enter in without accusing, defending, or otherwise inciting the walls to rise? Can we hold each twenty-first-century idea gently, thoughtfully, and wisely, listening for the markers of a culture downtrodden by unfulfilled expectations?

THE GOOGLE AGE

The air was cold as I stood in line outside the public high school, one of more than thirty teenagers waiting for the custodian to unlock the doors. It was our fourth week of class, and I knew the routine. If I arrived in time to be among the first ten kids in line, I would be fine; much past ten, and it could be a scramble. I heard the *thwack* of the first bolt sliding back, and we all stood a little straighter, blowing clouds of white into the cold morning air and waiting for the doors to swing open. As the left door began to open, I felt a kid behind me brush past, cutting ahead before I had a chance to stop him. "Hey!" I protested, and then we all pushed in, speed-walking down the waxed vinyl floors toward the typing room in the south hall. When I made it to the room, I beelined for the small electric typewriter under the far window. With a sigh of relief, I slid into the seat and pulled off my coat, looking with pity at the students who were still wandering in, rolling their eyes at the manual typewriters that remained. The goal was to claim a Smith Corona or a Brother Electric before the seats filled; otherwise, you were left to the slow press and carriage return of a manual typewriter, which always reduced your words-per-minute by at least a third.

We had both a manual and a Smith Corona in my childhood home, and I loved the clack and pull of the manual. Even in the 1970s, the manual typewriter carried a kind of nostalgia that echoed of tragic hours of writerly angst—something that appealed to me. What fun it was to yank partially filled pages from its carriage, relishing the whirl of gears as I crumpled the page and tossed it behind me, pressing a new page into place. As my school papers lengthened, I recognized the ease of the smooth-flowing Smith Corona; instead of tossing an entire page each time my thoughts shifted or I hit an inadvertent key, I could dab Liquid Paper artfully enough to erase the error and present a clean page.

In my undergraduate years, friends tried to wean me from my Smith Corona, persuading me of the brilliance of an IBM personal computer that eliminated the need for correction fluid and allowed for a more stream-of-consciousness approach to writing. I resisted until my Intercultural Communications professor lost a twenty-five-page term paper that I had turned in early in order to free my week for other projects. The professor apologized and was kind enough to assess me the grade he believed I would have earned, but I was crushed to have all of my hard work slide into oblivion so easily, without affirmation or feedback. For my next paper, I silenced my roommates by agreeing to compose my first paper on a borrowed IBM. Fourteen pages into my work, with footnotes painstakingly placed and library books stacked precariously across my desk, I heard an electrical click and watched my green glowing words and the blinking curser fade to black. "It must have crashed," my roommate said later. "It happens." The paper was lost, as was my faith in computers. It would be three more years before a newspaper editor insisted that I compose my stories directly onto the newsroom PCs rather than a yellow pad. In the 1980s and into the 1990s, a computer crash typically meant that the information lost was irretrievable—inextricably lost in an electrical glitch that wiped everything clean.

In 2003, thieves rummaged through every corner of our two-story home, smashing valuables, sweeping books to the floor, and stealing electronics. Gone was my 1990s laptop computer, which had been sitting on a living room desk with the first eighty pages of my PhD dissertation stored on its hard drive. When the police apprehended the thieves nearly a year later after they tried to similarly rampage a neighbor's home, our electronics were long gone—sold out of the trunks of sedans or in pawn shops, and likely wiped clear of any reminders that they once belonged to someone else. It was painful to have to rewrite those early chapters of my first dissertation, but the work was lost and it had to be duplicated in order for me to move forward with my degree.

When I first accessed in the internet in the 1990s, the rabbit trails of information were exciting but dangerous. Not only would X-rated material sometimes appear at inopportune times, but it could be difficult to recover information or patterns once a new trail began. Just as I feared the electrical click and black screen of a PC crash, I also was often anxious about clicking too far into something that I would not be able to find my way back out of. I still hold remnants of that anxiety now, and our five kids find it amusing. For me, the internet is an astounding tool brought forward in the late 1980s to bring millions of versions of my childhood *World Book Encyclopedias* to the forefront—volatile, fallible, and awe-inspiring. For our kids—none of whom were born "in the 19s," as they call the previous millennium—the internet is their worldview, their lens for discerning what is real and possible and true. When we ask a younger generation to stack their cell phones in a basket or unplug for a few days, we are ostensibly asking them to remove a portion of their brain that processes the world. Yes, limits are necessary, particularly when immature brains are involved, but as we learn to engage fully with a culture in need, how can we learn to say *yes* rather than *no*, or *let's imagine* rather than *never*?

In the 1990s, I watched Lieutenant Commander Data on the series *Star Trek: The Next Generation* with awe. When Captain Picard or other crew members asked Data a question, the human-like android would pause to compute and the results were astounding. A fellow crew member could ask Data any factual question, and he was able to answer with complete accuracy; here was my *World Book* come to life. The only hitch was time, which typically added to the drama of each episode. If Chief Engineer La-Forge needed critical information in order to know how to proceed without imploding the Starship Enterprise, Data would hear the question and first compute how much time it would take him to arrive at an answer. Sometimes the solution was immediate, but—more often than not—combing through the infinite amounts of data in Data's inner wiring took hours and sometimes days. Typically Data would complete his computations and arrive at the correct answer mere seconds before the ship was expected to crash or explode, narrowly averting whatever disaster was impending. While his artificial intelligence and synthetic construction affirmed his accuracy and immunity to biological weaknesses, Data was unable to conceptualize emotion or imagination, two deficiencies that added to the longing and complexity of his character.

Data, meet Siri, Alexa, Cortana, Bixby, and Google Assistant. What the writers of Star Trek imagined in the 1990s has fully entered our lives in the twenty-first century, and for many of us, it is the most astounding and frightening advancement of the Google Age. When we allow artificial intelligence (AI) assistants into our homes, cars, and workplaces, what ethical borders are we crossing as concepts that were once black and white muddle into gray? We enjoy the efficiency, but we fear a loss of control. We appreciate the immediacy, but we agonize over our personal boundaries. What about privacy? What about government control? What about AI infiltration or dominance or destruction? What about our own sense of who we are and why we are here?

Just as Data wrestled with emotion and imagination, wasting long hours in holographic recreational adventures, we are living in a cultural upswing that is venturing into similar territory: If the AI assistants on our wrists, in our pockets, or clipped to our ears are capable of computing data for us instantly, what space do we have for creativity, imagination, and embracing the depths of human emotion? Data did not long to erase his robotic abilities in order to acquire emotional intelligence. Instead he installs an emotion chip to allow himself a full range of human emotions, an addition that initially proves difficult for him to absorb. In time, however, he learns to identify and balance his emotions, including an occasional choice to deactivate the emotion chip in order to ensure his performance efficiency. Clearly the question is not about exclusion but balance. When we are overloaded with one, we tend to neglect the other. Now that we have access to Data-level information, how do we ensure that we are handling well our fullest range of human emotions, imagination, and creativity?

SOCIAL MEDIA

I watched my seventh-grade teacher with my interested, quizzical face: head cocked slightly to one side, eyebrows furrowed, lips pursed. He was pacing to and fro before the room-length black chalkboard, telling us something about exponents that meant little to me in that moment; beneath the desk that hid my hands, I folded the paper again and again until it was hardly more than a speck in my palm. Leaning slightly to the right with a stretch of the shoulder, eyes still on Mr. Cole as he droned on about our upcoming osmosis experiment, I passed the speck to the row behind me. A moment or two passed, and then I felt a nudge in my left shoulder blade. I stretched my arm behind me, coupling it with a well-timed half-yawn, and folded my fingers over a meticulously folded scrap of paper. I opened the note noiselessly in my lap, eyes on the teacher. A few words and a googly-eyed silly face looked up at me, a response to my earlier taunt about the white bits of dandruff that speckled across our teacher's broad shoulders. My friends and I had passed notes since we learned to write in the first grade, and our process was slick, careful, and rarely exclusive; we encouraged newcomers who would occasionally pass random silliness around the room, giving us all an excuse to think about something beyond mastering the loops of a cursive G or memorizing facts about the Byzantine Empire. In Spanish and science, our notes sometimes included test answers; in homeroom or choir, the notes typically gossiped about the teacher or some less-popular, unsuspecting peer. And the teachers rarely noticed—until this one day in seventh grade.

"May I see that, please?" Mr. Cole said, his eyes suddenly fully on me.

"See what?" I asked, instantly innocent—and willing myself to disappear. I pressed the paper deeper into my palm, praying it would magically disintegrate into dust.

"Hand it to me, please," Mr. Cole repeated, this time more sternly. I reached my hand toward him, palm up, eyes averted. He took the note and opened it slowly, fold after fold after fold. "Impressive," he murmured as he finally opened the note fully, pressing it flat against the desk.

I felt my cheeks begin to burn as I imagined him reading aloud my unkind words exaggerating the white dandruff flakes sprinkled across the shoulders of his dark suit. I stared at the blue rubber toes of my duck shoes and waited for his wrath. Instead I heard a low chuckle followed by a grunt. I looked up. "You think so, huh?" Mr. Cole said. He brushed his fingers across a shoulder, pretending to look for dandruff, dropped the note in the trash with a laugh, and turned to the chalkboard to continue his lecture about solvent molecules and high solute concentrations. I sunk a little lower in my seat that day and vowed never to pass another note . . . at least not about Mr. Cole.

As I have told my own kids many times, the challenge they face on social media is that the notes they pass are immortalized rather than tossed into a classroom wastebasket. In the 1970s and 1980s, our note-passing was frequent and not always kind, but the repercussions were fleeting. In the twenty-first-century, the note-passing is public, far-reaching, and permanent, and I am so sorry for a generation that must grapple with how best to manage their social relationships on a high, wide stage, with their parents, grandparents, teachers, and a cadre of other adults watching with arms crossed and criticism ready. When Data longed for emotional intelligence, his shipmates found his quest endearing, much like the Lion's search for courage or the Tin Man's quest for a heart in *The Wizard of Oz*. Why is it that we view social media as the unfortunate by-product of a generation led astray, rather than recognizing the enormous benefits of such a vast array of social connections, as well as the brain-numbing dangers of its all-consuming appeal? Why is the church more interested in conversations about the decline of American culture than linking arms with those who are seeking a yellow brick road?

Every Thursday morning, my inbox zings with five emails in a row from securely.com, a cloud-based web filtering service that our local public schools have employed to provide weekly parent reports on the Chromebook use of each of our kids. While I understand the need for the prevention of inappropriate internet use, particularly regarding pornography or bullying, I find the weekly flurry of emails disturbingly reminiscent of a dystopian novel. The emails are each divided into four quadrants: (1) Sites Searched, (2) Educational Sites Searched, (3) Words Searched, and (4) Videos Searched. When a quadrant does not have links to list for that week, a cartoon sketch of an unhappy piece of paper appears with the words "There's not enough data to display"; I always find that emoji-aided commentary amusing when it lands in the "Educational Sites Searched" box for one of my kids. How unfortunate to upset the school district's AI by not regularly searching education-approved sites, despite the binary codes that prevent the AI system from recognizing the learning that occurs outside of a finite lens.

What concerns me is that we are forcing our kids under nonstop plexiglass surveillance that we would never demand of ourselves. We seem to agree as a culture and as a church that failures and life struggles are character-building. Why, then, are we expecting perfection of a younger, Google-savvy generation? How are we stunting their ability to grow into healthy, forward-thinking, creative people when we are monitoring not only every step they take but every thought they think, redirecting and correcting until their actions are in line with our expectations and their souls are protected from the pain of loss? My prayer for our kids is that they fail well—preferably softly—while they are still living in my home. I delete the securely.com emails each week with an often-irritated click of the touchpad. Until adults are content to live under the same level of magnifying glass, expressing humility and living lives of intentionality, I will not frustrate my children with the sins they have yet to commit.

I recently taught a course at our university titled "The Facts and Myths of Social Media," and I was both startled and encouraged by the students' growth in our time together. In addition to their regular reading and writing assignments, I asked students each week to complete a different social media action and then share their results with the class. Some of the activities that garnered the richest discussions and realizations included the following:

- Track the time and frequency of your social media use for one twenty-four-hour period.
- Select a single event in human history that occurred prior to 1990 and discuss with at least one other person the following: If social media had been around at the time of the event, would things have turned out differently?
- Track social media use during at least one planned professional or social event this week: a staff meeting, a working lunch, a family dinner, a social outing, etc. How often do you check a device during the event? How often do the others at the event check devices? Do the occasional device-checks enhance or detract from the meeting?
- Find fifteen minutes to be bored—no internet, no texts, no email, no TV, no devices nearby. Sit outside, sit by a window, or sit in a cozy corner. Enjoy a cup of coffee or tea and a few moments of solitude.
- Choose an activity this week that is counter-cultural. For example, post a moment when life is not perfect, remind friends seeking affirmation that you appreciate them for who they are rather than their scripted images, or stick up for someone who is being shamed.
- Pick an action this week that you would ordinarily handle via social media or internet and instead reach out in person: a work message, a check-in with family or friends, a service industry contact, etc.

The learning students gained in our time together was twofold: (1) They learned that they individually spend far more mindless, unintentional time on social media than they realized, and (2) they learned that social media, when used well, is enormously beneficial for a seeking, longing, and hurting culture. As Christian pastors and leaders, how might we fare? Rather than dictating from on high, how do we, too, learn to enter in so we are able to appreciate the benefits of social media and offer guidance where older generations, in particular, may have diverted our attention to inconsequentials?

WORLDVIEW

My first realization of worldview came in my later toddler years, as it likely does for many people. We were living in an apartment in Detroit, Michigan, and a gaggle of neighbor kids were eating Kool-Aid powder straight from the rainbow-colored packets. I shudder now at the thought of dyed chemicals without the multiple cups of bleached sugar that made the drink palatable once it was mixed with water, but somehow this was appealing to kids in our apartment complex. I accepted when they offered, curious as usual, and while I don't recall the taste, I do remember realizing that my parents likely would not approve. Directions were to be followed, and surely we should not be dipping our fingers into packets of Kool-Aid powder that had not yet been mixed appropriately into a drink.

Later that day, I was startled when I heard my mother's voice calling to me from an upper story window when we dashed across the apartment building's courtyard. I paused and looked up to see what she needed, and I remember feeling deeply surprised that she had any ideas at all about Kool-Aid consumption. I don't recall her words, but I do know that she asked me several times whether I had been eating Kool-Aid powder. I told her "no" insistently, surprised that she would keep asking. I had resolved to keep it to myself, effectively rewriting reality in my own mind to clear my conscience, and I didn't understand why we needed to go back to something I had already moved beyond. I was later disciplined for my dishonesty, and I remember realizing in that experience that I must not hold as much power as I thought. While my worldview was now unique from my mother's, a fact I was enjoying as I was given increasingly more freedom to explore the world without her continual supervision, I realized with some disappointment that her worldview was equally unique from mine. And the fact that I had bright powder stains streaked generously around my mouth did not help my cause.

Those of us who have raised children know that an infant's worldview is firmly intertwined with his or her mother's—so much so that the infant does not view itself as uniquely individual and is daily startled when the mother does not anticipate the discomforts of life that she surely must be feeling as well: the stabbing pangs of hunger, the heaviness of fatigue, the cold dampness of a diaper that needs to be changed. As an older baby differentiates from the mother, an early understanding of worldview begins to form at its most basic level: My eyes are mine alone, which means I must point to or use words to describe the things that I see, want, prefer, or fear; those around me do not automatically see what I see. As a child grows and recognizes the power of storytelling, as I had begun to when I encountered Kool-Aid powder at nearly age three, worldview becomes something that is potentially pliable—both from my view and from yours. Or is it? The lines are gray, and as we mature, we subconsciously settle into the ethical, social, and cultural boundaries that most comfortably affirm who we are and who we hope to become. But when we are not aware of or intentional about the lines we draw, ethical quandaries can arise that surprise and confuse us.

The definition of worldview is simple: It is the lens through which we see the world. What becomes complicated is our ability to acknowledge the lens exists, our willingness to articulate what defines our unique lens, and our interest in encountering with grace, humility, and openness the lenses of those around us. Too often we assume that we have no lens, much as we have no discernible accent—everyone else has the accent. Or we assume that lenses come in like-colored packages, and ours matches nicely the lenses of the people we have chosen to live life alongside. But both assumptions are gravely, dangerously wrong: Everyone has a worldview lens, and everyone's lens is uniquely informed by his or her experiences, surroundings, and innate tendencies.

We had a discussion in our church recently about worldview and how best to engage those whose worldview may differ from ours—an admirable conversation but one that I found concerning when it overlooked the fact that an ability to articulate one's own worldview is the first essential step. In our church discussion, we weighed ideas of secularism, postmodernism, and Eastern religions and philosophies, but I began to hear an overarching assumption that a "Christian worldview" was something that the more than 100 of us gathered in that room shared in common. The reality in assuming we understand the worldview lens through which someone else encounters the world is that we will always, always be disappointed. While I may share a number of theological understandings with my pastor, for example, the fact that he is male, younger than I am, and grew up in another state is enough to shade our worldview lenses with remarkably different colors. I have no trouble with the differences—we should all embrace the richness of our differences—but I cannot expect to communicate with him as if our like-minded theology informs all of who we are; if I do, what nuance might I imply or words might I use that could mislead or offend? And if I mislead or offend and I am never aware that I have, what happens to our communication both in that moment and over the long term?

In the Christian Faith and Thought course, I often ask students to role-play various worldviews, answering challenging life questions from the lens of that worldview to see how it might differ from their own beliefs. The students each place a worldview name on a card before them: Individualism, Consumerism, Nationalism, Moral Relativism, Scientific Naturalism, New Age, Postmodern, Christian, etc. We then ask one another questions such as, "What happens when I die?" or "What is the purpose of human life on earth?" and work to answer as accurately as possible by our understanding of the worldview at hand. Students struggle and laugh their way through this exercise, typically defaulting to what sounds most rational and obvious in their own minds, but they walk away with an appreciation of the variety of lenses that surround us. I encourage them to recognize that the most problematic way to encounter life is to live it without examination. The hidden shades of our worldview lenses that we either don't see or refuse to recognize invariably are the particulates that dilute or infect our lives in deeply troubling ways that we may never realize.

A discussion about worldview should never begin with an assumption of solidarity and a vaguely condescending determination to understand the differing worldviews of those around us. It can take a lifetime to identify, articulate, heal, and teach from our own worldviews, and it would behoove us to start there. Some of the factors we each need to consider include age, gender, race, class, education, religion, culture, location, occupation, hobbies, friends, and family.

POSTMODERNISM

I was raised in a home that favored science over religion, rational thought over spiritual mysticism. We had one Bible in our home, and it sat mostly untouched on a shelf in the family room. We attended church fairly regularly throughout my childhood, but I was schooled to hold my discussions about faith and Jesus to Sunday mornings rather than spread religion across the week in a cultish, overbearing kind of way. When a group of "evangelists" visited a summer camp that I attended each year, I remember my family explaining to me that while they were likely very nice people, "evangelists" tended to be much too extreme in their approach to faith and religion, and that one should always be wary of the cost. As educated people, we could only carry religion a certain distance in our lives before it would start to impede our ability to think creatively and otherwise contribute intelligently to society. Religion compartmentalized to Sunday mornings was an organized way to assure our Christianity but leave ample room for intellectual gain, productivity, and achievement. The philosophy made sense to me at its most basic level, but as I grew older and explored Scripture on my own, I began to question how one could experience Christianity only slightly, retaining control and maintaining a careful distance; was it possible that this was not Christianity at all?

One Saturday afternoon when I had pulled pizzas from the oven and a number of neighboring kids happened to have mixed in with mine as we sat down for a late lunch, I asked everyone to pause briefly so my daughter could pray before our meal together. "Wait a minute," a twelve-year-old boy interrupted. "I'm atheist. I'm really not comfortable with this."

"Tim," I said quietly, "it will be painless. You don't need to close your eyes or do anything. Just hold tight for a moment, and before you know it, she'll be done." Tim's eyebrow arched with surprise as we continued despite his protest, and as we dished up the pizza a few moments later, I asked him how that felt.

"I guess it didn't really matter," he said. "I just believe in science instead of God."

"Instead of?" my son, also twelve, interrupted incredulously. "That's ridiculous. God created science. I believe in both."

Tim and my son continued a lively discussion over whether something can exist if it cannot be seen, touched, or validated scientifically, and I listened, relieved to hear my son's confident response and intrigued by Tim's questions. Here was the postmodern worldview encapsulated in a middle school boy's aversion to prayer, followed by an immediate challenge to rationally prove a belief system that Americans many generations ago took for granted as foundational. Just as I was raised with a notably postmodern worldview, the one lens that my students struggle the most to acknowledge, identify, and articulate is postmodernism—likely because we live so deeply entrenched in its assumptions that it is difficult for us to think beyond its limitations.

In the late nineteenth and early twentieth centuries, modernism emerged as a response to the vast cultural changes of the Industrial Revolution: a call for a movement that was fresh, engaged, and meaningful in a newly industrialized world. In the mid- to late twentieth century, postmodernism emerged as a response to modernism: an inherent rejection of unified movements of any kind, including religion, tradition, nationalism, and cultural expectation. Postmodernism is marked by deeply seeded skepticism and a reverence for scientific validation. Some critics have called for a movement beyond postmodernism into a kind of neo-postmodernism or neomodernism, which suggests that some of postmodernism's claims for equality, scientific authority, and non-conformity at all costs are self-defeating. While neomodernism raises effective questions, postmodernism is so deeply entrenched in our language and culture that it is difficult to conceptualize how a new way forward will rewrite our American worldview. A lasting revision of postmodernism will surely be driven by the far-reaching changes in technology and communication in the early twenty-first century.

As congregation members in our church discussion wrestled with definitions of worldview, the anchors of each definition emerged from a postmodern skepticism that most did not seem to notice: "Can the worldview be defined in a rational, discernible manner?" the pastor asked. And, "Are the tenants of the worldview supported by experience, whether by the individual or the group?" Our American culture has become so deeply mired in postmodernism since the mid-twentieth century that it is difficult for us to imagine a world where emotion is revered, adherence to the norm is preferred, and mystical experiences are the beacons of proof. Fredric Jameson argued in his 1972 book *The Prison-House of Language* that cultural swings are often indicative of linguistic limitations and unique modes of experience. Instead of standing in moralistic opposition, what if we analyze cultural phenomenon such as social media or a post-church trend, maintaining a sensitivity toward the markers and linguistic trends that limit our ability to imagine more fully? How do we help our culture resist the myopic limitations of us-versus-them and other non-biblical entrapments that smack of postmodernism?

Chapter 2

The Twentieth-Century Answer

The cool, hard wood pressed into my thighs as I sat on the edge of the pew, dangling my legs and peering between the adult heads in front of me as I wondered who would emerge from the mysterious door to the left of the pulpit. I knew the space behind the door was only a narrow hallway lined with wheeled garment racks, the polyester robes clicking on their wire hangers, but I liked to imagine a Lewisian portal into the snowy woods of Narnia or some other adventure-filled escape. When the door creaked open, what emerged was magical, just as I had hoped. I leaned into the center aisle for a better view, holding onto the hymn rack on the pew in front of me so I wouldn't fall. The man who walked out was stooped, his graying hair long and wavy across his shoulders. He wore a dark tunic that fell in folds around his heavyset frame, with a corded rope cinched around his belly. When he walked haltingly forward, I could see that his feet were bare beneath the tunic, and the clatter of chains cut through the sanctuary with each step. He shuffled to the pulpit and stood to one side, his left hand gripping the wood and his right hand outstretched. Chains shackled both his wrists and his ankles. When he spoke, his voice boomed to the back of the sanctuary and forward again, transporting us to the Mamertime Prison in Rome where Paul was waiting and writing.

I was mesmerized by our pastor's ability to become someone else for a time, presenting that individual to us in full costume and character rather than standing behind the pulpit to deliver yet another boring string of adult ideas knit together by long pauses and polite coughs in the audience. He didn't perform for us every Sunday, as I wished he would, but every month or two he would surprise us with some new storytelling adventure. Most Sunday mornings he could be found wandering the hallways in his black clergy robe and deep red stole, chatting with congregation members as they arrived. When he wasn't saying hello as we arrived, I knew we were in for a treat.

But something was amiss. Despite his thespian talent, he was one of those adults who looked slightly over one's head when he said hello—maybe not always in actuality, but always in sentiment. I semi-dreaded the close of church each Sunday when we would all file into the inner aisle between the pews, waiting to exit through the thick wooden front doors of the church as the pastor greeted each of us with an energetic handshake. His black robe covered my hand when he reached forward, and I was never quite sure whether he knew my name even though our family had attended that church for more than a decade.

As a child, I only half-listened from the back seat of our Jeep Wagoneer, pressed between two older brothers, as my parents discussed his sermons on the way home. Sometimes they agreed, sometimes they disagreed, and for a time, something deeper added an air of anxiety to our post-church drives. Much later in life, I learned that the pastor had an extramarital affair with a deacon in the church, and both he and the deacon chose to leave their spouses so they could marry one another. This news helped me to understand why my folks always had a difficult time sitting under this pastor when he preached about the sanctity of marriage, whether in a sermon or at one of our friends' weddings.

While I understood the fallibility of people and the complexity of life choices even at a young age, I have always had a difficult time witnessing untruth. I realized over the years that the reason my mother preferred our pastor's regular sermons to his dramatic monologues was that the former pressed him closer to humility and honesty, while the latter allowed the fiction that had threatened to dismantle the church around him. I am certain that the pastor preferred the drama, despite the preparations it must have required. When he was someone else, he no longer had to apologize or defend or pretend; each time he became someone else, he had a clean slate.

~

One of my most prized necklaces is a simple silver chain with a Chinese 50-yen coin hanging from it. The coin is a reminder of a lunch conversation my best friend and I had in our teen years with a woman who was a missionary to China. My grandmother had arranged the luncheon so we could meet the woman and hear her story, and we four sat together at a sun-dappled table eating BLTs and listening to this woman's tales of hard choices, painful sacrifices, and deep faith. Both my friend and I were startled by her practical sense of calling, coupled with a no-nonsense determination to continually move forward in the purpose she believed God had called her to. My friend and I were both searching, wondering about future jobs and future homes and future families, and this woman brought a compelling sense of mission as more than just a missionary's calling. As a parting gift, the woman gave my friend and me each a silver Chinese coin, and my friend later gave me a necklace on which to hang the coin as a reminder of the purpose and inspiration we experienced that day.

When my friend was tragically murdered many years later, the necklace became an even more precious reminder of the miraculous gift of peace, joy, and hope that we are called to share with all we are privileged to encounter. In both the missionary's story and in my friend's horribly premature death, the fanfare is stripped away until what remains is our humanity against a backdrop of God's brilliance. The older I got, the less I understood the showmanship of my childhood pastor and the more I longed for the intentionality and humility of a missionary's life. But did that always mean an airline ticket to somewhere across the globe, or was Jesus suggesting something more?

REDEFINING THE MISSION FIELD

The earliest roots of the missional movement began with necessary conversations in the early twentieth century about missionary methods that were deemed too reliant on Western superiority.[1] As this healthy look at missionary ecclesiology spread, writers such as Darrell Guder, Ed Stetzer, Tim Keller, and Alan Hirsch carried the conversation into a broader church context in the late twentieth century, calling for a missional church. And

1. Aniol, "A Brief History."

while the missional movement was founded on good intentions, its efforts have not met twenty-first-century secular sensibilities in sustainable ways. Some critics suggest that the movement's definitions lack clarity—an ongoing omission that could lead to the movement's demise unless we step forward with practical, assessable tools. Consider, for example, J. Todd Billings' call for a clearer articulation of purpose in his 2008 *Christianity Today* article titled "What Makes a Church Missional?"

> Some use *missional* to describe a church that rejects treating the gospel like a commodity for spiritual consumers; others frame it as a strategy for marketing the church and stimulating church growth. Some see the missional church as a refocusing on God's action in the world rather than obsessing over individuals' needs; others see it as an opportunity to "meet people where they are" and reinvent the church for postmodern culture. Clearly, we need to examine the range of perspectives hiding under the term *missional* if we're to make use of insights learned in the missional-church discussion.[2]

Editor Darrell L. Guder's multi-authored 1998 volume *Missional Church: A Vision for the Sending of the Church in North America* is typically considered the focal point from which today's definitions of "missional" have emerged. In *Missional Church,* we find a discussion of Christendom-focused Christianity, cultural privilege at play in the church, internal-focused church structure, *mission dei*, Lesslie Newbigin's missional focus, and a new emphasis on believers sent into the world to share the gospel. Guder notes in Chapter 9 that the movement of this new church should be ever-outward: "The theological formation of the missional connectedness of the church should be centrifugal in nature."[3]

In their book *The Missional Church in Perspective,* Craig Van Gelder and Dwight J. Zscheile attempt to bring clarity to the muddled definition of "missional." Their answer, generally speaking, is to allow the fluidity for a broader application in a variety of situations: "Some argue today . . . that the word 'missional' has become vacuous and has thus lost its definitional value. We are proposing a different argument in this book, namely, that 'missional' displays an inherent elasticity that allows it to be understood in a variety of ways."[4] Perhaps, although how will a nonbelieving audience encounter such elasticity, particularly when they are predisposed to skepticism, hurt, and even hatred? In *Introducing the Missional Church,* Alan J.

2. Billings, "What Makes a Church Missional?"
3. Guder, ed., *Missional Church,* 249.
4. Van Gelder and Zscheile, *The Missional Church,* 3.

Roxburgh and M. Scott Boren include a subheading that reads, "How the Missional Church Transcends Categorization."[5] Roxburgh writes in his 2011 book *Missional: Joining God in the Neighborhood* that part of the missional movement centers on a new way of seeing the world around us: "An important part of joining with God in mission-shaped life is learning to see again with fresh eyes, to wake up to the fresh and not-so-obvious ways God is present. How might we learn to see our neighborhood through God's eyes and become detectives of God's life in our neighbors and the activities of the streets where we live?"[6] The missional movement has done well to redefine the mission field as far more than a life dedicated to work in China, as my necklace reminds me, or a morning spent serving spaghetti with meatballs at a local soup kitchen. When Jesus commands us to "Go, therefore, and make disciples of all nations,"[7] he does not suggest that we leave our neighborhoods in order to begin; nor does he command that we stay in our neighborhoods and worship together in large, vacuous, ornate, pious buildings. Jesus simply commands that we go.

In *The Forgotten Ways: Reactivating the Missional Church,* Alan Hirsch argues that the church's step "to the edge of chaos" may actually be a positive move:

> There are signs of real movement going on. One of the more obvious signs is the sense of holy discontent among Christians of all ages and classes—it's not just the younger generations that are asking questions. Even the boomers are asking, "Has it all come down to this? Attending church services, singing songs to God, and attending cell groups? Is this really what Christianity is all about?" But more disquieting perhaps is that there is a mass exodus from the church: remember the research of David Barrett and Todd Johnson that there are 111 million Christians without a local church in the world today. These people claim to take Jesus seriously but feel alienated from current expressions of church. We all know them, don't we? My own experience tells me that there are more Christians aged twenty-something outside the church than inside the church at any given time. The statistics and premonitions must say something to us, and they are not unnecessarily gloomy. What they tell us is that there is a search going on. This search for alternatives is a sign that the

5. Roxburgh and Boren, *Introducing the Missional Church,* 49.

6. Roxburgh, *Missional,* 183.

7. Matt 28:18.

> system is responding, and it has led to significant experimentation, and eventually to some genuine innovation.[8]

What the missional movement has allowed is a recognition of our privileged position as we seek to follow the Great Commission. The advent of both the Google age and a post-Christian worldview, however, demand a new kind of conversation that is keenly direct, transparent, and genuine. As we encourage the missional movement, are we adequately preparing pastors and disciples for a twenty-first-century society that eschews muddled reasoning and hypocrisy even more than its predecessors?

REDEFINING THE MISSIONARIES

If we step more fully into the twenty-first century continuing our discussions of clarity, defending our intentions and ideals but never really gaining any traction, Mike Breen's aptly titled 2011 article could come to fruition: "Why the Missional Movement Will Fail." Breen argues that the missional movement is repeating the doomed slide of so many previous efforts in the Western church; while the ideals are admirable, the inner workings are not primed for traction: "They are a car without an engine," Breen writes. "A missional church or a missional community or a missional small group is the new car that everyone is talking about right now, but no matter how beautiful or shiny the vehicle, without the engine, it won't go anywhere."[9] Breen calls for more intentional discipleship training. Missional work sends people into a spiritual war zone, Breen argues, and without both a boot camp for training and a hospital for recovery, it's no wonder that the movement itself is spinning its wheels: "When we don't disciple people the way Jesus and the New Testament talked about, we are sending them out without armor, weapons or training. This is mass carnage waiting to happen. How can we be surprised that people burn out, quit and never want to return to the missional life (or the church)? How can we not expect people who will feel used and abused?"[10]

In his foreword to Hirsch and Catchim's *The Permanent Revolution*, Darrell Guder acknowledges that the term *missional* gained popularity after the publication of his 1998 compilation *Missional Church* but quickly blew astray: "The term immediately became a cliché that today means everything

8. Hirsch, *The Forgotten Ways*, 268.
9. Breen, "Why the Missional Movement Will Fail."
10. Breen, "Why the Missional Movement Will Fail."

nothing.”[11] Interestingly, it is Breen who attempts to bring some clarity to the conversation by contributing a section to Hirsch and Catchim’s 2012 book. In his introduction of the APEST ministries, Breen suggests that these ascension gifts are a means of clarifying New Testament language in a way that is accessible and assessable for contemporary ministry efforts. Breen defines the APEST ministries as follows:

- The *apostle* is tasked with the overall vigor, as well as extension of Christianity as a whole, primarily through direct mission and church planting. As the name itself suggests, it is the quintessentially missional ministry, as “sentness” (Latin *mission*) is written into it (*apostello* = sent one).
- The *prophet* is called to maintain faithfulness to God among the people of God. Essentially prophets are guardians of the covenant relationship.
- The *evangelist* is the recruiter to the cause, the naturally infectious person who is able to enlist people into the movement by transmitting the gospel.
- The *shepherd* (pastor) is called to nurture spiritual development, maintain communal health, and engender loving community among the people of God.
- The *teacher* mediates wisdom and understanding. This philosophical type brings comprehensive understanding of the revelation bequeathed to the church.[12]

Breen’s efforts have proven helpful to many who are seeking better definitions for Christian purpose, but like any attempts we make to articulate God’s plans, our definitions can morph into a prison-house of Holy Spirit-sanctioned good. The conclusions in *The Permanent Revolution* echo the same circular searching-for-definition we have seen since Guder’s *Missional Church*. If, for example, a prophet is called to maintain faithfulness, or an evangelist is “the naturally infectious person,” who will more precisely define these terms to prevent the infighting that invariably will follow? If we agree to divide into roles, who will decide who fits into which, and how will we heal the wounds of those who do not fit at all?

Like many, I was raised believing that a “missionary” was someone who went on mission somewhere far away from home, sometimes for a week or two and sometimes for a lifetime. Interestingly, the people I have admired most in my life have nearly always been missionaries in the classic

11. Hirsch and Catchim, *The Permanent Revolution*, xv.
12. Hirsch and Catchim, *The Permanent Revolution*, 8.

sense: from the woman who dedicated her life to rural villages in China; to a couple who spent a lifetime serving a small village in Ethiopa, translating the Bible into the Anuak language; to parents who raised their children in both Tartarstan, Russia, and the United States; to a family who left the comforts of their home in the lower continental United States to move to a remote village near the southern tip of the Kenai Peninsula in Alaska to serve the Alutiiq people. I initially thought I admired the sacrifice of traveling far from home, risking a loss of comfort, structure, and familiarity, but I have since realized that these allowances are not the more difficult piece of the equation. While opening ourselves to physical discomfort can be admirable, the greater challenge is living a life of intentionality, humility, and complete reliance on a Creator who has far greater plans than we can ever devise. What complexities are we reinforcing when we encourage our pastors and Christian leaders to memorize Scripture, recite the confessions, and learn to manage mission-driven, orderly church systems, when really what the Great Commission is calling us to is the barest humanity that we can imagine? When the discomfort is not just physical but psychological and emotional as well, are we up to the task?

~

In the late 1980s, I spent a month living on a Dunkard Brethren mission on a Navajo reservation in north central New Mexico. The couple who were called to start the mission had lived there for thirty-some years at that point, raising their three children and then welcoming grandchildren as the mission field that was once foreign had firmly become their family's home. When we ate meals together, alternating between serving and receiving, Anglo and Navajo, there were no pretenses or spaces for hiding. If there were ideas to discuss or stories to share, we talked as we ate, sometimes laughing and sometimes debating. And if there was little news since the previous meal just a few hours prior, we ate silently, rising to help with dishes when everyone had finished.

When we went sledding together one brisk January night, I was relieved to join the women in adding trousers beneath our ankle-length skirts for protection against the frigid desert air. There was no tension among the twenty or more people who traveled to the sledding hill together, as emotional responses were handled quickly and directly until all were appeased. Instead the missionaries and the Navajo people alike had an enormous capacity for joy in the moment, and a deep-set, peace-filled confidence in their purpose on the earth. And when a friend and I were trapped in our fifteen-passenger van by an enormous guard turkey who threatened to attack each time we began to open a door, we did not think to blame the residents who owned the turkey and let him run wild, or the turkey itself for its surprising aggression, or the woman who had sent us out to hogans to take a census of the people on the reservation. Instead we laughed and tapped at our windows and wondered aloud how a turkey could possibly stretch himself taller than five feet high in order to intimidate us back into the van; instead we enjoyed the moment and left the errant details up to God. And while my blood pressure likely shot up a bit each time that turkey widened its grisly eyes and ran straight towards the van door, I so appreciated my friend's ability to be humble, transparent, bold, and joyful without even the slightest bit of pretense. We have little need to fear or defend when we believe that each next moment is the Creator's gift to us.

AN ELUSIVE GOSPEL

The fender-bender looked inconsequential to me, but it was enough to bring both drivers out into the road, arms raised and shouting. I could not hear what the woman whose car had been hit was saying, but her fists were clenched and her cheeks were flushed as she berated the other driver. The young man who had caused the accident had raised his voice to match hers, and I heard him repeat again and again as I slowly drove by, "But I have to get to work. I have to get to work." They were arguing with each other about a minor car accident from which I could see no damage to either car, and yet the heated conversation was not about the accident at all. The young man was responding from the anxiety of a job that likely paid necessary bills, and the woman was expressing her own anger and fear about whatever was going on in her life in and around that moment. Both individuals were looking directly at one another, but neither could hear or see the other with any clarity. The moment was fleeting as my line of westbound traffic inched along, but it troubled me. How often do we speak to one another with no knowledge or recognition of the other's backstory? More importantly, how often do we speak to one another with no recognition of our own backstory?

Pope Francis acknowledged this danger in a recent homily about hypocrisy: Catholics who follow their ritual observances mindfully but neglect to behave biblically in their daily lives are living a double life that is scandalous, he said. "It's better to be an atheist" than a hypocritical Christian.[13] In his book *The Bad Habits of Jesus*, Leonard Sweet challenges readers to recognize the supernatural brilliance of what others might consider Jesus'

13. Zauzmer, "Pope Francis Suggests."

"bad habits": "The religious establishment of Jesus's day were good—no, they were great. In fact, there was nobody better at keeping a list than the Pharisees were. The problem was they were so good, they thought they had it all wrapped up."[14] In what ways do we, as Christian leaders, operate from a hypocritical assumption that we, too, have it "all wrapped up," never pausing to recognize the backstories contorting the shoulders of our listeners and creating a grotesque malformation on our own? How can we speak to one another, let alone listen, when we have not yet learned to live the authentic lives that Jesus calls us to? And yet we do speak, as we have for generations since Jesus was crucified, spreading a gospel that seems elusive to us as we continually seek new and more progressive ways to spread a problematic kingdom.

BY MIGHT

The first way the Reformed Church has sought to share the gospel is by might—an ironic effort given the foundations of the Protestant Reformation. As Bruce Gordon writes in his chapter about religious life on the eve of the Reformation, the true character of Christianity in the early 1500s was confusing and deceptive: "The Church in the world, Christ's bride, was everything her contemporary advocates and critics claimed—fervent in worship, devout in prayer, rich in sacramental reverence, fearful of the afterlife, and zealous in pious works and gifts. At times, the Church was poisoned by corruption and venality in her highest offices and drained of life by indolence in her lowest."[15] And while the Reformation brought spiritual freedom from a hierarchy of Catholic doctrinal dictates and depravity, the fathers of the Reformation developed their own doctrines that birthed a new church marked with new ill-defined backstories. Martin Luther's ideas about marriage and women, for example, were decidedly demeaning and androcentric: "For example, as early as 1520 he wrote that if a woman could not have a child by her husband then she should take her husband's brother aside and contract a secret marriage with him, an idea which [Luther] repeated in his treatise on marriage in 1522."[16] The authors of *If Eve Only Knew* echo this concern when they remind readers that the Bible ultimately is a book about Christ-inspired freedom, and yet the evangelical church has done much to subjugate women who should otherwise feel unrestrained by secular rules:

14. Sweet, *The Bad Habits of Jesus*, 192.
15. Gordon, "Late Medieval Christianity," 1.
16. Roper, "Martin Luther," 64.

> The Bible is, after all, the ultimate grand story of liberation. Mixed with this journey to freedom are voices that doubt, voices that call women and men away from deeper truths, voices that tempt us to question who we are and why we are here. These messages perpetuate the false notion that women are created to be less than and subjugated to men; that their value lies in a sexuality that is controlled by men; that women are most godly when they are wives and mothers, serving their husbands and families with little consideration of their own autonomy and individual callings. But these are false assumptions that are not consistent with the biblical call of liberation.[17]

Luther and others entered the Reformation with a premise of liberation, but somewhere along the way we become distracted by the mundane quandaries that demand our wisdom and rule-declaring abilities—often to the detriment of those we most want to bless with the gospel.

According to writer Ta-Nehisi Coates, the chasm is wide. Americans too often subscribe to irreducible truths that are not truths at all but social mythologies propagated by a dominant culture: "Difference in hue and hair is old. But the belief in the preeminence of hue and hair, the notion that these factors can correctly organize a society and that they signify deeper attributes, which are indelible—this is the new idea at the heart of these new people who have been brought up hopelessly, tragically, deceitfully, to believe that they are white."[18] So if the lines of subjugation are false and Jesus came to earth in human form to tell us to stop pouring ourselves into legalisms that separate us from authentic relationships with one another, why do we continue to do what he asked us not to do? Coates's bestselling book is a letter to his teenage son, a brave tumble into social and political history that has resulted in generational chains that Coates hopes to loosen with his words: "I wanted you to have your own life, apart from fear—even apart from me. I am wounded. I am marked by old codes, which shielded me in one world and then chained me in the next."[19] If we consider the son in Coates's story, the women in Irons and Mock's book, and the man and woman whose cars collided on the neighborhood street, we see the "old codes" of both daily life and former generations that make it difficult for us to speak to one another. Despite its efforts to ensure spiritual freedom, the Reformed church reverberates with these aging chains, insistent that

17. Irons and Mock, *If Eve Only Knew*, 186.

18. Coates, *Between the World and Me*, 7.

19. Coates, *Between the World and Me*, 125.

women are more fulfilled in subservient roles and Jesus had fair skin and a radiant smile.

In *The Culture Map*, Erin Meyer describes the implicit communication in Japanese culture that demands an adept ability to gauge how a listener is receiving the words we are speaking: "Every year in Japan there is a vote for the most popular new word. A few years ago, the word of the year was 'KY.' It stands for *kuyuki yomenai*, which means 'one who cannot read the air'—in other words, a person sorely lacking the ability to read between the lines. In Japan if you can't read the air, you are not a good listener."[20] Americans are decidedly KY people, Meyer quips, and yet our notably low-context culture is marked by a highly idiomatic language that relies on metaphor and mythology, simile and story. Rather than the might of a state-sponsored church that demanded one-tenth tithes, offered priestly forgiveness, and threatened excommunication, the Reformed church has presented the gospel with the forceful might of a culture that refuses to acknowledge interpersonal nuance and a language that hinders even the most earnest attempt to speak a simple reality to one another. If we don't acknowledge the backstories of our own lives, the generations that have come before us, the culture that surrounds us, and the church that informs our faith, how do we expect to share the gospel in a way that is joyful, truthful, and genuine?

BY REASON

A second way the Reformed church has attempted to share the gospel is through reason, an approach that emerges in part from the profound economic influence of doctrinal convictions on the emergence of capitalism in the Western world. Alexandra Walsham reminds us of the reasonableness of the "Protestant work ethic" with its emphasis on "industriousness, self-discipline, and thrift," alongside "frugality, self-denial, and a dogged commitment to labour above leisure and pleasure."[21] Compared to Catholics who wore their crucifixes and rosary beads boldly and who depended on priests for sanctification, the Protestants of the seventeenth century were a curious anomaly of simple dress, high moral standards, and intellectual prowess. In his 2015 book *How We Learn*, Benedict Carey describes well our propensity for the patterns and satisfactions of reason:

> Learning scientists like embedded hierarchy problems because they model the sort of reasoning we have to do all the time, to

20. Meyer, *The Culture Map*, 33.
21. Walsham, "Reformation Legacies," 240.

> understand work politics as well as math problems. We have to remember individual relationships, which is straight retention. We have to use those to induce logical extensions: if A > B and B > C, then A must be > C. Finally, we need to incorporate those logical steps into a larger framework, to *deduce* the relationships between people or symbols that are distantly related. When successful, we build a bird's-eye view, a system to judge the relationship between any two figures in the defined universe, literary or symbolic, that's invisible to the untrained mind.[22]

As scholars and scientists have studied the brain and our capacity to learn, Christian apologists have met those developments with an increasingly complex understanding of how we understand Scripture and the supernatural power that embodies it; consider G. K. Chesterton, C. S. Lewis, Richard Swinburne, Lee Strobel, Alister McGrath, N. T. Wright, and others. But logical reasoning is not the enormity of what Jesus calls us to. As Paul reminds us in 1 Corinthians 2, without the Holy Spirit, our church-led reasoning makes little sense to the nonbeliever anyway: "This is what we speak, not in words taught us by human wisdom but in words taught by the Spirit, explaining spiritual realities with Spirit-taught words. The person without the Spirit does not accept the things that come from the Spirit of God but considers them foolishness, and cannot understand them because they are discerned only through the Spirit."[23]

Consider, for example, Dallas Willard's discussion of Nietzsche and moral goodness: "Friedrich Nietzsche is usually thought of as a bitter opponent of Jesus. But he clearly saw his indispensable role in the civilization into which Nietzsche himself had been born."[24] In other words, the impact of Jesus' teachings on the world was so profound that it redefined the philosophical axis on which we balance conversations about good, evil, truth, longing, relationships, and authenticity. Jesus was a master of using the particular—specific moments grounded in the social and cultural context of his listeners—to bring us to the universal: comprehensive moral theory that reverberates through the writings of such influential thinkers as Augustine, Aquinas, Wesley, and Bonhoeffer.[25] But when the Western Reformed church relies on reason to forward the truth of the gospel, the effect is stagnant, uninspired, and unlikely to convince a skeptic whose reality is a scaffolding of worldly logic and sometimes errant emotions. While Christian apologet-

22. Carey, *How We Learn*, 203.

23. 1 Cor 2:13–14.

24. Willard, *The Divine Conspiracy*, 131.

25. Willard, *The Divine Conspiracy*, 130.

ics has its place, particularly among nonbelievers who are seeking, rational theology cannot explain well the miracle of the Holy Spirit, as Paul suggests in 1 Corinthians 2.

BY SPECTACLE

The third way American churches attempt to entice newcomers through their doors is by spectacle: the bigger and bolder, the better. As church attendance began to wane in the United States in the tumultuous 1960s, the concept of "megachurches" emerged alongside an intensifying dependence on colorful mediums such as television:

> American businessmen discovered, long before the rest of us, that the quality and usefulness of their goods are subordinate to the artifice of their display; that, in fact, half the principles of capitalism as praised by Adam Smith or condemned by Karl Marx are irrelevant. Even the Japanese, who are said to make better cars than the Americans, know that economics is less a science than a performing art, as Toyota's yearly advertising budget confirms.[26]

When pastors join the fray in an attempt to bring forward a gospel that is culturally relevant, the result can be disastrous. Neil Postman continues in *Amusing Ourselves to Death* with a memory of watching Billy Graham exchanging quips with George Burns, the comedian who was revered in his later years for his role in the *Oh, God!* movies: "Although the Bible makes no mention of it, the Reverend Graham assured the audience that God loves those who make people laugh. It was an honest mistake," Postman continues. "He merely mistook NBC for God."[27] When we fall into the programming/entertainment trap, we assume that our ability to capture an audience's attention with colorful, comical, memorable visuals is the best way to bring new believers into the kingdom; and we forget that Jesus did none of this. In fact, his approach was quite the opposite: He visited with untouchables, he washed others' dirty toes, he asked his disciples to give up all worldly goods to become itinerant preachers, and he rode into Jerusalem on the back of an unbroken donkey.

In their book *The Permanent Revolution*, Alan Hirsch and Tim Catchim warn against the "superpastor" or "hotshot CEO type."[28] Little

26. Postman, *Amusing Ourselves to Death*, 4–5.

27. Postman, *Amusing Ourselves to Death*, 5.

28. Hirsch and Catchim, *The Permanent Revolution*, xx.

good can come of pastors who quote Scripture handily and put on an impressive show but have no theological depth. In fact, the displays that come from program-focused ministries often become the "easy straw man" that others call upon to point to the simplicity, irrelevance, and untruth of the gGospel: "At best, these writings are highly unlikely to convince the unconvinced, and at worst, they hinder the cause in the broader church."[29] Much as Postman suggests in his critique of media culture, the spectacle of a performance-driven church entices followers for precisely the wrong reasons, leaving eventual empty pews or, worse yet, the hypocritical Christians that Pope Francis bemoaned. When we rely on human agency to spread the gospel and build the church, the Holy Spirit has little room to enter in. The challenge, according to Hirsch and Catchim, lies with our willingness to risk: "We have huddled and cuddled, taught and preached, the church to near death. It's time to grow up! It's time to allow some holy chaos to enter so we can break loose from the iron cages of oligarchy and engage the missional challenge to extend the gospel in this century."[30] The goal, they continue, is "inviting disequilibrium."[31]

Hirsch continues this discussion in *The Forgotten Ways* with a push for churches to move beyond the stage and spectacle to an acknowledgement of the cultural barriers they have left unacknowledged and unaddressed. Rather than focusing on performance, we should be looking at people—as Jesus did—and pondering the most effective ways to step outside of the inherent cultural reach that is most readily apparent. The institutional church has failed notably in sharing a gospel that expresses the peace and joy Christ embodies: "[W]hen surveyed, the average non-Christian described a high degree of alienation. It seems that at present, most people report a 'God? Yes! Church? No!' type of response."[32] Later in his book, Hirsch points to the organic systems necessary to grow the church as the living system Jesus intended. If we are all irreducibly interconnected by the Holy Spirit—and the propensity for the Holy Spirit in those who are seeking or soon-to-be-tapped—how can we engage the authenticity of the Gospel with the conversations we have, the decisions we make, and the Sunday services we host? If a broader view is required of an American church that has become overly insular in its efforts to open its doors wide and entice people inside with colors and fancy words, what will it mean to reimagine a Reformed church that is motivated by mission and loving in character?

29. Hirsch and Catchim, *The Permanent Revolution*, xx.

30. Hirsch and Catchim, *The Permanent Revolution*, 271.

31. Hirsch and Catchim, *The Permanent Revolution*, 271.

32. Hirsch, *The Forgotten Ways*, 34.

BY ALLURE

Inspired by Hirsch's ideas, the fourth way the Reformed church has sought to spread the kingdom is by the allure of Jesus' sage and loving example. According to Alan Roxburgh and M. Scott Boren in their book *Introducing the Missional Church*, the missional church seeks to turn on its head the approach that has informed church practices for generations: The approach should not be a church that seeks a mission but instead a church that seeks to recognize that God is a missional God who sends his people: "Rather than the primary question being, 'How do we attract people to what we are doing?' it becomes, 'What is God up to in this neighborhood?' and 'What are the ways we need to change in order to engage the people in our community who no longer consider church a part of their lives?' That is what a missional imagination is about."[33] Roxburgh echoes this call to community in his book *Missional: Joining God in the Neighborhood*, coupling the call with a sense of twenty-first-century impending doom:

> This book articulates what might be involved in rethinking Christian life in an unthinkable world. It comes out of my own wrestling with questions about what God might be about in our neighborhoods, cities, towns, and villages. It seems to address questions about how we can faithfully engage during a time when so many of our churches have lost their capacity to engage the people in their communities.[34]

The point is to stop focusing our planning on the church, Roxburgh argues, and instead focus our discussions on the people in our surrounding communities: Who are they? What are their needs? What are their hurts, aspirations, ponderings, longings, and relationships? What has their experience with the church been, and how might a new kind of church speak into their lives?

In *Missional Church*, Darrell Guder affirms our need for both a new approach and a new image: "The calling of the church to be missional—to be a sent community—leads the church to step beyond the given cultural forms that vary dubious assumptions about what the church is, what its public role should be, and what its voice should sound like." The missional church movement is grounded not in recruitment inward but sending outward, Guder argues; it is in the going that we will find Holy Spirit-led moments to share the promises of the kingdom.[35] In *The Missional Church Perspective*,

33. Roxburgh and Boren, *Introducing the Missional Church*, 20.

34. Roxburgh, *Missional*, 16.

35. Guder, ed., *Missional Church*, 109.

Craig Van Gelder and Dwight J. Zscheile suggest that a missional approach will help us to redefine our most basic idea of who God is: "Relational trinitarian theology gives us a vision that makes space for others to participate."[36] But is this shift to a missional-minded, community-focused church enough to spread the gospel in a Jesus-honoring way? If we enter into the communities around us to share the allure, will the kingdom spread?

J. Todd Billings argues that the "incarnational ministry" arm of missiology can be as dangerously misleading as the façade of might, reason, or spectacle:

> I was told that just as God became flesh in a particular culture 2,000 years ago, my job was to become "incarnate" in another culture. Eight months later, equipped with training in cultural anthropology, I set about learning the language and culture in Uganda. But I quickly ran into doubts about the "incarnational" method. Would the Ugandans necessarily "see Jesus" as a result of my efforts at cultural identification? Was I assuming that my own presence—rather than that of Christ—was redemptive? Is the eternal Word's act of incarnation really an appropriate model for ministry?[37]

Donald Miller writes at length about the danger of the allure in his book *A Million Miles in a Thousand Years*. In a chapter titled "The Reason God Hasn't Fixed You Yet," Miller reminds us that God never intended to bring everything here on earth to perfection;[38] that kind of other-worldly peace and joy will come in heaven one day, and it can be dangerous when we send our church missionally out to extend promises that ultimately could smack of hypocrisy and deception in a way that mimics the state-run church that inspired the Reformation.

STAGNANT WATERS

As we continually look outward, seeking the approach that will make our work most effective and meaningful, most in line with the Great Commission of Matthew 28, is it possible that we are neglecting the essence of our salvation? If the aforementioned solutions are not spreading the gospel in a way that is lasting and true, what should we be doing differently? The answer, I believe, is simple: It lies in our ability to look at ourselves with

36. Van Gelder and Zscheile, *The Missional Church in Perspective*, 109.
37. Billings, "The Problem with 'Incarnational Ministry.'"
38. Miller, *A Million Miles*, 203.

honesty and humility, acknowledging our own backstories before we begin to speak into the lives of those around us. The gospel is a story of atonement, N. T. Wright reminds us in *The Day the Revolution Began*, and it is up to each of us to embrace our faith wholly and unabashedly:

> We have gone wading in the shallow and stagnant waters of medieval questions and answers, taking care to put on the right footwear and not lose our balance, when only a few yards away is the vast and dangerous ocean of the gospel story, inviting us to plunge in and let the wild waves of dark glory wash us, wash over us, wash us through and through, and land us on the shores of God's new creation.[39]

In Matthew 7:5, Jesus tells us to check our own eye for blemishes before we look to pluck the excess out of someone else's. Unlike us, Jesus had an unmatched IQ, an impeccable EQ, and a keen sense of AQ. Perhaps it would behoove us to follow his example more closely, seeking to improve our EQ before we step out into the world and assume that others will have the inclination and fortitude to listen.

CONSIDERING THE PARADOX

In his 2010 book *Nudge,* Leonard Sweet argues for a new kind of missional church:

> The church has been more prone to "take a stand" on issues or "take a vote" on programs than touch. Touch is a centripetal force that includes and embraces. Taking stands is a centrifugal force that separates and divides. While the rest of the world is moving, the one taking a stand is frozen in time like kids playing freeze tag, waiting for the sign that says it's okay to move again. Christ ran around touching people and tagging them. Every Jesus tag offered freedom. Every Jesus tag let the person tagged know they had been touched by God.[40]

The Pharisees operated by centrifugal force; Jesus perpetuates a centripetal force. As a church, we know this, and yet our efforts to stand for truth in the twenty-first century invariably repel rather than attract. According to Dan Kimball, we are at a point where we need to offer both an apology and an apologetic: "While we need to stand strong on what we believe and need not be ashamed of the gospel in any way, we need to make sure we are

39. Wright, *The Day the Revolution Began*, 416.

40. Sweet, *Nudge*, 242.

presenting a biblical picture of the church and not perpetuating negative stereotypes. We need to offer an apologetic to correct misperceptions."[41]

In 1989, I toured the Portland, Oregon Mormon Temple before it was formally dedicated and closed to non-Mormons. The Temple sits on seven acres in Lake Oswego with six spires rising from a marble exterior and green slate roof with a gold-leafed statue of the angel Moroni on top of the 170-foot eastern spire. To enter through the south doors, we pulled paper slippers on over our shoes and were asked not to touch anything as we were guided through the hallways of the nearly 80,000-square-foot interior. We wandered through room after room of dramatic white marble, chandeliers, full-wall tapestries, and gold statues. Our guide told us that once the building was dedicated and operational, not only would non-Mormons be forbidden entry, but only Mormons of particular stature according to age, gender, and accomplishments would be permitted to step into many of the rooms of the temple.

It was difficult not to emerge weighted by both the exorbitant cost and the focus on exclusive works-based admission. I drove away relieved to not be entrapped by the assumptions, dictates, and prophecies of a belief system that did not align with biblical truths. Yet was my relief any different from a nonbeliever who has engaged with a Christian? Perhaps the most challenging paradox we face is the biblical call to both share the gospel and extend love that surpasses the language we use to describe who Jesus was. Do we tell the story? Do we love our neighbor and our enemy? Do we know how to do all of this at once without self-consciousness or personal baggage or erroneous assumptions about the people we encounter? Do we know how to live in the psychological and emotional discomfort of Christianity's paradox?

As Sweet argues in *Me and We,* the world's structural problems will remain as long as the individual human heart is ailing: "The [social gospel] movement's demise has been the subject of vast speculation and scrutiny, but it can be seen perhaps best this way: social gospelers tried to save an ailing turtle by switching out its shell, one embossed with the name 'Christianity.'"[42] The missional movement is in danger of a similar end. If we don't pause in our discussion of the core ideas of missiology to consider how individual hearts can be strengthened and encouraged, missional ideas will never rise from rhetoric to reality. According to Gillian Tett, understanding the "messy gaps between rhetoric and reality" is critical: "Life does not always fit into the official descriptions of what people are *supposed* to do.

41. Kimball, *They Like Jesus*, 250.

42. Sweet, *Me and We*, 3.

Much of the time we ignore these messy realities."[43] How, then, do we ensure that our discussion of missional church adequately prepares, equips, and strengthens the hearts of those who are sent to disciple? Are we embarking on missions—both around the globe and across the street—without properly training disciples? Peter Scazzero writes that a healthy understanding of self is essential: "The vast majority of us go to our graves without knowing who we are. We unconsciously live someone else's life, or at least someone else's expectations for us. This does violence to ourselves, our relationship with God, and ultimately others."[44] In an effort to extend the missional conversation and keep the movement alive, an examination of individual EQ and AQ is an essential next step.

43. Tett, *The Silo Effect*, 224.

44. Scazzero, *Emotionally Healthy Spirituality*, 66.

Chapter 3

The Jesus Problem

"Do you believe in God?" Tom Hanks asks Meg Ryan's character Patricia in the 1990 cult classic *Joe Versus the Volcano*. Joe Banks and Patricia Graynamore are floating on a private luxury yacht in the South Pacific, reclining alone under the stars and pondering the purpose of life.

"I believe in myself," Patricia answers.

"What does that mean?" Joe asks.

She smiles. "I have confidence in myself."

Joe nods. "I have been doing some soul searching lately, been asking myself some pretty tough questions. And do you know what I found out?" he asks. Patricia smiles and shakes her head. "I have no interest in myself," Joe says. "I start thinking about myself, and I get bored out of my mind."

Patricia laughs. "Well, what *does* interest you?"

"I don't know," Joe says, pondering. And then, with a look of surprise, he realizes his answer: "Courage," he says firmly. "Courage interests me."[1]

As the picturesque ocean scene swells into chaos, sinking the yacht and leaving the two afloat under the hot sun on four steamer trunks, Joe's interest in courage becomes an uncompromising obsession. He had demonstrated little courage in his years working in a dreary factory on Staten Island, and now that he has tapped into it, courage becomes the purpose that drives every decision he makes. As per Patricia's self-confidence, she later bemoans a life lived not by her own choices but by the promises and bribes of her father; the self-confidence she proclaimed so quickly is clearly a farce.

But together the two are seeking, and together they discover an initial awareness that is such a critical part of the journey: "My father says that almost the whole world is asleep—everybody you know, everybody you see, everybody you talk to," Patricia tells Joe as they float beneath the stars. "He says that only a few people are awake, and they live in a state of constant total amazement."[2] The edginess of this curious, Beckettesque film demands that we wake up to the oddities, the pressing questions, and the curious humor of a life lived with intentionality rather than in a daze.

As we have moved into the twenty-first century and technology has allowed us to communicate with and observe one another in ways that we never imagined possible, is it possible that our most jarring realization is that we have been asked to wake up? For generations, cultural facades have answered for us the questions that we naturally ask as we mature and encounter life: Why am I here? What is my purpose? What is my place? Who are my people? What do I have to offer the world? Am I worthy? When we bolt our front doors closed each evening, settling into concentric circles of sometimes erroneous understanding, assuming the answers that we have been taught are the only recourse—or choosing to battle those answers with our reputations, our strength, our lives—we can be lulled to sleep by the *no's* that knock down our dreams and hold us captive to daily necessities.

When the internet began to crash through the walls of our homes in the 1990s, opening our lives in ways that both excited and terrified us, we were asked to awaken to the realities of the world and of the choices we make. But the sleepy lull is instinctive and, in many ways, easier, which means many of us have not yet realized that we are called to wake up to purpose and moment-by-moment intentionality. Instead we cling to our defensiveness and excuses, walking through our days in a state of anxiety as

1. *Joe Versus the Volcano.*
2. *Joe Versus the Volcano.*

we scroll through social media feeds and wonder why the reality around us does not match the filtered photos and pithy memes.

When we seek the disconnect, we find it is easiest to blame: the internet, the younger generation, the older generation, the people close to us, our circumstances. Life has been gamified by the technology explosion of the past two decades, and we are increasingly more surprised that the joysticks we hold don't have the same results on the world around us that they do when we manipulate the world in Minecraft, Super Mario Bros., Candy Crush Saga, Facebook, or Snapchat. Our answer is to wake up, and waking up means that we will need to make decisions we may not want to face and stand up in situations that demand our voice. When we sleep, our body relaxes into trusting comfort; when we awaken, we are opening ourselves to the extremes of comfort, discomfort, and any realm of possibilities in between.

At just before 4 a.m. on New Year's Day morning, 2018, a teenager died from a self-inflicted gunshot wound after inadvertently shooting himself in the head during a game of Russian roulette. According to a local police captain, the teenager had brought the .357 double-action revolver to a friend's home and, although there were other people present at the time, he was the only one playing the game: "At some point, he took it out and began to play—as we know it—Russian roulette. Spinning the cylinder of the gun and placing it to his head. He did this all on his own accord, and there were no other people who were involved with the incident as far as that goes. One of the rounds did fire, which killed him."[3]

As startling as the tragedy itself were the Facebook posts that followed: "Where were the parents in this?" some community members accused. "Way to start the New Year with a bang!" one man wrote, and his comment was tagged with smiling, laughing, and thumbs-up emojis multiple times. Not only had life become a game for this teenager, whose brain was hardly developed enough to conceptualize the enormity of the game he had chosen to play, but life is a game for the observers as well. Most would never have the gumption to approach the grieving family of this poor young man, let alone accuse, ridicule, or degrade them. Where is the courage in a culture that is waking up to a surprising reality of the enormity of life? Where is the intentionality, morality, compassion, and grace? If our remarkable ability to see, hear, and engage with one another is informing our culture in groundbreaking ways, how can the church enter in rather than step away?

Our American culture has been curiously obsessed with *self* since the social revolution of the 1960s, and the introduction of the internet in

3. Heye, "Police."

the 1980s and 1990s has intensified that fascination. As we consider the trends and ramifications of self-help, self-awareness, self-image, and self-actualization, it is important to recognize that fear and shame often lurk in the shadows of a search for self, threatening to overwhelm and encouraging the seeker to simply go back to sleep. How can we call for courage, as Joe Banks suggests, and enter in with the humility, passion, and purpose of missionaries?

SELF-HELP

If we critically consider how *self* has become a linchpin of twenty-first-century American culture, we must begin with the generations-old genre of self-help books. I remember visiting bookstores as a child and eyeing the shelves titled "self-help" with a mixture of curiosity and trepidation—much like an inadvertent encounter with *People Magazine* or *Cosmopolitan* in the dentist's office. The section was clearly marked, and the books that lined those shelves addressed issues of personal insecurity, financial struggle, parenting quandaries, leadership issues, and so on. Classics such as Dale Carnegie's *How to Win Friends and Influence People*, Harold Kushner's *When Bad Things Happen to Good People*, and John Gray's *Men Are from Mars, Women Are from Venus* helped to edge the self-help genre into an increasingly more widespread market, and today publishers identify categories such as "willpower," "vulnerability," "psychology," or "business" rather than "self-help." As Boris Kachka writes in "The Power of Positive Publishing," self-help snake oil is no longer contained on those singular eclectic shelves where it once rested.

> Today, every section of the store (or web page) overflows with instructions, anecdotes, and homilies. History books teach us how to lead, neuroscience how to use our amygdalas, and memoirs how to eat, pray, and love. The former CEO of CNN writes the biography of an ornery tech visionary and it becomes a best seller on the strength of its leadership lessons. The Nobel-laureate psychologist Daniel Kahneman writes a subtle analysis of our decision-making process and soon finds his best seller digested and summarized in MBA seminars across the country. Philosophical essayist Alain de Botton launches a series of self-help books called "The School of Life," whose titles will begin with "how to." Even before books are written, their advances are often predicated on strong "takeaways" targeted to proven demographics. More like a virus than MacDonald's frogs, self-help

> has infiltrated and commandeered other fields in its drive to reproduce.[4]

From a biblical standpoint, the self-help genre is dangerously unmoored. Much like New Age mysticism or eclecticism, self-help aids and abets as the feel-right winds will blow, laying out steps for accomplishment that are not too painful and not too compliant. In other words, if it feels right, it is right, and if it feels wrong, it either means that more self-correction is necessary, or it is wrong. The slippery rationale is enough to make most educated people shudder, and yet the self-help trend pulls in billions of dollars as an industry each year. The market demand is explosive, and it feeds on people's weaknesses. Agree or disagree, the cultural grounding is clear.

What concerns me the most about the self-help industry is that it tends to engender self-congratulatory back-pats rather than forward movement, an unfounded sense of accomplishment rather than actual production. Much like someone who feels as if she or he has accomplished a task merely by announcing the need to do it, not by actually doing it, these books fill readers' minds with a sense that they have accomplished something new and unique when in actuality they have done little more than indulge themselves in some light and mostly forgettable reading. But the desire for light and forgettable is unmistakable. Rhonda Byrne has grossed hundreds of millions with her bestselling *The Secret* book series. The crux of her philosophy is that positive thinking will help us to achieve our goals. Deepak Chopra also makes millions each year with his books, teas, herbal supplements, lotions, shampoos, and other products; his theories emphasize the importance of listening to our hearts and taking responsibility for our actions. Stephen Covey sold millions after publishing *The 7 Habits of Highly Effective People,* and his books outlines a series of progressive habits that are built on what he calls "The Character Ethic," which attempts to ground our decision-making in a universal ethical standard. Many have suggested that *The 7 Habits* is a secular interpretation of Mormon principles. Interestingly, Covey studied American self-help books in his doctoral work at Brigham Young University, although I suspect his studies helped him to enter more fully into the industry rather than rise above it.

In *The 7 Habits of Highly Effective Teens*, Sean Covey, one of Stephen Covey's eight children, argues from a progression that moves from "The Set-Up" to "The Private Victory" to "The Public Victory" to "Renewal," and the seven habits he outlines are:

(1) Be proactive.

4. Kachka, "The Power of Positive Publishing."

(2) Begin with the end in mind.

(3) Put first things first.

(4) Think win-win.

(5) Seek first to understand, then to be understood.

(6) Synergize.

(7) Sharpen the saw.[5]

Throughout the book, Covey offers anecdotes, illustrations, checklists, and encouragement, and the reader likely will feel affirmed and encouraged in the process of reading. But the book—like most self-help books—does not encourage the reader to dig deeply into the who, what, where, and why of *self*. The book does not ask the reader to look closely in the mirror, and not just any mirror but a high-powered magnifying mirror, to see and begin to acknowledge what is reflected in the glass. The book does not challenge the reader to understand the reflected image first without hesitation, shame, anger, or hurt, and then learn to articulate what is there so that others might learn from his or her experiences. In other words, the book does not ask the reader to dig deeply, which typically suggests that the meaning, in time, will be lost. While the self-help industry may be explosive and culturally all-consuming, it has not challenged us to step much beyond a simple acknowledgement of the word *self*.

SELF-AWARENESS

The first step is an awareness of self. If I exist as an individual who is unique from the other brains around me, from the landscape that surrounds me, and from the context where I find myself, how do I understand that differentiation? Do I measure myself by defining and judging what lies around me, and assuming that I am the norm around which all else revolves, rather than beginning by defining myself? There is a narcissism that underlies a lack of self-awareness, as those individuals would rather see the rest of the world take the time to understand and describe them than vice versa. Self-awareness also can be muddied by past hurts and abuse, loss, insecurity, anger, or sorrow. Many people become increasingly more self-aware in their late teens and early twenties as they begin to interact with the world as adults, making decisions and setting personal boundaries. When these changes come with foresight and intentionality, self-awareness can be healthy; when

5. Covey, *The 7 Habits of Highly Effective Teens*.

these changes come by happenstance or situation, an individual may not develop a sense of self-awareness at all.

According to British organizational psychologist Adrian Furnham, self-awareness is "the accurate appraisal and understanding of your abilities and preferences and their implications for your behavior and their impact on others."[6] While some may begin with the "accurate appraisal and understanding of your abilities and preferences" and feel rather self-satisfied about their level of self-awareness, the greater challenge comes at the end of the definition: "and their implications for your behavior and their impact on others." Furnham tucks two key points in here: both the implications for our own behavior and the implications for the kind of impact we will have on those around us. Without a deep-set understanding of self at this level, most behavior becomes reactionary and sleepy rather than intentional and wide awake. Self-aware individuals are "more resilient, more realistic, and for others more predictable."[7]

In an article for the *Harvard Business Review*, writer Anthony Tjan writes that strong leadership is impossible without an astute sense of self: "You can't be a good leader without self-awareness. It lies at the root of strong character, giving us the ability to lead with a sense of purpose, authenticity, openness, and trust."[8] Unfortunately, the sheer expanse of the internet and the speed with which we must react in order to appear efficient have eroded self-awareness in our twenty-first-century American culture. When we cannot take the time to reflect on our own needs or ponder purpose or make creative mistakes, we lose the sense of ourselves amidst the monolith. How do I remember to distinguish myself when I am always plugged into the larger mass, always responding and always present? Where do I make space for solitude, for rabbit trails of thought, for healthy failures?

When I asked my university students recently to set aside fifteen minutes in their week for boredom as the week's homework assignment, some were excited and embraced the activity, and others were decidedly flummoxed. Regardless of their individual reactions, their responses were thoughtful and interestingly indicative of a culture struggling to incorporate technology in a comfortable, productive way:

- **Student 1**: For my fifteen minutes of solitude, I took a bath. After about five minutes, I reached for the book I brought with me and read the book jacket. After I read the book jacket, I checked the clock and realized I still had several minutes to go. I wanted to spend this time

6. Furnham, "Self Awareness."
7. Furnham, "Self Awareness."
8. Tjan, "5 Ways to Become More Self-Aware."

truly distraction-free, so I put the book down. At first, I spent my time thinking about how I was going to fill my time. I checked the time a lot, and I started to panic when I saw that I had seven whole minutes left. So I downed my Moscato and poured myself another glass. I started reading the back of the shampoo bottle, and then the conditioner. I thought about what my dog might be doing, and then I heard her snoring. By the time the fifteen minutes were up, I was completely over the bath. Usually when I take a bath, I either read or watch TV. Baths are pretty relaxing for me, and I go to the tub to unwind. This experience was anything but relaxing.

- **Student 2**: I often spend time in prayer, meditation, and yoga several times a week. During those times, I put away electronics and practice clearing my mind. For purposes of this exercise, I wanted to challenge myself a bit more. I left home without my phone and walked to a nearby park. Once there, I found a bench close to the river and sat quietly. Not having my phone was daring for me and produced an initial sense of nervousness. I took me a little longer to let go of restless thoughts, but once there, I felt a sense of openness that allowed me to receive. For that moment in time, I could let go of expectations and enjoy the beauty of nature. It was different than some sort of prayer or meditation time because I gave myself permission to let go and feel the moment without expectations. My electronics were not an option, and I wasn't anticipating future needs but was present in the moment. It felt fabulous.
- **Student 3**: I personally think of myself as someone who will wait in the ridiculous drive-up line for a single cup of coffee. But this day, I went inside Starbucks to order. After I had ordered my coffee, I waited eagerly for my coffee like everyone else, but this time was different. As I waited, I purposely left my phone in my car so I wouldn't be tempted to scroll through my feed, and the most miraculous thing happened. This middle-aged woman (also not looking through her phone like everyone else we were standing with) asked me how my morning was and what I had planned for the day. I responded with a quick overview of my work day and then politely asked her for her agenda for the day. We were in the same line of work, but she was working with a temp agency. Before either of us received our morning coffee, a gentleman approached her asking if she was looking for a full-time position with her line of work. Seriously so astonishingly mind blowing. If I had chosen to be on my phone during this time period, she would not have expressed her temp work with anyone surrounding us, this gentleman

would not have overhead our in-person conversation, and she would not have been offered a full-time position.

- **Student 4:** I spent thirty minutes taking my dog for a walk though my neighborhood. I put my phone away, but my brain seemed to be stuck in overdrive. My thoughts were scattered and racing. I wondered if this was a side effect of my constant technology usage throughout the day. I couldn't stop thinking about school assignments that were due, issues that I'm facing at work, what I want to accomplish in the future, recent news stories, and a plethora of other things. I couldn't help but think it was no wonder that people use social media as a distraction. I felt anxious at times like I needed to hurry up and get back so that I could get things done. However, by the end of the walk, my mind started to clear up a little—not completely, but noticeably. I plan on continuing to examine this as I go for walks. By actively noticing the way my thoughts were scattered and chaotic, I was able to wrangle them in a bit. I may be able to use this as a tool to relieve anxiety and meaningfully disconnect for a bit each day.
- **Student 5:** What I found when trying to make myself sit still and listen for fifteen minutes is that it's incredibly hard. Unless I'm thinking about going to bed and giving myself a focused you're-going-to-sleep-now pep talk, it's hard not to reach for my phone, my computer, my iPad, my video games, or any number of the other items that are sitting around me. I think I am going to work on incorporating this more into my morning routine because almost one of the first things I do when I wake up is to start checking email (which usually is just deleting junk emails first thing in the morning). Maybe I can give myself a few minutes to sit, think, plan, and contemplate before I jump in to what the rest of the world wants to place on my plate.

In an era when the world appears to be demanding more and more of each of us each day, it is difficult to remember who we are. While the twenty-first century is marked by a decided search for self, self-awareness is disappearing into a demanding swirl of Snapchat streaks, Instagram likes, and Facebook emojis. How can we ensure self-awareness among the leaders and twenty-first-century missionaries in our churches?

SELF-IMAGE

While self-awareness can provide a first glimpse beneath the surface of differentiation from the world that surrounds us, self-image moves a step closer to careful introspection. Thirty years ago, self-image was an autological phrase: We carried an *image* of how we perceived our *self* in the world. In the twenty-first century, on the other hand, self-image is frequently defined in one of two ways: (1) by the self in a false, idealistic manner or (2) by the friends, family, and strangers who surround the self. In other words, even if an individual has an astute sense of self-awareness, his or her self-image could be tattered by the internet waltz that can carry us within seconds from alarming news story to self-affirmation to odd pet photos. According to a survey reported in CNN by Common Sense Media, many teens who are active on social media worry daily about how their image is received:

- 35 percent are worried about people tagging them in unattractive photos.
- 27 percent feel stressed about how they look in posted photos.
- 22 percent felt badly about themselves if their photos were ignored.[9]

A 2013 Microsoft Research study suggests that seasonal patterns of depression in high-income nations such as the United States correlate directly with a crowd-sourcing social media index that tracks social activity, emotion, and language on Twitter. More than 27 million Americans suffer from depression, and more than 30,000 suicides in the United States each year are directly associated with a depression disability; in the twenty first century, the World Health Organization began ranking major depression as "one of the most burdensome diseases in the world."[10] Because of the study, its authors and others are working to develop individualized predictive models that are able to analyze a person's social media feeds in order to provide early warnings of potential issues of depression or other disorders.[11]

Paradoxically, the images and videos that go viral are often those that expose something more richly human than perfection—a celebrity's error or an ordinary person's struggle. Consider the self-deprecating Twitter video posted by University of Texas student Ann Mark in December 2017. In the video, Mark is walking across UT's vast campus, describing her experience with her first final exam as a college freshman:

> Mark tells viewers that she showed up to her exam room without a "blue book," a thin journal of notebook paper used primarily for essays. After acquiring two blue books, she admits she hasn't been to class in nearly a month and realized she was

9. Knorr, "How Girls Use Social Media."
10. De Choudhury et al., "Social Media as a Measurement Tool."
11. De Choudhury et al., "Social Media as a Measurement Tool."

> in the wrong test room. After thinking she found the correct room, she's told her exam is in another building that shares the same name as one of the auditoriums on campus. She managed to make it to her exam for World Cinema History and wrote an essay about the film *Napoleon Dynamite*.[12]

Within just two days, the video went viral on Twitter, with more than 100,000 retweets and 300,000 likes. UT-Austin President Gregory L. Fenves even responded to Mark with a Tweet, offering to buy her four years' worth of blue books. Other community members posted words of gratitude for Mark's transparency and encouragement for her journey.[13] Several days later, the video went viral on Instagram as well. For Mark, the video was a means of venting her frustration in a way that affirmed her experience, excused her errors, and helped her to move forward. Depending on her own level of self-awareness, Mark may have considered the experience an affirmation of her poor preparation as a student or an opportunity to move forward into a higher level of excellence.

From a biblical standpoint, God assures as again and again throughout Scripture that we are esteemed and worthy:

- **Joshua 1:9**: "Have I not commanded you? Be strong and courageous. Do not be afraid; do not be discouraged, for the Lord your God will be with you wherever you go."
- **Isaiah 41:10**: "So do not fear, for I am with you; do not be dismayed, for I am your God. I will strengthen you and help you; I will uphold you with my righteous right hand."
- **Jeremiah 29:11**: "'For I know the plans I have for you,' declares the Lord, 'plans to prosper you and not to harm you, plans to give you hope and a future.'"
- **Matthew 10:31:** "So don't be afraid; you are worth more than many sparrows."
- **Luke 12:7:** "Indeed, the very hairs of your head are all numbered. Don't be afraid; you are worth more than many sparrows."
- **2 Corinthians 5:17:** "Therefore, if anyone is in Christ, the new creation has come: The old has gone, the new is here!"
- **Ephesians 1:4:** "For he chose us in him before the creation of the world to be holy and blameless in his sight."

12. Molina, "If You've Ever Taken a College Final."
13. Molina, "If You've Ever Taken a College Final."

- **Hebrews 10:35:** "So do not throw away your confidence; it will be richly rewarded."
- **1 Peter 2:9:** "But you are a chosen people, a royal priesthood, a holy nation, God's special possession, that you may declare the praises of him who called you out of darkness into his wonderful light."
- **1 John 4:4:** "You, dear children, are from God and have overcome them, because the one who is in you is greater than the one who is in the world."

If we are missionaries to our family, friends, neighbors, and strangers, how can we carry this level of Scriptural peace and confidence into an internet world that both affirms and destroys, encourages and dissuades?

The twenty-first century has introduced a new level of fleeting but permanent nuance that makes it exceedingly difficult to discern our own worth beneath the online identity we are obliged to create and the assumptions about us that others encourage. Is the answer to insist that people unplug and recenter themselves, or is the answer to step more fully into the internet milieu in order to bring levity or clarity? Likely both.

SELF-ACTUALIZATION

The fourth and final *self* in our consideration of the uniquely twenty-first-century search for self is self-actualization, which is the admirable goal of bringing a healthy self-awareness and a healthy self-image to bear in the world. Self-actualization is the fulfillment of an individual's potential, or—in biblical terms—the ability to step fully and mindfully into God's plan. Many of us would prefer to bypass the difficult work of self-awareness and self-image and move directly into self-actualization, jumping into the spotlight without the hard work behind the scenes or accepting the promotion without working our way diligently up through the ranks. But shortcuts rarely lead to success. The most admirable individuals and leaders are those who have fought to earn their place, lifting others along the way and earning the trust, respect, and appreciation of their peers. Abraham Maslow's hierarchy of needs points the individual from (1) basic needs such as food, water, and shelter, to (2) psychological needs such as belonging and a sense of accomplishment, to (3) self-actualization, which he defines as achieving one's full potential. According to Steven Joseph, Maslow identified the first two levels as deficit-filling, which means each defines a state in which an individual is lacking or seeking something.[14] The final level, self-actualization, is not about a lack but a natural pre-wiring that allows us to rest comfortably in this default state. According to Maslow, the self-actualization level allows us to be the following:

- efficient in how we perceive reality
- accepting of ourselves and of other people
- able to form deep relationships
- appreciative of life
- guided by our own inner goals and values
- able to express emotions freely and clearly[15]

What if we moved ahead in our twenty-first-century internet-infused culture with the Maslowian assumption that we are each hard-wired for self-actualization? What if the default belief in our churches, schools, workplaces, and communities was that each of us is not only fully capable of self-actualization but that is our presumed end result? What if we acknowledge those who are still struggling with self-awareness and self-image, and we offer them tools and guidance to move beyond their own sticking points?

Consider the complexity of the Logan Paul "Suicide Forest" scandal, which pushed social media to a heightened level at the close of 2017. Paul, an American YouTube vlogger and actor, filmed a third part to his "Tokyo Adventures" in Aokigahara, a forest on the slopes of Japan's Mt. Fuji known as "suicide forest" for the hundreds of people who have tried to take their own lives there. While hiking into the forest with his entourage, Paul encountered the body of a suicide victim hanging from a tree. He continued filming, wearing a green googly-eyed hat and later posting close-ups of the victim's body with the face blurred out. "This is not clickbait," Paul said in an introduction to his video. "This is the most real vlog I've every posted to this channel."[16] Paul's disrespect for the victim, the victim's family, and the gravity of the situation smacks of a gamified life and a deep lack of self-awareness. "Yo, are you alive?" Paul calls out to the victim, then draws closer. "His hands are purple. He did this this morning," he says to his viewers.[17] Members of Paul's crew joined him in their astounding inability

14. Joseph, "What is Self-Actualization?"
15. Joseph, "What is Self-Actualization?"
16. Matsakis, "The Logan Paul Video."
17. Matsakis, "The Logan Paul Video."

to grasp the gravity of the situation; one friend posted his own video titled "WE FOUND A DEAD BODY!!!"

In only twenty-four hours after it was loaded, Paul's "suicide forest" video had already hit 6.5 million views on YouTube; soon after, Paul himself voluntarily removed the video. Reaction on Twitter was quick and pointed, denouncing Paul for his insensitivity and calling for a boycott.[18] Louis Matsakis from *Wired* and other writers asked YouTube to bear some responsibility for encouraging young vloggers to overstep social boundaries: "YouTube takes 45 percent of the advertising money generated via Paul and every other creator's videos," Matsakis writes. "According to SocialBlade, an analytics company that tracks the estimated revenue of YouTube channels, Paul could make as much as 14 million dollars per year. While YouTube might not explicitly encourage Paul to pull ever-more insane stunts, it stands to benefit financially when he and creators like him gain millions of views off of outlandish episodes."[19]

Paul's individual understanding of self-awareness, self-image, and self-actualization is youthful and egregiously limited, suggesting someone who likely bypassed much of the first two levels on his way to the third. As Maslow himself suggests, the first two levels represent a search for something that is missing, and those who neglect to fulfill what is missing will continue to experience the lack even as they move on to other things. While Paul's apology video is heartfelt and sincere, the vlogger's ability to conceptualize his own error is limited to an understanding of the immediate situation rather than the broader scope of a cultural swing or a deeper moral dilemma. And Paul is far from alone. As we seek to engage with the world with a twenty-first-century sensibility that acknowledges the complexity of a new digitized, gamified landscape, how will we train pastors, leaders, and educators to encounter our American culture with the empathy, compassion, wisdom, and purpose of a new kind of missional church?

THE JESUS PROBLEM

If we are to step forward as a missional church, mindful and unshakeable in our knowledge that (1) we, too, have been anointed by the Lord, (2) our purpose is to share the good news, and (3) we have come to free the oppressed and offer sight to the blind, how will we equip leaders to first locate and then maintain this kind of Jesus-inspired steadfast confidence? For more than a century, our understanding of human intelligence has been

18. Matsakis, "The Logan Paul Video."

19. Matsakis, "The Logan Paul Video."

misled by our inability to articulate well an individual's capacity to function within emotional constructs—even though the Bible clearly acknowledges that God created us as emotional, relational beings. Since the 1990s, we have begun to see studies emerge that examine an individual's emotional quotient (EQ) rather than IQ in assessing potential job performance success. As we consider Jesus' reading in the synagogue in Nazareth in Luke 4, how might we use EQ assessment strategies to help guide missional leaders and disciples into the God-given confidence that Jesus embodies?

As Andrew Farley writes in *The Naked Gospel*, Christianity today is seen as a cancer as often as it is seen as a crutch. "Many non-Christians whom I know have purposely opted not to contract the Christian disease," Farley writes. "Outsiders are growing wise to the fact that many Christians are dissatisfied with their church or their personal relationship with God. Their faith just isn't working for them anymore as they can't seem to maintain their end of the 'bargain' with God."[20] But what if the works-motivated "bargain" were eclipsed by emotional intelligence, purpose, and confidence?

As he moves into his ministry, Jesus offers us a supernatural example of perfect EQ. When confronted with a crisis, he does not ponder his own personal motivations, childhood scarring, long-held resentments, or misled assumptions. He does not tamp down his emotions with guilt or shame, trying to be something he is not. He does not question whether he is good enough, whether his purpose is clear enough, whether he will appear to his audience as precisely as he hopes to appear. Jesus is unfailingly focused on his Spirit-anointment, his good news, and his purpose. In addition to his flawless example of what EQ should be, Jesus demonstrates a remarkable Holy Spirit-guided sense of his audience.

This third quotient is best described as an "audience quotient" (fro IQ to EQ to AQ), and in Jesus we see it exemplified perfectly. When the men lower the paralytic on a mat through the roof tiles, Jesus' response is focused wholly on the men themselves: "When Jesus saw their faith, he said, 'Friend, your sins are forgiven.'"[21] When Jesus sees Matthew at his tax booth, he does not ponder what those around him will think or whether Matthew will receive his words; instead, Jesus focuses his attention on Matthew and offers exactly what his disciple-to-be needs to hear: "'Follow me,' Jesus said to him."[22] When Matthew holds a great banquet of tax collectors in his home and Jesus joins the feast, the Pharisees complain to the disciples, questioning Jesus' allegiances. Jesus' answer to them is neither defensive nor self-

20. Farley, *The Naked Gospel*, 31.

21. Luke 5:20.

22. Luke 5:27.

effacing. He focuses on the questioners themselves, offering an answer that is solely about his audience and the state of their hearts: "Jesus answered them, 'It is not the healthy who need a doctor, but the sick. I have not come to call the righteous, but sinners to repentance.'"[23]

When Jesus meets the centurion and later the widow with her dead son, his compassion for those encounters is genuine, unencumbered, and Holy Spirit-guided.[24] Other examples of Jesus' perfect EQ and AQ include the following: Jesus' time with John the Baptist,[25] his forty days and nights in the desert,[26] his greeting of the first disciples,[27] his Sermon on the Mount,[28] his encounter with the man with leprosy,[29] his meeting with Peter's mother-in-law,[30] his reminder at the lake,[31] his healings of the demon-possessed men and the paralytic,[32] his commissioning of the twelve,[33] and the brilliance of his parables.[34] Even when he reprimands the Pharisees[35] and gently confronts Judas,[36] Jesus has a keen sense of both his own emotions and the ability of his audience to receive what he has to say.

As humans mired in complicated histories and worry about the future, the health of our relationships can be critical in affirming our sense of self, particularly if our EQ is underdeveloped: "We live in a culture that now prioritizes belonging over believing. Pastors and key leaders sense that they need to adjust their language in order to adapt to this cultural shift. The question is, 'How?'"[37] Joseph Myers asks in *The Search to Belong.* Jesus knew how. Jesus knew how to set aside self and focus on the Father, to step forward with clarity and confidence, to hold fast to purpose, to articulate his own emotions and use them for good rather than confusion, to see and hear his audience in a way that was unfettered by self, to proclaim freedom for

23. Luke 5:31–32.
24. Luke 7:1–10, 11–17.
25. Matt 3:13–17.
26. Matt 4:11.
27. Matt 4:18–22.
28. Matt 5:1—7:29.
29. Matt 8:1–4.
30. Matt 8:14–17.
31. Matt 8:18–22.
32. Matt 8:28—9:8.
33. Matt 10:1–42.
34. Matt 13:1–58, 18:10–14, 20:1–16, 21:28, 22:1–14.
35. Matt 23:1–39.
36. Matt 26:23–25.
37. Myers, *The Search to Belong*, 6.

the oppressed and sight for the blind, to offer his listeners the word or deed that spoke to their soul, to hold steadfast to his God-given purpose in every crisis, challenge, and quandary.

Part of our problem, John Haught suggests in *Resting on the Future*, is that our perspective is marred by a post-Enlightenment reliance on what is tangible and a postmodern skepticism that dismantles anything that smacks of the supernatural. But Haught argues that a new church movement must press for something more: "In a post-Copernican age, therefore, can the spiritual quest discover windows to perfection that may stir us anew to lift up our hearts? Are there any natural openings to a transcendent sacred reality that can explain our souls, heal our anxieties, and give us peace? In the age of science, is there any inspirational equivalent to the flawless heavens that in ages past pointed so palpably to the infinite?"[38]

Jesus offers us himself. How can we recalibrate the church in such a way that we embrace, absorb, and embody his gift?

JESUS' INTELLIGENCE QUOTIENT (IQ)

Consider the wisdom of the Messiah: From what we see in the New Testament, Jesus did not brood over his own IQ, wondering whether he was equipped to speak before others or wise enough to ponder the questions of those who were trying to trip him up. He did not bow out of opportunities to teach and lead, begging for more time to prepare, or sidestep difficult concepts, suggesting that his brain did not have the cognitive flexibility needed. Jesus knew that God had created him purposefully and perfectly, and while the challenges he faced were daunting, he did not waste time wondering whether his intelligence could be an impediment. That said, he also did not walk blindly into his role as rabbi, assuming innocently that he could fumble his way forward; instead he spent thirty years living a life of study, work, and family.

As a child, Jesus traveled with his parents each spring from his home in Nazareth to Jerusalem for the Festival of the Passover, a seventy-mile walk that likely took four or five days. When Jesus was twelve, his parents began the return trek to Nazareth at the close of the festival without him, not realizing that their son was not among their traveling group of relatives and friends. When Joseph and Mary recognized his absence, they returned to Jerusalem to find him: "After three days they found him in the temple courts, sitting among the teachers, listening to them and asking them questions. Everyone who heard him was amazed at his understanding and his

38. Haught, *Resting on the Future*, 44–45.

answers."[39] Even at the youthful age of twelve, Jesus demonstrated his foundational IQ. And while his mother was clearly upset that she could not find him for a time—"Son, why have you treated us like this? Your father and I have been anxiously searching for you"[40]—she carries from the experience a realization of her son's exceptional intelligence: "But his mother treasured all these things in her heart. And Jesus grew in wisdom and stature, and in favor with God and man."[41]

As Jesus began teaching from village to village at the age of thirty, many were unnerved by his unshakeable wisdom:

> When the Sabbath came, he began to teach in the synagogue, and many who heard him were amazed. "Where did this man get these things?" they asked. "What's this wisdom that has been given him? What are these remarkable miracles he is performing? Isn't this the carpenter? Isn't this Mary's son and the brother of James, Joseph, Judas, and Simon? Aren't his sisters here with us?" And they took offense at him.[42]

Jesus' wisdom was such that others were threatened by it, and yet he stood firm in his purpose and timing, never deviating from his God-ordained path either in fearful anxiety or in reckless presumption. As Paul reminds us in his first letter to the Corinthians, Jesus' wisdom was God's wisdom: "It is because of [God] that you are in Christ Jesus, who has become for us wisdom from God—that is, our righteousness, holiness, and redemption."[43]

JESUS' EMOTIONAL QUOTIENT (EQ)

But Jesus' wisdom ran deeper than mere intellectual finesse. As we witness throughout the New Testament stories, Jesus understood his own emotions in an innate way that both affirmed his intellect and avowed his heart for the world around him. Jesus did not emote in a reactionary way, wreaking unintentional havoc and pronouncing follow-up apologies to excuse his behavior. Instead Jesus experienced a familiar range of healthy human emotions—from anger to sorrow to joy—and expressed them in appropriate and productive ways. While our postmodern sensibilities sometimes lead us to assume that wisdom is one's ability to memorize and reproduce vast

39. Luke 2:46–47.
40. Luke 2:48.
41. Luke 2:51–52.
42. Mark 6:2–3.
43. 1 Cor 1:30.

quantities of information, or to merge familiar ideas in unfamiliar, creative ways, the Apostle Paul reminds us in his letter to the Colossians that Jesus' wisdom was something far more complex: "My goal is that [all who have not met me personally] may be encouraged in heart and united in love, so that they may have the full riches of complete understanding, in order that they may know the mystery of God, namely, Christ, in whom are hidden all the treasures of wisdom and knowledge."[44] Later Paul refers to Christ's wisdom as "all the fullness of the Deity," a profound reminder that our postmodern insistence on separating intellect from emotion or the right hemisphere from the left hemisphere is myopic and dangerously limiting.

Consider, for example when the teachers of the law bring an adulterous woman before Jesus in the Temple in Judea. The Pharisees remind Jesus that by Jewish law, the woman should be stoned to death for her sinful behavior. Angered by the hypocrisy of Jesus' teachings, the Pharisees bring the woman to the Temple in order to trick Jesus into saying something that will reveal his heretical behavior or, at the very least, the humanness of his emotions. Instead Jesus' calm is infuriating for the teachers who are understandably threatened by this itinerant rabbi who says he is the Messiah but who bears no resemblance to the king they are hoping to one day see:

> They were trying to trap him into saying something they could use against him, but Jesus stooped down and wrote in the dust with his finger. They kept demanding an answer, so he stood up again and said, "All right, but let the one who has never sinned throw the first stone!" Then he stooped down again and wrote in the dust.[45]

As an individual with exceptional emotional intelligence, Jesus has unfailing impulse control. He does not succumb to the Pharisees' anxious pressing or match their increasing anxiety with a reprimand or irritation. Jesus is not concerned about besting his opponents in an academic argument or shaming them for their surreptitious attempt to discredit him publicly. Jesus demonstrates a masterful adherence to the Law of Moses coupled with an EQ-infused understanding of the complex human emotions at play: those of the Pharisees and teachers of the law, those of the woman herself, those of his disciples, and those of the many onlookers who had gathered to hear him teach that day.

If we equate IQ with knowledge of the Law of Moses and EQ with our belief that God is love, Jesus came to earth to rewrite our understanding of both: "Do not think that I have come to abolish the Law or the Prophets; I

44. Col 2:2–3.

45. John 8:6–8.

have not come to abolish them but to fulfill them."[46] So if rational thought is not in opposition to emotional reaction, just as science is not in opposition to faith in God, how do we learn to view our world not as binary but with the rich complexity that God intended?

JESUS' AUDIENCE QUOTIENT (AQ)

Because Jesus had perfect confidence in his own IQ and EQ, he was able to focus his attention fully on those he encountered, whether a single individual or a crowd of thousands. Without the weight of insecurity, the pang of self-consciousness, or the mere ignorance that most of us shoulder, Jesus was able to step fully into each new moment, unfettered by his own erroneous assumptions and fully prepared to receive the complexities of those around him. As he was teaching throughout Galilee and a paralyzed man was brought to him, for example, Jesus was able to ascertain the hearts of all who were involved: both the men who carried the paralyzed man to him and the teachers of the law who questioned his proclamation that their sins had been forgiven. As the men carried the paralyzed man to Jesus on a mat, Jesus responded with assurances because he "saw their faith"[47]; without an exceptional ability to move past IQ and EQ and into full AQ, Jesus would not have been able to witness the sincerity of their actions. As the teachers of the law turned to one another in distress, Jesus' response emerged from "knowing their thoughts": "Why do you entertain evil thoughts in your hearts?" he asked.[48] Without full confidence in his own IQ and EQ, Jesus likely would not have had the capacity to hear the negative thoughts of those who were watching his every move, waiting from him to slip.

Jesus was not strident in his evangelism, nor was he shaming. He instead acted from a deeply grounded sense of self that allowed him to love in a way that both embodied and extended the laws he came to fulfill. Perhaps our greatest affirmation of this complexity comes when Jesus explained his authority in John 5.

> Very truly I tell you, the Son can do nothing by himself; he can do only what he sees his Father doing, because whatever the Father does the Son also does. For the Father loves the Son and show him all he does. Yes, and he will show him even greater works than these, so that you will be amazed. For just as the Father raises the dead and gives them life, even so the Son gives

46. Matt 5:17.

47. Matt 9:2.

48. Matt 9:4.

> life to whom he is pleased to give it. Moreover, the Father judges no one, but has entrusted all judgment to the Son, that all may honor the Son just as they honor the Father. Whoever does not honor the Son does not honor the Father, who sent him.[49]

When we hold truth like this so deeply within that it seeps from our very pores, there is no room for anxiety about worldly trivialities or fear that we are not enough. And if we believe that we are not capable enough for the next moment that God has called us to, what does that say about our faith in our Creator? Jesus knew, Jesus embodied, and Jesus loved fully and well.

The Jesus Problem that overlays our twenty-first-century myopic approach to church is that Jesus did not come to empower us to focus on growth, timelines, programming, missional outreach, strategic plans, connectedness, numbers, membership, mission statements, vision statements, objectives, capital campaigns, budgets, social media usage, or small groups. While many of these concepts can lead us down the right path, too often the paths replace the key commandments, about which Jesus was indubitably clear: (1) Love the Lord your God with all your heart, soul, and mind, and (2) Love your neighbor as yourself.[50] The Jesus Problem is that despite our best intentions, our deepest Holy Spirit connections, and our most heartfelt prayers, we still don't get it. Jesus did not ask us to reach farther and wider and with greater success; he asked us to love well—first God and then one another. And perhaps because it is difficult to love and it is even more difficult to assess whether we are really loving at all, we have chosen to bypass Jesus' two greatest commandments and slide back into the habits of the Sadducees and Pharisees, repeating the errors of our fathers and mothers before us. The solution, then, cannot lie in the mathematics of our management processes or the depth of our passion for what is righteous. The solution lies first and foremost in our ability to love without letting ourselves get in the way.

49. John 5: 19–23.

50. Matt 22:37, 39.

Chapter 4

Intelligence Quotient (IQ)

I WAS AT WORK when my oldest brother died. I was teaching a prior learning assessment course, and we were discussing learning outcomes that evening. The students were struggling to articulate professional and personal life experiences in academic lingo, tightening their learning into crisp, single sentences that encapsulated a worldview change, and my cell phone was tucked deep inside my shoulder bag. After the last student had left and I had turned off the classroom lights, I reached for my phone to check for messages. I was surprised to see that I had three phone calls and several texts from my brother Randy. I dropped my bags on my office floor and tapped "return call" on my phone.

"Randy," I said when he answered. "I was teaching. What's up?"

"Are you sitting down?" he asked. "I have bad news."

In that moment—as time became a long, slow inhale—I thought of my grandmother, who had just celebrated her one-hundredth birthday several weeks prior; of my father, whose genetic propensity for cardiac issues was unusually high; of my mother, who had been plagued by lung infections since her childhood years. I thought about my close childhood friend Piper, who had been murdered many years prior, and my good friend Ed, who was run over by a cement truck as he biked to work in the 1990s. I didn't want to hear the words that would announce loss, carving a new hole that would take days, months, sometimes years to repair. And I wasn't ready to hear that my forty-nine-year-old brother Robert had left his home to go for an afternoon run earlier that day and never returned. We later learned that the cause of death was hypertrophic cardiomyopathy: a heart that had grown to nearly twice the size and thickness of a normal heart until it no longer had capacity to pump blood through the body. He died mid-stride, his six-foot-two frame crumpling to the sidewalk when his heart seized and then froze, unresponsive even to the EMTs who soon appeared

I have my brother's sunglasses—the pair he was wearing when he died. The right hinge is cracked where his head struck the pavement, his spirit already gone and his body unresistant as he fell to the pavement. I wonder what it felt like to die standing up, your brain focused on the pull of your hamstrings, the ache in your lungs, the breeze on your face as you propel your body forward. I wonder what damage a headlong fall like that would incur. Surely the impact concussed his brain, interrupting the electrical currents snapping from neuron to neuron. The sunglasses are still intact, and when I slide them on, I can imagine how his brain worked—pondering the next project to bring to completion, the next skill to learn, the next problem in need of a creative solution.

Robert was "the smart one" in our family, or so my other brother and I were raised to believe. I don't think our parents or anyone else intended harm with that statement, but it does carry a weight worth pondering both for the recipient himself and those around him. If Robert was "the smart one," what additional pressure did that place on him? I know as his sister that the vast majority of Robert's drive to succeed was innate, wired into his DNA in inexplicable ways that pushed him to work without sleeping and to assume success in areas that others would never consider.

Robert was valedictorian of his high school class of more than 400 in an era when only one valedictorian stood at the graduation podium, and he fought hard for that honor. He earned a four-year ROTC scholarship to the Massachusetts Institute of Technology (MIT), where he earned first a bachelor's and then a master's in aeronautical and astronomical engineering. He served as an officer in the Air Force Reserves and later earned an MBA from Harvard Business School. In the early 1990s, he was vice president and general manager of Aurora Flight Sciences Corporation, where he secured a contract with NASA to build an unmanned research aircraft designed to measure damage to the earth's ozone layer. In the late 1990s, he was one of the founding vice presidents and first employees of XM Satellite Radio, where he created and designed the first portable satellite radio receiver and earned a patent for some of the key features still standard in portable satellite radios. Robert's work in writing the XM Radio business plan and launching the service was written up in two Harvard Business School case studies that are still taught in business schools around the country. In the 2000s, Robert served as general manager, CEO, and president of several innovative start-up companies from Seattle to Silicon Valley, and it was always fun at family gatherings to grill him on his latest projects.

I don't know if Robert ever took an IQ test, but I'm confident his results would have been favorable. I always heard at home about his off-the-charts test scores and superior intellectual aptitude, but when I would ask him about it, he would shrug with some embarrassment and say that he simply made it a priority to work harder than anyone else in the room. And that hard work always paid off in the long run.

"It's not rocket science" is not a phrase we used in our home, because when your brother is a rocket scientist and you are the younger sister, you don't want to feed his ego too readily. I grew up believing that rocket science is a field of study like any other. High IQ or not, it demands the hard work of pressing forward and expecting of yourself a mental acuity that many assume is simply too much effort.

Did our family assumption that Robert was "the smart one" have an impact on my brother Randy and me? Probably. We considered ourselves "average," subpar in comparison to Robert, and I sometimes wonder how life might have been different if one of us had walked under the title of "the smart one." How would life be different? How do these words come to define the very core of who we are?

"EVEN A 'B' STUDENT"

When I was a senior in high school, I took an accelerated English class with a teacher who decided early on that I was a B student. I worked hard in that class, memorizing the prologue to Chaucer's *Canterbury Tales,* a soliloquy from Hamlet, and poems by Gerard Manley Hopkins. I wrote papers that sparkled with new vocabulary and yet were carefully grounded in an appropriately narrow thesis statement. I pushed myself to contribute in class discussions, and I even thought of questions to ask the teacher before and after class to ensure that she knew who I was. One morning she asked the twenty-five of us to circle our chairs so we could discuss *The Merchant of Venice*. I angled so I could sit near her, hoping that she would witness my wisdom as I turned the pages of the play, my patience as I waited for other students to muddle through their half-baked ideas, and my finesse as I raised my hand and pronounced the very point of New Historical literary criticism that she had been waiting for the class to realize.

I was a second-string player on our high school's varsity basketball team that year, and our early-morning practices meant I often raced to class after a high-speed shower, hair wet and clothes untucked. On that particular morning, I had forgotten to bring the granola bar I typically zipped in my backpack for breakfast, and I could tell that my stomach was not going to let me get away with a water-only morning. As I sat there, I leaned forward strategically, hoping to cover a potential growl, and then stretched to the right as I felt the gurgle sliding across my abdomen. Just when I thought I was safe, my stomach betrayed me and squeaked out a whining protest of hunger.

My teacher glanced my way when she heard it, catching my eye before what I assumed would be a continuation of her discussion of Shylock's "pound of flesh" penalty. Instead she stopped talking, laughed, and turned to the class.

"Well! Did anyone else hear that?" she asked. "That was certainly impressive!"

I spent the rest of class pressing my right hand into my belly to prevent further noises, sunken deep in my seat and longing for the bell to ring. With that pronouncement, I decided to agree with her. I would be a B student; it was probably easier anyway.

In the spring of that year, after many, many B essays and B vocabulary tests and B oral presentations, I joined my peers in sitting for the AP Composition exam. I was anxious during the exam, cognizant of the second hand sweeping quickly around the clock face above the door and wondering whether any of my ideas were even AP-worthy at all. But the prompts were straightforward and logical, and the essays I wrote marched to the same simple math of composition that I had discovered long before.

The school year was over when I received my score, and it surprised and excited me: a perfect 5 out of 5. I remember feeling relieved and grateful that my impression of the exam was not mistaken. And I also looked forward to the apology that my teacher would surely extend when she realized that she had typed me incorrectly for an entire year, never viewing me with an accurate lens or allowing me to rise to the fullness of what I could become. But that apology was not to be.

A year later, after I had graduated and was enjoying the benefits of my high exam score by bypassing all composition courses at the university I attended, I heard from a friend that my teacher indeed had announced my perfect score to her class: "You see," she told the class. "Even a B student can do exceptionally well on the AP exam."

On one level, I knew she was wrong; I believed I was an A English student, and she was a teacher who simply wouldn't listen to my determination and give me a fair chance. But on another level, I believed she was right. Just as my family saw me as subpar alongside my genius oldest brother, perhaps she had typed me correctly and I should relax into a semi-mediocre existence that would surely carry fewer stressors than an upper-echelon life of innovation and achievement. Was I a B student or an A student, and—more importantly—whose grading rubric were we using anyway?

DEFINING IQ

The IQ assessment is a measure that has been around for just over a century, and its capability of defining both individuals and whole populations is both indelible and, at least in the Western hemisphere, a cultural norm. Most trace our current intelligence quotient testing to the work of French psychologists Alfred Binet, Victor Henri, and Théodore Simon. In the early 1900s, the French government commissioned Binet to help identify students who were likely to experience difficulty in school. Binet and his colleagues began developing an assessment tool that posed questions on areas not specifically taught in the schools, such as the ability to problem-solve, remember, and focus. The initial Binet-Simon test focused on children's verbal abilities; scores were used to identify children who needed specialized assistance in order to be successful in school rather than sent to a mental asylum.

Binet was the first to consider a difference between a child's chronological age and "mental age," and he built into the assessment a tool to measure intelligence based on the average scores of children in a particular age group. The Binet-Simon Scale became the basis for intelligence tests used today, although Binet himself emphasized the inherent limitations of the test. He believed that intelligence was a broad concept influenced by a variety of factors and capable of changing over time. What this tool allowed was a means of using approved psychometric instruments to measure general inborn levels of intelligence determined in comparison with children of similar backgrounds. It should not become a determinate of character, ability, success, longevity, and happiness.

American psychologist Henry Goddard published a version of the assessment titled "The Binet and Simon Tests of Intellectual Capacity" in 1908, and he worked diligently to promote the tool among American psychologists: In 1911, Goddard introduced the assessment in public schools. In 1913, he began using the assessment on immigrants at Ellis Island. And in 1914, Goddard was the first psychologist to use the Binet-Simon Scale as evidence in an American court of law.[1] As Goddard's work popularized psychological testing in the United States, Stanford University psychologist Lewis Terman standardized Binet's original assessment using a sample of American participants. Terman published the results of his adapted tool in 1916, and the Stanford-Binet Intelligence Scale soon became the chief assessment for intelligence testing in the United States.

While the Stanford-Binet intelligence test has been revised many times over the years, its initial psychometrics remain foundational: An individual's score on the test is a single number known as the intelligence quotient or IQ. The score is found by dividing the individual's mental age by his or her chronological age, and then multiplying that number by 100. In the 1950s, the Wechsler Adult Intelligence Scale (WAIS) modified the reliance on chronological and mental age by directly comparing an individual test taker's score to the scores of other test taker's in the same age group. The average score was fixed at 100, and a normal range was established at between 85 and 115. Current popular charts rank IQ ranges as follows[2]:

145–160	Very gifted or highly advanced
130–144	Gifted or very advanced
120–129	Superior
110–119	High average
90–109	Average
80–89	Low average
70–79	Borderline impaired or delayed
55–69	Mildly impaired or delayed
40–54	Moderately impaired or delayed

1. Benjamin, "The Birth of American Intelligence Testing."
2. Roid and Barram, *Essentials of Stanford-Binet.*

A dark side of IQ testing in its early years and into the mid-twentieth century is that many of its proponents were eugenicists who favored sterilization of certain intrinsically inferior segments of the population:

> Goddard's work at Vineland [New Jersey] led him to conclusions about the origins of "feeblemindedness." He expressed those views in his most popular book, *The Kallikak Family: A Study in the Heredity of Feeble-Mindedness* (Macmillan, 1912). Using a fictional family name, Goddard shared the story of a family begun by an American Revolutionary War soldier who married a "worthy Quakeress," but also "dallied with a feeble-minded tavern girl." According to Goddard, descendants of the marriage produced generations of normally functioning people, whereas the union with the "tavern girl" produced inferior descendants, even criminals. The book sought to illuminate the role of heredity in "feeblemindedness" and provide a moral lesson emphasizing the societal harm that can result from casual sex. In fact, Goddard argued that society should keep feebleminded people from having children, either through institutional isolation or sexual sterilization.[3]

When Goddard encouraged IQ tests to screen new immigrants arriving at Ellis Island, the results were often used to make sweeping generalizations about specific populations of people. As humans, educated or not, we prefer to identify patterns among inconsistencies, imposing definitions on the world around us in order to create policies, laws, and social systems. But even Binet himself recognized the dangers of deifying a tool above the individual. Binet created the assessment in answer to a call from the French government. France had recently declared it compulsory for children ages six to sixteen to attend public school, and officials were seeking a tool to ensure the all children received the aid necessary to be successful.

While most psychologists would disagree, today's popular culture assumes that "IQ" is a fixed reality that an individual is born with, an assumption that suggests the tool itself is infallible and constant. In his blog on *Psychology Today*, psychologist Brian Roche questions the cultural assumptions surrounding the IQ score:

> [P]sychologists have made a "construct" out of intelligence, or more fairly they have (what clever-sounding philosophers of science call) "reified a construct." Put simply, an idea such as intelligence that was meant only to help us describe arbitrary but interesting differences we see among people, becomes

3. Benjamin, "The Birth of American Intelligence Testing," 20.

> something that is real and somehow possessed by people, fixed for life and as real as our bones, our hair and eye color. Constructs, however, are only supposed to be used like metaphors, as ideas or guiding models to represent something abstract.[4]

While the IQ assessment is still an industry standard, psychologists and cultural critics are beginning to question the dangers of its presumed infallibility, coupled with the potential of its use by modern-day eugenicists. In a scholarly study analyzing IQ, socioeconomic status, and criminal behavior, for example, the authors open by citing Goddard's 1914 argument that "at least 50 percent of all criminals are mentally defective," acknowledging that current studies must climb through a mire of dangerously minimizing metrics. When the authors introduce IQ, they describe it as "a term typically treated as synonymous with the concept of intelligence," a definition that suggests a need for a broader view.[5]

MODERN REVISIONS

When Annie burst into my class on the first day, she was fifteen minutes late, out of breath, and apparently joyful to see me.

"Oh, I was hoping I would get *you*," she pronounced as she trounced across the front of the classroom, bringing the entire class to a halt with her entrance.

I laughed inwardly at her announcement, wondering if she presumed flattery would excuse both her tardiness and her inappropriate interruption. From the moment I met her, Annie was a bundle of enthusiastic joy complicated by culturally imposed definitions that locked her firmly in a cycle of inspiration, first steps forward, and then self-defeat. It was as if she were jogging on a treadmill, sometimes sprinting ahead joyfully and other times recognizing the futility of her efforts when she could see the colorful world beyond but the machine itself prevented her from going anywhere.

Annie stayed after class that first day to apologize for her tardiness and chat about her aspirations. She was engaging and enthusiastic as she talked about the limitations of the Americans with Disabilities Act (ADA). She lived with two family members who were confined to wheelchairs, and it had become her life's passion to ensure that their access to the wider world was assured and protected. She told me stories of professional sporting events where the organizers rolled their eyes when they saw her coming,

4. Roche, "Your IQ May Not Have Changed."
5. Mears and Cochran, "What is the Effect of IQ on Offending?," 1280.

pushing a wheelchair and joyfully seeking an entrance; while their websites assured ADA compliance, most facilities did not provide an adequate experience—from dark, winding tunnels that were otherwise locked to seating that was crammed, narrow, and far from the excitement of the event.

Fierce and focused, Annie wondered about seeking justice for those with physical disabilities. Where could she focus her energies in hopes of effecting change? How might her studies help her one day? To whom would she need to appeal if she expected any kind of response? We talked about the challenges of ADA renovations in the 1990s, the long battle to get the civil rights law enacted in 1990, and the difference between honoring the letter of the law and honoring the spirit of the law.

When we parted ways that first night, Annie seemed determined to complete the work necessary to finally finish her bachelor's degree. She had a history of starting and stopping university-level work, and the degree had eluded her for years. While Annie presented as an energetic, creative soul, her mother had told her many years prior that she had been born with severe academic disabilities: ADHD, ADD, and possibly dyslexia. I assured her that her energy and her faith would carry her through, and she laughed and waved as she ducked inside her car to call her mother.

The next week in class, Annie was excited and engaged, interrupting me from time to time to ask how the concepts we were covering would apply to her current paper or her week at work. I didn't mind the interruptions, but it was clear that Annie had little awareness of how her peers were responding to her. She was friendly and asked questions of the other students sitting close by, nodding as they answered and laughing when something struck her as funny. During the larger group discussions, her peers smiled at her jokes but were increasingly impatient with the frequent tangents. I did what I could to keep our discussion focused, but I also appreciated Annie's ability to push beyond the confines of linear thinking. Higher-level intelligence rarely manifests as mere rule-following, and Annie exemplified unharnessed intellectual creativity.

For the next two weeks, Annie was gone. She did not come to class, she did not answer my emails, and she did not respond to my phone messages. The health of family members in her household was tenuous at best, and I worried that something might have happened. When she reappeared on a Thursday, breathless and apologetic in my office doorway, I ushered her inside and asked her what had happened.

"It's my mother," she said.

"Oh no," I said. "Is she all right?"

"She can be a little mean, but otherwise she's fine," Annie said with a smirk. "Oh, I'm sorry," she said when she saw my confusion. "I didn't mean that she is ill or dead or anything like that. I just meant that she's the reason I haven't been to class."

"What do you mean?" I asked.

"She thinks your essay assignments are too difficult," Annie said, "and I think I agree with her. With my disabilities, it's difficult for me to sustain thought for as long as you are asking. Is there another assignment I can do instead? Could I write my own prompt, and then have you approve it?"

"Annie, you sustain ideas wonderfully well. I've watched you in class."

"Yes, but did you notice how I jump from place to place, asking crazy questions at the wrong time? That's part of my disability. I can't stay with one thing like the rest of you can."

"I don't see that as a disability, Annie. I see that as creativity. If you don't mind my asking, have you been diagnosed by someone in the medical field? And what were you diagnosed with?"

"Not exactly," Annie said. "My mother never thought it necessary, since she was an elementary school teacher for years and has seen this kind of thing. She homeschooled me most of my way through high school anyway. It was just easier."

"When is the last time you followed a school assignment just as it was written?" I asked.

"I don't know," Annie said. "I don't usually. Because of my disabilities."

"I want you to try," I said. "Start with just this first essay, and let's see how it goes."

I met Annie in my office three times after that so we could work through her ideas together. Each time we met, we would build on her passion for ADA compliance, narrowing in on single stories that she could tell and regulations within the Disabilities Act that needed revision. Her ideas were fresh, her energy was high, and her focus was excellent. But each time she left my office, she shrugged her shoulders at the fifteen or twenty texts from her mother, who needed her home to help care for their invalid family members.

The last time I saw Annie, she met me in the hallway before class and apologized that she couldn't do it any longer.

"My brain is all in a swirl," she said, laughing as she tried to make light of her withdrawal from school. "I just can't think straight like the rest of you can. My mom is worried that I'm forming bad habits that will be difficult to undo. I don't know if she's right or not anymore, but everything is easier if I just do what she asks."

"Annie, do you think you have disabilities?" I asked.

Annie looked at her shoes, pondering. "I think I'm just me," she said with a smile.

"And so do I."

~

When Jeff asked for his third extension of the semester, I asked him to come see me in my office so we could talk about whether this was the best time for him to be in school. He was a nice guy and always very respectful, but I was concerned about his ability to dedicate the time needed to be successful. It is frustrating to watch students sign up for courses, pay their tuition, and then begin sliding into a mire of missed deadlines and late assignments until the tuition dollars become little more than a bruised ego and an unfortunate F on the transcript.

When Jeff arrived, I could tell he was anxious. He began by apologizing—again and again—for missing the most recent essay deadline.

"It's the rain," he said.

We were in the midst of the wettest winter we had seen in years, and the rain was indeed taxing. But a deterrent for accomplishing homework? "Jeff, I know the rain can be depressing for some people, but it's really not—"

"My laptop got wet," he interrupted. "My tent is usually fine in the rain, but this is so much more than usual, and I just can't keep my things dry. I don't mean to make excuses, but I need this rain to stop, even just for a day or two, so I can get everything dried out."

"You're living in a tent?"

"It's only temporary," he said. "My wife asked me to leave, and I can't afford another place. She said I wasn't pulling my weight, and she's right. The kinds of jobs I was getting were embarrassing. I never realized how important education is, and now I really, really need this degree so I can make things work."

When Jeff began to describe the tent property he had built for himself on a half-acre just outside of town, as well as his passion for family, integrity, and hard work, I heard a wisdom that is generally hard to come by. Jeff had made tactical errors in his relationship with his wife, landing him in the wet outdoors rather than the warmth of his rented duplex, but his resiliency and creativity were exceptional. Where most would collapse in despair, Jeff tucked his head and worked harder. Where most would lash out in anger or hide in sorrow, Jeff stepped forward with hope and joy. I asked him why.

"Probably my education," Jeff said. "Pardon me—my *un*-education." And then he told me his story.

Jeff was in third grade when his teacher called his parents in to discuss the doodles in the margins of his notebook. The teacher was concerned that the cartoon-like sketches of ninjas battling could be indicative of some kind of concerning inner turmoil; Jeff's parents left disgusted by the teacher's narrow-mindedness. The next day, Jeff's parents told him that he no longer needed to go to that school, if he didn't want to. With visions of sleeping as long as he wanted in the mornings and carefree afternoons on his bicycle, Jeff agreed.

Jeff's mother said that she would homeschool him, and for the first two weeks, Jeff awoke each morning to a homework packet on the kitchen counter. Excited by the freedom of this new life, he sat diligently at the counter and completed his daily work, then rode his bicycle gleefully around the neighborhood until his friends were released from school and able to join him.

After two weeks, there were no more packets. At first, Jeff was thrilled. Then he assumed his mother must have forgotten in the busy-ness of getting to her job at the restaurant each day, and he waited for a catch-up pile of exercises. But there was nothing. The freedom was exhilarating, but Jeff soon realized that when all of your friends are in school and you're not, there's a loneliness that begins to grow.

Years passed, and Jeff felt himself growing further apart from the friends he once knew well. When he should have been in seventh grade, he had a conversation with a friend's dad that alerted them both that something was wrong. The dad asked Jeff his thoughts on some basic pieces of American history—George Washington's presidency, maybe, or something about Abraham Lincoln—and Jeff had no idea what the man was talking about. When Jeff got home that evening, he asked his parents to let him go back to the public school, but his parents said no. They were concerned that Jeff would be embarrassed to join his peers so belatedly, or perhaps they were concerned that they would be found negligent for not providing their son with a proper education. And so Jeff continued the pattern of his school-age years: sleeping late, waking to an empty house, eating meals alone at the counter with the television for company, and riding his bike through the streets of his neighborhood until the other neighborhood kids were released from school. He never learned math, or history, or science, or health, or how to read. Jeff was illiterate, and he was convinced that his IQ was abnormally low.

"I had a third-grade education for most of my early adulthood," Jeff said. "Do you know how hard it is to get a job when you can't even prove that you went to high school or middle school."

"I can't" became Jeff's stock phrase for a time, letting him off the hook when some task or another seemed too daunting.

"I've watched you in class," I told Jeff. "You can as well as anyone else, if not better. It's time you found a new life mantra."

CONSIDERING MADNESS

> *Brothers and sisters, think of what you were when you were called. Not many of you were wise by human standards; not many were influential; not many were of noble both. But God chose the foolish things of the world to shame the wise; God chose the weak things of the world to shame the strong. God chose the lowly things of this world and the despised things—and the things that are not—to nullify the things that are, so that no one may boast before him. It is because of him that you are in Christ Jesus, who has become for us wisdom from God—that is, our righteousness, holiness, and redemption. Therefore, as it is written: "Let the one who boasts boast in the Lord."*[6]

Twelve of us waited until fifteen minutes past the hour for our Latin professor to arrive. We were doctoral students seeking to study classical Latin together for a year to satisfy one of our three language requirements, and other professors had told us we were in for a treat. When our professor came bursting through the door with her books and boxes of flashcards clutched under her arm and red lipstick drawn at an upward angle across her upper lip and out toward her cheekbone, we all wondered what we had gotten ourselves into.

Dr. P. was breathless that first afternoon, apologizing for her tardiness and murmuring something about not feeling well. She had us open our *Wheelock's Latin* books to the first chapter, and she began reciting verb conjugations and describing the careful precision of translation as opposed to mere etymological considerations. She moved quickly, almost nervously, and it was obvious that her mind was operating on a plane we could only aspire to one day reach. She was intimidating.

At our second weekly lesson, only seven of us returned. By the third week, only five, and by week seven, it was down to two of us.

"It's not unusual," Dr. P. told us that week. "Few students are up to the challenge of true classical Latin."

And then she peered at each of us over her glasses: first Jim and then me. This week her lipstick was drawn carefully along the outline of her lips,

6. 1 Cor 1:26–31.

although the pink seemed rather bright for a university professor with a mind like hers. "Are you sure you want to stick this out?" she asked pointedly.

"Yes," I told her quickly. I wasn't sure at all, as the work was difficult, the course was far more time-consuming than I had anticipated, and her genius was overwhelming. But I needed this course if I was going to move closer to earning my PhD, and at this point I saw no other route than to press ahead.

"Me, too," Jim said. I knew he felt the same as I did, but we had assured one another that we would keep going together, rather than leaving the other one to study alone with our unpredictable, eccentric professor.

Dr. P. held a special faculty position at the university. She didn't seem old enough for retirement, but her position carried the respect of a professor emeritus. Each week, Jim and I sat in that classroom unsure what her mood would be when she entered the room—sometimes anxious, sometimes calm, sometimes hurried, and sometimes oddly carefree. She was always careful to cover precisely the materials promised for the day at hand, and her impatience with us as we struggled to rearrange Latin into recognizable English patterns was amusing.

It wasn't until halfway through our year together that Jim and I were told what ailed Dr. P., causing her to sometimes appear frazzled or to show up fifteen, thirty, even sixty minutes late: schizophrenia. In her own words, schizophrenia is a mental illness that is unfathomably all-consuming:

> Schizophrenia defies the mind in every way. It is the ultimate disease of our ultimate possession: the human brain. To the researcher or clinician, schizophrenia is an amazingly resilient opponent. To those of us who painfully experience it, schizophrenia subverts the ability to think, as we try to sift our way through the mud and to sort through the snakelike coilings that the disease makes of our minds.[7]

From what other professors told us, Dr. P. indeed was brilliant, but her mind would unexpectedly turn inward on itself, distracting her from her teaching responsibilities or publication deadlines as it pulled her into worlds where darkness reigned and reality danced elusively across a backstage that was always in sight but never in reach, always flirting its silhouette across a backlit night sky but never stepping into the light. The university entrusted her with the one-year weekly Latin course because administrators knew that its students could opt out at any point, and only the truly dedicated would stick it out. And, of course, they were right.

7. Payne, *Speaking to My Madness*, xiii.

If she canceled class entirely, she never told us why, and she always gave us additional homework to make up for this missed time—lots of additional homework. We could tell by her demeanor that she was irritated by the delays—not with herself in a self-pitying or browbeating kind of way, but with the demons that lived inside her brain, threatening to press the normalcy from her routine at ill-defined moments. For Dr. P., the logic of the Latin language helped to realign her missed days, reminding her that control was possible, at least for a little while. And she had grown accustomed to this thorn in her flesh many, many years prior.

> My roommate at Stanford [saw] in hindsight that I was already mentally ill when I came back to Palo Alto at 20, after spending sophomore and junior years studying in Europe. Then—months in a private hospital at 22; then—Harvard. A year of being lost in San Francisco, three years of being horribly lost in New Orleans, then years of blackness, first alcoholism, then schizophrenia. A slow, slow circling through nowhere, balancing on a spider's thread of right thinking. Journeys through medications, each a different country. Languages—Latin, Greek, Italian, French, Spanish, Hebrew—and the rigorous logic of translating were a swaying bridge back to my own mind. Today, I have a foot in each world, but I lean as far as I can into your world. Even the bizarre glamour of gleaming psychotic reality and its terror calls like a Siren.[8]

As Jim and I neared the end of our year with Dr. P., we worried about what our final exam would be. While the year of Latin was a pass/no pass course rather than a letter grade, neither of us was convinced that we would pass her lofty expectations of what an accurate translation should be. As the homework grew more complex and the translations more intricate, we would each spend hours weaving and unweaving parts of speech until we thought we had made sense of a passage, only to learn from Dr. P. that our attempts had grossly misconstrued the writer's intentions and our comprehension of even the most basic Latin grammar was questionable at best. How in the world would we satisfy her expectations for a passing final grade?

When Dr. P. shared with us the Cicero passage that she expected us to mechanically render into colloquial English, I initially relaxed into what I thought was a reasonable pattern of verb-subject, verb-subject, verb-subject—until I reached the end and realized that I had misconstrued Cicero's entire meaning with a single mistranslated pattern. So I started over. And then I did it again. And then a third time. By the time I had arrived at what

8. Payne, *Speaking to My Madness*, xv.

I thought was a proper English translation of Cicero's musings, I no longer knew what language we were studying and what degree I thought I wanted to earn. When Jim and I arrived in class with our frustration-crinkled final translations, I had no idea what would happen next.

The next week, Dr. P. telephoned and invited both Jim and me to lunch at her fourth-floor apartment. We accepted, of course, but we both wondered whether this meal would be celebratory or conciliatory. Thankfully, it was the former. Dr. P. met us with glee at her door and informed us that while both of our work would have earned a C- or so had she graded it on a traditional scale, it was enough for a pass, which meant that both of us had satisfied one of our language requirements. Because of our success, she had bought us a cake at the local grocery store, and her eyes sparkled with excitement as she showed us the way the baker had written our names in curly red frosting, circling the cake as if "Jennie" and "Jim" were a two-worded Southern name, like Bobby Joe or Billie Jean: Jennie Jim.

Her apartment was mostly white and notably sterile, and on the counter sat three white Styrofoam containers that held thick pastrami sandwiches for lunch. Dr. P. was clearly pleased to have us visit her home, and she walked us from room to room, showing us the pictures that hung on the walls and the afghans that her great aunt and grandmother had crocheted. As we ate, we talked about Cicero and Latin and PhDs and the university we attended. Dr. P. watched us carefully as we ate, inquiring about the food with each bite, and when our time with her neared the one-hour mark, she became increasingly more agitated. Taking the cue, Jim and I thanked her profusely for the sandwiches and the cake, and we walked together to the street below.

Much like Annie and Jeff were dominated by others' definitions, Dr. P. walked a life where the definitions resided in her own brain, controlled by a disease that defied even the MDs who sought to care for her. The language that defines us is critical, whether it emerges from the culture that surrounds us or the biology within us, and it can limit our ability to view the world around us and—most importantly—the people who walk alongside us. While some of us carry burdens that are as visible as the examples here, others shoulder misconceptions about intelligence, wisdom, and IQ that are unseen and even subconscious, defining our worlds in ways that even we don't realize. As we move toward the Jesus Quotient, a Christ-informed capacity to love others boldly and well, we must first acknowledge and accept the wisdom that God gifted to us, as well as the capability we each have of progressing every day toward something broader, larger, and continually improving.

POSTMORTEM

We had two funeral services for my brother Robert: one in Menlo Park, California, that was attended by more than 300 family and friends less than a week after his death, and a second service a month later in Tigard, Oregon, for those who were unable to travel to the first. At the Menlo Park service, I read a favorite passage, Isaiah 55:12–13:

> You will go out in joy
> and be led forth in peace;
> the mountains and hills
> will burst into song before you,
> and all the trees of the field
> will clap their hands.
> Instead of the thornbush will grow the pine tree,
> and instead of briers the myrtle will grow.
> This will be for the Lord's renown,
> for an everlasting sign,
> which will not be destroyed.

While the words still speak to me now of joy out of pain and growth out of struggle, I remember the shock of why I was there overcoming me like a stranger's gloved hand, pressing into my throat and onto my chest until I wasn't sure if I could stand. I steeled myself to be strong in my brother's memory, but the suffocation still arises from time to time in unsuspecting moments—a song on the radio, a product in the grocery aisle, a memory while I'm driving.

At the Oregon service, enough time had passed that I felt better equipped to speak, and it was important to me to attempt to share my brother's definition of intelligence. For Robert, IQ was not a marker of worth; integrity, authenticity, and honesty were. I don't know where his faith stood when he died, but I have peace knowing that he was reading a book about the life of Jesus when he passed. Whether he realized it or not, Robert's life principles were Jesus principles. Perhaps it is time we let go of the constrictive definitions of the twentieth-century IQ exam and embrace something broader-thinking and quintessentially more Jesus-like. Here is what I shared at Robert's Oregon service:

(1) **When you "live life to the fullest," that does not mean that you follow every rule or that you blindly break rules; it means that you study the rules until you know them better than the rule-makers themselves.** When I studied for the SAT way back in high school, Robert made sure I understood his algorithm of multiple-choice exams:

Number one, study. Number two, have enough context in your brain that you can make educated guesses. Number three (and only arrive at number three if you absolutely have to), if you really don't know, always always always pick B. Did it work? I don't know. But we both have gotten where we needed to go, so I suppose it held some merit.

(2) **Always work harder and longer than anyone else.** When you are in a competitive situation, don't ever presume you are smarter than anyone else. While you can exercise your brain—and Robert and I shared many books over the years about how to do that—you only have so much control over how intelligent you are. What you do have control of is your work ethic. So if you walk into a room of competitors, always tell yourself that you can and will be the one to emerge having worked harder and longer. At the height of a rather difficult work transition when Robert was clearly exhausting himself with the minutiae, I remember a late-night conversation with Robert, Randy, Robert's wife Gigi, and me. Our families had gathered at Pacific City, and our eleven kids were all in bed. Robert was telling us a story about work, I believe, and at one point his dramatic pause seemed a little long. We waited, and it continued. The light was dim in the room, and when we looked more closely, we realized he had fallen sound asleep, mouth agape, in the midst of his own story. As an English professor, I use that example—with Robert's blessing, of course—as how not to bore your audience: If your own story puts you to sleep, must we listen? Fatigue aside, he was pushing himself for a purpose at that point, and it did prove successful.

(3) **Failure is necessary and always a step toward something bigger.** When my brothers and I would downhill ski together as kids, we always said that whoever didn't fall wasn't really doing it. And whoever had an epic fall—as my kids would say—was really doing it well that day. But it's not just about skiing; it's about school and work and life. When you have an epic fall, you never lie there in the snow, because if you do, the snow will soon begin to melt and your clothes will get all wet. Instead you jump up, gather up, and consider what you will do differently so it doesn't hurt as much the next time.

(4) **The world is full of disagreeable, unethical people. What can you learn from them?** When I was in third grade and Robert was in seventh, I remember a moment on the Bridlemile Elementary School playground when the yellow line that separated middle school-age from primary-age loomed larger than it ever had. I was running with friends when I spotted Robert on his side, clearly being taunted by a

kid we all tried to avoid. I stood there watching as this kid—who was shorter than Robert; they always were—jabbed his hands in Robert's direction and sang in a mocking, sing-songy voice. Robert stood with his shoulders squared and just stared. I could tell by the way Robert held himself that he wasn't angry and wasn't going to do anything, which was befuddling to me. I was angry, I could do something, although I wasn't sure what kind of horrible punishment would ensue if I crossed that yellow line. So I stretched my toes as far as I dared into that daunting yellow line, leaned forward into the opposing playground, and yelled, "Hey!" to get their attention. They both turned toward me, and now Robert looked angry. He waved me away with the irritation of an older brother, while the bully laughed and proceeded to tease Robert about his little sister who was going to come save him. I now know that Robert was studying that guy. It never solves anything to fight with a bully—or, at the adult level, a disagreeable or unethical person—but we can learn from them. Every bad boss that Robert had was not a reason to complain but a catalyst for studying human nature and determining how not to be like that person.

(5) **Always wonder.** Wonder about the world, about life, about possibilities—and when other people tell you your ideas are too big or too new or not possible, go back to #1, 2, 3, and 4 above and quietly, carefully prove them wrong.

Chapter 5

Emotional Quotient (EQ)

HUMANS HAVE LONG SOUGHT an optimal means of assessing intelligence: Before the Binet-Simon Scale, the French tool used to identify the abilities of French school children who were underperforming, human intelligence was measured through observation and other less-exact mechanisms. Psychologist William Stern, a German-born philosopher who fled to the United States during Hitler's regime, first introduced the German word *Intelligenzquotient*, a term later used by Terman and others as they sought to measure the elasticity, adaptability, creativity, and speed of the human brain as precisely as possible. But as the science of psychology has morphed into cultural assumptions, how have we allowed a psychometric tool to become an exact measure of human character and worth? And what role has the church played in inculcating these erroneous mythologies?

Surely Jesus embodied the intelligence we seek: "It is because of [God] that you are in Christ Jesus, who has become for us wisdom from God—that is, our righteousness, holiness and redemption."[1] We see Christ's wisdom most overtly in the gospels, where the Jews question the source of his intelligence: "Not until halfway through the Feast did Jesus go up to the temple courts and begin to teach. The Jews were amazed and asked, 'How did this man get such learning without having studied?' Jesus answered, 'My teaching is not my own. It comes from him who sent me.'"[2] How curious, then, that even Christian leaders seek wisdom through a postmodern survey of evidence rather than turning to the source of all wisdom.

In her book *Changing Signs of Truth*, Crystal L. Downing acknowledges that Christ's wisdom is present and active: "[I]f we genuinely believe that the Holy Spirit still moves among God's people, we should believe that the Spirit enables us to identify truths that transcend the biblical inconsistencies identified by C. S. Lewis and the manuscript errors identified by Bart Ehrman," Downing writes. "Nowhere does the Bible proclaim its own scientific inerrancy, but everywhere it demonstrates the (re)signing of truth."[3] How have we used enlightenment and a postmodern reliance on physical evidence to entrap ourselves in the Pharisaical assumptions of the first-century teachers of the law?

Popular self-help-type books boast simple formulas for exercising the brain to increase IQ scores, as if the century-old assessment tool boasted factual inerrancy and spiritual truth beyond its capability. Consider the current top five IQ books on Amazon.com: *The Complete Book of Intelligence Tests: 500 Exercises to Improve, Upgrade, and Enhance Your Mind Strength*, by Philip Carter; *Your Miracle Brain: Maximize Your Brainpower, Boost Your Memory, Life Your Mood, Improve Your IQ and Creativity*, by Jean Carper; *1000 Hard Word Search Puzzles to Improve Your IQ*, by Kalman Toth; *IQ Baby—Facts and Tips to Improve the IQ of Your Child: From Conception to School*, by Gabriel Morales and Dr. Julie Harvard; and *50 Picture Puzzles to Improve Your IQ*, by Kalman Toth. Interestingly, however, current business theory has begun to step away from individual IQ toward a recognition that collaborative group work is far more creative and productive than the inspirations of a single individual.

1. 1 Cor 1:30.
2. John 7:14–16.
3. Downing, *Changing Signs of Truth*, 83.

Consider the words of Linda Hill in *Collective Genius,* for example: "Innovative companies value collaboration and take conscious, proactive steps to build it into the way they work. They understand that the best, most innovative work happens when diverse people interact closely and integrate their ideas. They know individuals working by themselves can only take an idea or project so far."[4] This emphasis on shared intelligence as superior to individual wisdom is antithetical to the self-reliant American ideal, and yet its internet-inspired foundation is both notable and enduring; why not share ideas and move further faster in our increasingly capitalist world, particularly when the internet promotes sharing that is instantaneous and no longer geographically constrained? The shift is both counter-cultural and biblical.

As Harvard MBA-inspired business theories are beginning to focus more on group work than on individual IQ, so, too, are the case studies that emerge. In books such as Kerry Patterson's *Crucial Conversations,* the organizational matrix is shifting from an individual's climb up the corporate letter to a rather befuddled realization that we should find better ways to relate to one another: "Despite the importance of crucial conversations, we often back away from them because we fear we'll make matters worse. We've become masters at avoiding tough conversations. . . . But it doesn't have to be this way. If you know how to handle crucial conversations, you can effectively hold tough conversations about virtually any topic."[5]

The quintessential American upward climb boasts a control that is lost when one begins to rely on others for growth and progression. In the close of *The Silo Effect,* Tett calls the messiness of reaching outside of the safety of one's own experience "The Curse of Efficiency": "Letting people 'roam' in an undirected way tends to seem like a self-indulgent luxury. So is the idea of creating cultural translators, conducting social analysis, or—dare I say it—looking at life through an anthropologist's lens. There is a constant tendency for people to organize themselves into silos in the name of hyper efficiency, accountability, and effectiveness."[6] But if we are to step boldly away from an emphasis on individual IQ and into the world of relationships, how do we quantify whether we are doing it effectively or assess how we might improve? Here is where we find the shift from IQ to EQ.

As Reuven Bar-On and Rich Handley write in *Optimizing People,* our assumptions about human intelligence for the past century have been misled by our inability to articulate and measure an individual's capacity

4. Hill et al., *Collective Genius,* 103.

5. Patterson et al., *Crucial Conversations,* 3.

6. Tett, *The Silo Effect,* 254.

to function well within the constructs of emotional, personal, and social understanding. Bar-On differentiates between cognitive intelligence and non-cognitive intelligence, acknowledging that the latter is in need of more specifically defined operational models in order for us to accurately measure one person against another.[7]

But since the 1990s, Bar-On writes, we have begun to see studies emerge that suggest the necessity of gauging EQ rather than IQ when predicting successful job performance. Bar-On points to a 1998 study by a graduate psychology student that affirms a direct correlation between high EQ and high job performance, as well as an insignificant correlation between high IQ and high job performance: "[T]his is the first scientific study that has proven that EQ is more important than IQ. This shows that the truly intelligent human being is one who is not only *cogtelligent* (cognitively intelligent) but *emtelligent* (emotionally and socially intelligent) as well."[8]

In a similar quest to differentiate cognitive intelligence from emotional intelligence, Daniel Goleman points to trends in the study of psychology. In the mid-twentieth century, behaviorists such as B. F. Skinner insisted on a modernist understanding of reality: The only behaviors that can be studied with scientifically acceptable objectivity are those behaviors that are visible to an observer. Cognitive scientists in the 1960s opened the studies to such inobservable elements as the nature of intelligence and the pathways by which the brain stores and retrieves information, "but emotions were still off-limits. Conventional wisdom among cognitive scientists held that intelligence entails a cold, hard-nosed processing of fact. It is hyperrational, rather like *Star Trek's* Mr. Spock, the archetype of dry information bytes unmuddied by feeling, embodying the idea that emotions have no place in intelligence and only muddle our picture of mental life."[9]

Using more affirming semantics than Bar-On, Goleman differentiates between cognitive understanding and meta-cognitive understanding, arguing that emotional and relational abilities are critical, measurable factors of human intelligence. Continuing his science fiction analogy, Goleman reminds his readers of the Spock-like character Data in *Star Trek: The Next Generation,* a character who recognizes that his own inability to fully experience human emotions is a detriment to his quality of life not just as a relational being but as an intelligent, progressive decision-maker as well. Logic alone is not enough to lead one to the best human solution.

7. Bar-on and Handley, *Optimizing People*, 2.
8. Bar-on and Handley, *Optimizing People*, 4.
9. Goleman, *Emotional Intelligence*, 40.

> Our humanity is most evident in our feelings; Data seeks to feel, knowing that something essential is missing. He wants friendship, loyalty; like the Tin Man in *The Wizard of Oz*, he lacks a heart. Lacking the lyrical sense that feeling brings, Data can play music or write poetry with technical virtuosity, but not feel its passion. The lesson of Data's yearning for yearning itself is that the higher values of the human heart—faith, hope, devotion, love—are missing entirely from the coldly cognitive view. Emotions enrich; a model of mind that leaves them out is impoverished.[10]

Note the echoes of biblical longings here in Goleman's reference to "the higher values of the human heart": "And now these three remain: faith, hope, and love. But the greatest of these is love."[11] As pastors and church leaders, how have we neglected to recognize the enormity of this shift in the field of psychology from cognitive to metacognitive? Are we so caught up in bemoaning the skepticism of postmodern thought that we have missed an opportunity to agree with this new cultural standard of articulating and measuring relationships, affirming an inner longing that every individual has for relationship?[12]

DEFINING THE TERMS

Psychologist and *New York Times* journalist Daniel Goleman opened his 1995 book *Emotional Intelligence* with an Aristotelian challenge:

> Anyone can become angry—that is easy. But to be angry with the right person, to the right degree, at the right time, for the right purpose, and in the right way—this is not easy.
>
> Aristotle, *The Nicomachean Ethics*[13]

The challenge is both simple and undeniably Herculean: Are we as individuals able to identify, own, manage, and act on our own emotions? Shouldn't this be a measure of intelligence as much or more than our capacity to think with creativity and flexibility? In an era when violence and devastation dominate our news feeds, is it possible that our cultural adulation of high IQ is hugely problematic?

10. Goleman, *Emotional Intelligence*, 41.

11. 1 Cor 13:13.

12. Isa 26:9, Ps 119:20, Ps 73:25, Ps 42:2, Ps 63:1, Ps 143:6, John 6:35, John 7:37, Rev 22:17.

13. Goleman, *Emotional Intelligence*, ix.

Consider some of the most highly publicized killers of the past few decades: John Wayne Gacy, Ted Bundy, Theodore Kaczynski, Jeffrey Dahmer, Dylan Klebold, and Eric Harris. If we are a culture that reveres high IQ scores, how do we justify the violence that emerges from individuals like these? Clearly a high intelligence quotient is not the answer to our cultural woes, despite the self-help books that might suggest otherwise.

Goleman defines "emotional intelligence" as the ability to identify one's most innermost feelings and to curb emotional impulses: "This expanded model of what it means to be 'intelligent' puts emotions at the center of aptitudes for living."[14] While we are each genetically inclined to a particular temperament, one that can also be fueled by our environment, character is not a fixed reality. Our brains are extremely malleable, Goleman argues, and we can all work to improve our EQ by learning to identify our own emotions and act on them appropriately.

In my earliest years of parenting, I was surprised by the intensity of my own emotions—particularly those that seemed inherently conflicting. If I loved my child with a depth that surpassed all else, how could I possibly feel irritation, let alone anger, for this trusting, helpless creature? And yet I did, and I was horrified by my own emotions. I ordinarily am a patient, flexible person, especially when children are involved, and I began to suspect that I might have deeper issues that had never before come to the forefront. Was I an angry person underneath my mostly calm exterior? Was this a development of age that no one warned me would come? I was unhappy with myself, and I did not see things improving as I had first three, then four, and finally five children ages seven and under.

Desperate for tools to help soothe the surprise of my own emotions, I bought the book *Anger* by Thich Nhat Hanh, hoping that Hanh's deep message of inner peace would remind me of my own Christ-inspired calm. Hanh's words were affirming, but I was surprised—more than anything else—by the simplicity of his advice. Rather than offering a miracle cure or a brilliant foundational cause, Hanh's chapters suggest again and again that we must recognize our emotion, name it for what it is, and decide what effect we will impart on the world with our response. Anger is not a psychological ailment; it is a natural emotional response that demands impulse control, self-awareness, and wisdom.

After a late night of reading *Anger* as I nursed, changed, walked, and soothed my babies, I determined the next morning to pay keen awareness to my own physiological responses to each new occurrence. We stayed home that day, which helped to incubate my experiment, and I was relieved to

14. Goleman, *Emotional Intelligence*, xiii.

realize that I did not randomly awaken each morning angry at my children and the world. I awoke calm, measured, and mostly normal as I helped children dress, prepared food, and changed diapers. As I was whirring baby food in the blender with the youngest in my left arm, I heard the five- and seven-year-olds begin to bicker at the table and felt the inner festerings of irritation. I tried to ignore the feeling, focusing instead on the peas in the blender, but when the three year old began to fuss as well, I felt the heaviness of the emotion begin to seep upwards from my gut and into my chest. I finished the baby food, tucked the youngest in his table-top sling, and asked the oldest two whether they wanted to pull out Play Doh for the morning. Distracted by an activity, their bickering stopped, and I felt the darker emotion wash away as if I had swallowed a cool drink. Was it really this simple? Yes and no.

Yes, the act of (1) recognizing, (2) acknowledging, and (3) acting was simple enough, but I was not always successful when things moved quickly, or when I myself was tired or hungry or already feeling frustrated. I learned in time that my tipping point as a parent was not a single fussy child and not necessarily two. I found my tipping point at three or more children needing me to help, soothe, or creatively divert at once. Something about the number three was simply too much, and I needed to learn to warn those around me once we hit two that I could not successfully manage much more. I learned to use my words well, just as we were teaching our kids, and in their younger years, my kids would sometimes hear me say, "That's going to make me angry" or "I'm starting to feel irritated." I found that simply speaking the words when I felt the beginnings of the physical emotion could prove helpful, maybe for the kids but moreso for me as I admitted my own weakness and began to seek a solution.

According to Travis Bradberry, EQ is critical—in the home, at work, and in society in general.:

> When emotional intelligence (EQ) first appeared to the masses, it served as the missing link in a peculiar finding: people with average IQs outperform those with the highest IQs 70% of the time. This anomaly threw a massive wrench into the broadly held assumption that IQ was the sole source of success. Decades of research now point to emotional intelligence as begin the critical factor that sets star performers apart from the rest of the pack. The connection is so strong that 90% of top performers have high emotional intelligence.[15]

15. Bradberry, "Are You Emotionally Intelligent?"

Goleman and his team have identified eighteen competencies organized into four clusters[16]:

Self-Awareness: Knowing one's internal states, preferences, resources, and intuitions.	• **Emotional Awareness:** Recognizing one's emotions and their effects. • **Accurate Self-Assessment:** Knowing one's strengths and limits. • **Self-Confidence:** A strong sense of one's self-worth and capabilities.
Self-Management: Managing one's internal states, impulses, and resources.	• **Emotional Self-Control:** Keeping disruptive emotions and impulses in check. • **Transparency:** Maintaining integrity, acting congruently with one's values. • **Adaptability:** Flexibility in handling change. • **Achievement:** Striving to improve or meeting a standard of excellent. • **Initiative:** Readiness to act on opportunities. • **Optimism:** Persistence in pursuing goals despite obstacles and setbacks.
Social Awareness: How people handle relationships and awareness of others' feelings, needs, and concerns.	• **Empathy:** Sensing others' feelings and perspectives, and taking an active interest in their concerns. • **Organizational Awareness:** Reading a group's emotional currents and power relationships. • **Service Orientation:** Anticipating, recognizing, and meeting customers' needs.

16. Goleman et al., *Primal Leadership*.

Relationship Management: The skill or adeptness at inducing desirable responses in others.	• **Developing Others:** Sensing others' development needs and bolstering their abilities. • **Inspirational Leadership:** Inspiring and guiding individuals and groups. • **Change Catalyst:** Initiating or managing change. • **Influence**: Wielding effective tactics for persuasion. • **Conflict Management:** Negotiating and resolving disagreements. • **Teamwork & Collaboration:** Working with others toward shared goals. Creating group synergy in pursuing collective goals.

EQ assessments typically drill into each of the eighteen competences, posing related questions with a scale of one through six:

1 = Never

2 = Rarely

3 = Sometimes

4 = Often

5 = Consistently

6 = Don't Know

While EQ tests organize assessments of brain plasticity and emotional awareness into definable clusters, EQ traits are not acquired or improved in a linear progression. Most assessments, such as the Emotional Competency Inventory (ECI) scored by HayGroup, cluster the competencies so that a single overall score for the tool does not make sense. Instead an individual receives EQ scores within each cluster that may suggest optimal levels in some competencies and lower-range scores in others. Published materials by Goleman, Bradberry, and others offer tools for studying the various competencies in order to achieve individual improvements.

MEASURE THE COST

If we neglect to recognize the importance of EQ, particularly in today's internet-connected, social-media-dominated culture, we could find ourselves traveling deeper into the mire of depression, unrest, and social strife. Consider the headlines from CNN on a summer's day in 2018:

- YouTube star is wrong-way driver in fatal crash
- Final hours of 3-year-old boy's life at a New Mexico compound revealed
- Police chief stands by reenactment video
- Mom accidentally locks child in car, calls 911; dispatchers don't help
- Explosion erupts at coffee shop
- Trump divide could spill into streets
- Child punished for calling teacher "ma'am"
- 4 in stable condition; students hit by car at LSU
- Love triangle sparked double stabbing
- Police find body of young child inside duffel bag
- 10th cat found mutilated; cases may be connected
- Woman 'viciously mauled' to death by dog
- Man accused of kidnapping, assault
- Man uses chainsaw to cut down political sign
- Catholic Charities phasing out foster care
- School Superintendent accused of using racial language
- Hospital guard accused of having sex with corpse
- Police find body of young child inside duffel bag
- NBA champ arrested in Hollywood
- College football's most polarizing coach is a Twitter menace

If we are not self-aware enough to turn away when the negative news surpasses our personal threshold or to at least appropriately recognize and name the emotions we are experiencing, the downward spiral becomes as visible as the headlines that fill our news feeds: negativity perpetuates negativity, so at what point are we intelligent enough to call a halt? In our current twenty-first-century culture, we tend to blame others and defend ourselves: blame the media, blame politicians, blame poor parenting, blame the internet and social media, blame the younger generations. The secular world does this, and the church does as well. And as we blame, we justify our own positions, articulating a separation from the object of our blame and creating a personal reality that often does not match the reality that others would name for us. A person of high EQ will recognize that blaming outwardly is typically futile when we bear responsibility for the cultural forces that surround us. Someone who blames has something to protect—an inner insecurity that would be embarrassing or crushing to reveal. Someone who blames will rarely be helpful in working toward a solution, and someone with high EQ knows to (1) recognize and accurately name inner responses first, and then (2) seek the most effective means of action.

As we seek to achieve the "cogtelligence" that Bar-On references, key emotional skills that EQ assessments identify are as follows:

- Identifying and labeling feelings
- Expressing feelings
- Assessing the intensity of feelings
- Managing feelings
- Delaying gratification
- Controlling impulses
- Reducing Stress
- Knowing the difference between feelings and actions[17]

Goleman coined the term *emotional intelligence* before school shootings became stories of teenaged snipers with multiple victims, before the internet became commonplace in many American households, and before social media encouraged people to respond impulsively, affirming false ideals and shaming those who falter. Goleman bemoans a new generation that has not been taught proper skills for identifying and resolving emotional conflicts, and he calls for courses in emotional literacy at all levels of education.[18] The cost of ignoring the importance of EQ are the generations of young adults and kids who have grown up with internet communication as a key facet of their realities. Life for them is not about dropping a smart phone into an adult's basket when you walk into the classroom in order to assuage some kind of fear of the unknown. Life is about stepping fully into the quagmire, phone in hand and internet data available, ideally equipped with the skills necessary to react appropriately and effectively.

CONSIDERING THE CULTURE

With the internet has come a new way of thinking about intelligence, creativity, and business, along with a new way of building space to promote

17. Goleman, *Emotional Intelligence*, 301.
18. Goleman, *Emotional Intelligence*, 286–87.

creativity. Built in the early 2000s, the corporate headquarters for Google in Mountain View, California, is iconic with its swimming pools, sand volleyball courts, eighteen cafeterias, free laundry rooms, winding pathways, and giant artwork. The campus is designed for self-sufficiency, variety, and to empower innovative thinking. With more than two million square feet of office space in the original complex alone, Googleplex is a model of twenty-first-century collaborative work. As Gillian Tett writes in *The Silo Effect*, intentionality has been our greatest weapon against an increasingly fragmented world, and that intentionality has pushed us towards a new kind of teamwork: "[I]n today's complex twenty-first-century world, we are all faced with a subtle challenge: We can either be mastered by our mental and structural silos or we can try to master them instead. The choice lies with us. And the first step to mastering our silos is the most basic one of all: to think how we all unthinkingly classify the world around us each day. And then try to imagine an alternative."[19]

The Nike World Headquarters in Beaverton, Oregon, is another example of a business that encourages innovation with its nearly 300-acre campus of more than seventy-five buildings, multiple playing fields, reflecting ponds, museums, trails, restaurants, shopping, memorabilia, statues, art, workout rooms, swimming pools, footbridges, and track. When employees are encouraged to discuss business and have difficult conversations while on a morning jog or kicking a soccer ball, EQ is essential. A team member who denies his or her emotions or who operates passive aggressively will likely struggle in such an open, competitive environment. Gone are the privacy walls of the twentieth century; today's culture operates in a fast-moving digital cloud that demands authenticity, integrity, and high EQ.

In the winter of 2003, Harvard University psychology sophomore Mark Zuckerberg began toying with computing code to develop a program that would answer the innate human need for interaction. In its earliest stages, Zuckerberg hacked into protected areas of Harvard's computer network to find photographs of each Harvard student. Together with junior Eduardo Saverin, Zuckerberg launched first "Facemash" and then "The Facebook" in 2004. As Zuckerberg and Saverin added other colleges and then developed the "Wall," a feature that allowed students to write comments on one another's profile pages, the site began to grow. Zuckerberg dropped out of Harvard that year and moved to Palo Alto, California, in the heart of Silicon Valley, and Sean Parker began raising money from area venture capitalists

19. Tett, *The Silo Effect*, 254.

and investors. By 2006, Facebook was open to the public, and by 2009, it was ranked as the most popular social media site in the world.[20]

What Zuckerberg and the other founders of Facebook have faced from the beginning is a twofold challenge: how to effectively manage external growth as the number of members grows and how to effectively manage internal growth as the number of employees grows.[21] For the engineers at Facebook, the underlying patterns of both users and employees are best viewed as statistical probabilities: "Because of our computing training, we tend to think of human organization problems as graph problems—we look at systems, nodes, and connections. And when you look at the world like that, it can get some really interesting results."[22] Rather than waiting for the pangs of growth to demand change, an error that could prove fatal as the social media giant managed user interactions, Facebook continually experimented with social engineering to determine the best way forward. Zuckerberg and others wanted to avoid the destructive silos and tunnel vision of companies like Sony, Xerox, Microsoft, General Motors, and UBS.; Instead they wanted to create an internal environment that mimicked the success of the silo-busting networking and social intimacy that marked the company's success.

As Facebook built its 430,000-square-foot headquarters in Menlo Park, California, the company sought to reduce bureaucracies and encourage dynamic creativity. The campus includes a nine-acre roof garden planted with 400 native trees intended to attract local birds, custom artwork, and unique but sparse architecture. Architect Frank Gehry said Zuckerberg wanted him to create a space that would foster innovation and allow for movement: "He did not want it overly designed. It also had to be flexible to respond to the ever-changing nature of his business, one that facilitated collaboration and one that did not impose itself on their open and transparent culture."[23]

As a metaphorical nod to the vast infrastructure of the Facebook site itself, Zuckerberg had architects connect the upper floors of varying buildings with walkways painted in the same orange-red as the Golden Gate Bridge. Doors at the ends of the walkways open automatically, much like supermarket doors, allowing engineers to keep walking without pause. Both Zuckerberg and Sheryl Sandburg, the company's high-profile CEO, work in glass-enclosed offices in the center of the open plan space, visible to all:

20. Tett, *The Silo Effect*, 169–70.

21. According to www.statista.com, Facebook boasted 2.23 billion monthly active users in the second quarter of 2018, and 25,105 employees as of December 2018.

22. Tett, *The Silo Effect*, 171.

23. Stone, "Inside Facebook's Futuristic New Campus."

"The Facebook managers were determined to present the company to the employees as a single, open mass, where everyone could—and should—collide with everyone else, in a free-wheeling, irreverent way."[24] Rather than the cattle-pen-style cubicles of the latter twentieth century, One Hacker Way exemplifies structural and social shifts of the twenty-first century. While every model has its faults, what Facebook has done well is to continually turn the lens back on itself, pondering new ways to bring humans together in productive, invigorating ways. Integrity, authenticity, and a healthy EQ are essential in an era when human interactions can be fast and fleeting, allowing little time for counting the cost of past missteps.

WHAT MAKES IT HARD

We live in an era when emotions are seen as a problematic distraction. Since the latter half of the twentieth century, we have revered characters like Spock and Data from *Star Trek*, assuming that their logical minds allow them to access intellect at a rate that is uncluttered and efficient. But why do we unquestioningly presume a dialectical opposition between human emotion and rational thought? Isn't it likely that the two work better together?

Consider the cultural swings that have pulled these assumptions to and fro in recent generations: With the Industrial Revolution of the late eighteenth century, we witnessed the miracle of machines that accomplished routine tasks at a higher speed and without the human distractions of injury, illness, laziness, or interpersonal conflict. The changes that came like fast-clicking dominoes were global, irreversible, and immensely freeing. Human were fallible, distractingly emotional, and replaceable.

The reverence for machines left artists thirsting for something more, and the early nineteenth century ushered in the cultural backlash we now remember as Romanticism—a period that revived a focus on human intellect, creativity, and artistry. As Industrial Revolution-inspired inventions continued bursting forth in the background, Romanticism gave way in the latter nineteenth century to modernism, a cultural movement that affirmed both the innovation of industry and the creativity of the Romantics. Archetypal modernists like Sigmund Freud and Friedrich Nietzsche introduced a fascination with human psychology, and characteristics such as irony and self-consciousness arose as a response to a newly industrialized world.

In the mid-twentieth century, postmodernism emerged as a rejection of the presumed constraints of modernism. Postmodernism is often characterized by a deep-set skepticism and an irreverence for all things

24. Tett, *The Silo Effect*, 181.

sociologically organized or smacking in any way of compulsory structure. Deconstructionism and post-structuralism are two schools of thought typically associated with postmodernism. Postmodern critical methodologies often revere philosophy, psychology, and sociological studies, and most postmodernists eschew organized religion and anything grounded too overtly in human emotions. This skepticism of human emotions, spirituality, and anything that cannot be held and beheld runs so deep that most Americans do not recognize the ways that postmodern thinking has shaped our world.

Our first challenge, therefore, is to step outside of the postmodern worldview long enough to recognize that human emotions may not stand in opposition to intellect. Is it possible that human emotion, when intentional rather than reactionary, could actually make us more intelligent people in this twenty-first-century era of mass social interaction?

Our second challenge is simply recognizing that the work is hard. When we first learn to acknowledge our own emotions, we can feel embarrassed, ashamed, and out of control. While postmodern thought has taught us to maintain individual control at all costs, emotions often take us by surprise, making us feel out of control and vulnerable. The easiest response is to learn superior impulse control, shoving unpleasant emotions deep beneath the surface, but that response nearly always leads to a harmful outburst—harmful both to us and to those around us who have to endure the slings and arrows of our tamped-down frustration.

Some of us were taught as children to hide our emotions rather than announce them, which can lead to confusion about when emotions are occurring and which emotions are which. Goleman lists the following families of emotions in his work:

- **Anger**: fury, outrage, resentment, wrath, exasperation, indignation, vexation, acrimony, animosity, annoyance, irritability, hostility, and sometimes pathological hatred and violence
- **Sadness**: grief, sorrow, cheerlessness, gloom, melancholy, self-pity, loneliness, dejection, despair, severe depression
- **Fear**: anxiety, apprehension, nervousness, concern, consternation, misgiving, wariness, qualm, edginess, dread, fright, terror, phobia, panic
- **Enjoyment**: happiness, joy, relief, contentment, bliss, delight, amusement, pride, sensual pleasure, thrill, rapture, gratification, satisfaction, euphoria, whimsy, ecstasy, mania

- **Love**: acceptance, friendliness, trust, kindness, affinity, devotion, adoration, infatuation, agape
- **Surprise**: shock, astonishment, amazement, wonder
- **Disgust**: contempt, disdain, scorn, abhorrence, aversion, distaste, revulsion
- **Shame**: guilt, embarrassment, chagrin, remorse, humiliation, regret, mortification, contrition[25]

Some of our inherent postmodern ignorance of these basic human emotions stems from (1) our inability to acknowledge our own physiology as we experience good moods, bad moods, or other reactionary responses; (2) traumatic experiences that have made it difficult for us to access or face these emotions; (3) childhood patterns that encourage avoidance; (4) personal insecurities that lead us to a place of defensiveness, fear, or self-protection; (5) a lack of impulse control and little awareness of ways to improve self-management; (6) a life lived in unintentional stress; (7) a fear of other people's opinions; (8) a skepticism of all things intangible and mysterious, including our own physical responses; (9) a fear of the conflict that may arise if emotions are shared; and (10) a belief that temperament is destiny and therefore unchangeable. But, as Goleman argues throughout his work, our character indeed is malleable if we choose to do the work. An excellent first step is to simply acknowledge that we are not always able to anticipate or understand our own emotional responses. Much like an addict must first admit that he or she has an ailment and needs help, we must admit our inability to detect or predict our own emotional responses and then seek the resources necessary to learn, practice, and make changes.

I had a friend who would shrug his shoulders and say something like, "You chose to be friends with me!" when I expressed concern about the ethics of something he had done, particularly when it included an inappropriate emotional response. His refusal to acknowledge or master his own emotions eventually led to a ruptured relationship, and I realize now as I look back over the several decades I have known this person that his inability to maintain friend or family relationships clearly ties to his inability to recognize his own emotions. While his IQ is high and he can be *friendly* in normal social situations, his ability to be a *friend* or a congenial employee is hugely stunted by poor EQ.

I later had a coworker who insisted that "everything is great" any time I inquired about her well-being, her interactions with others, or the stressors I knew she was facing. I could tell by her inability to sustain eye contact

25. Goleman, *Emotional Intelligence*, 289–90.

and the way her hands stayed in motion that she was not offering an honest answer, and further pressing only brought continued insistence that all was well. Her avoidance eventually led to depression and her choice to leave our place of employment. I was sorry to see her go since her skills added depth to our workplace, but her low EQ greatly hampered her ability to be successful or relate in an honest way with other people.

We've all known people whose emotions erupt in explosive outbursts once in a great while, a clear symptom of avoidance and bottled-up frustration. The better we are able to pause and ponder the emotions that challenge us the most or the situations that are most likely to bring on an unexpected or unsavory emotion, the more wisely and intentionally we will be able to live our lives.

HOW JESUS DID IT

Jesus walks in the humility and confidence that his wisdom and his emotions are from God. What would it look like if leaders of the twenty-first-century church were trained to walk similarly—humble but confident in God's plan to (1) create each of us with the perfect IQ and (2) equip each of us with the desire and means to continually improve our EQ? Consider, for example, the blind men hollering and begging along the highway leading to Jericho:

> As Jesus and his disciples were leaving Jericho, a large crowd followed him. Two blind men were sitting by the roadside, and when they heard that Jesus was going by, they shouted, "Lord, Son of David, have mercy on us!"
>
> The crowd rebuked them and told them to be quiet, but they shouted all the louder, "Lord, Son of David, have mercy on us!"
>
> Jesus stopped and called them. "What do you want me to do for you?" he asked.
>
> "Lord," they answered, "we want our sight."
>
> Jesus had compassion on them and touched their eyes. Immediately they received their sight and followed him.[26]

As Jesus is leaving Jericho and anticipating his prophecy-fulfilling entry into Jerusalem, he had every right to be self-focused and anxious. He has told his disciples just a few verses prior that he will be betrayed by the teachers of the law and condemned to death, and while the disciples may not believe or understand what he is telling them when he predicts the course of the next few days for the "Son of Man," Jesus knows. As he approaches the blind

26. Matt 20:29–34.

men on the roadside, a large crowd is following him, likely clamoring for more teaching and healing. The highway is dry and dusty, Jesus is walking to his public mocking, torture, and crucifixion, and the press of the crowd behind and around him is likely overwhelming. Most leaders in this situation would succumb to anger, fear, defensiveness, or even egoism. But Jesus hears the two men calling from the side of the road for mercy, and he stops.

A fearful leader would have been too focused on his inner pain to even hear the men. An angry leader would have shamed either the blind men or the crowd or both, demanding that the conflict stop. A sorrowful leader would have been too inwardly focused to hear the men. A disgusted leader would have turned away from both the men and the large crowd, seeking respite among his disciples from the messiness of the world. And an ashamed leader also would have been too inwardly focused to hear the men. While he acted on none of them, Jesus likely experienced all of these emotions during his final days. Instead of ignoring or not hearing the blind men as he walks toward his impending death, Jesus hears them and stops to speak with them.

Here again, most leaders would not respond as Jesus does. Assuming a leader were able to hear the men, a likely response would be to either tell the men how to shoulder their fate well or announce to the men that their sight has been restored. But Jesus, whose perfect IQ and EQ allow him to focus fully on those around him, is calm, wise, and empathetic enough to ask the men what it is that they want from him. Rather than ignoring them or assuming he knows what they need—which surely he does—Jesus assures the men that he sees them and that their voices matter. He empowers them with his simple question, and he is able to empower the men on the roadside because he does not carry the burden of insecurity about his own IQ or an underdeveloped EQ. When the men answer that they want their sight, Jesus "had compassion on them" and "touched their eyes." Because of his secure IQ and EQ, he is able to take the time needed to hear the men's voices, stop in the road to see the men, empower the men with his question, have compassion for the men's blindness, and touch the men physically when he extends healing.

I was raised with a flannelgraph Jesus whose face was serene and whose character was disappointingly milquetoast. It was a relief, therefore, to realize in my early teen years that Jesus experiences a variety of emotions in the Gospels, demonstrating the fullness of his humanity as well as the authenticity of his emotional intelligence: anger at the teachers of the law, in the Temple, and with the fig tree[27]; impatience with unbelief[28]; sorrow over the death of Lazarus and over the city of Jerusalem[29]; compassion for the sick and needy[30]; eagerness to be with his disciples[31]; extreme distress in the garden of Gethsemane[32]; and the joy of his Father.[33] Jesus warns continually against fear, anxiety, hatred, anger, greed, lust, envy, and gluttony,[34] and he calls on his followers to love God and love their neighbors as themselves.[35]

Roy Oswald and Arland Jacobson argue that a key marker of Jesus' emotional intelligence is found in his ability to heal in a culture where sickness was common: "Since Jesus is portrayed as an exceptional healer, it seems fair to conclude that he had an unusual capacity for eliciting healing trust in ill persons. We regard this as evidence of emotional intelligence."[36] As we saw with the two blind men, Jesus' ability to prioritize the needs of others above his own is an exceptional example of his humble confidence in his own IQ and EQ. If he were tentative as he approached others, would the sick have the comfort and confidence to meet him? Illness was something to be avoided in the germ-ignorant first century, and it is unlikely that those with ailments would take the risk of approaching an itinerant rabbi who is unsure of himself and his God. A God-ordained security in his own IQ and EQ is what allowed Jesus to love others well. Wouldn't it behoove us to seek a similar path in order to step boldly forward in the two greatest commandments: to love the Lord your God with all your heart, soul, and mind, and to love your neighbor as yourself?[37]

EQ AND THE CHURCH

John Lee West and his coauthors attempt to redirect church leaders in their 2018 book *Emotional Intelligence for Religious Leaders*, walking a sometimes tenuous line between the helpful and hubris. In a chapter about emotional self-awareness, for example, the authors state that although religious leaders

27. Mark 3:5, Mark 11:15–18, Mark 11:12–14.
28. Luke 9:41.
29. John 11:35, Luke 13:31–35.
30. Luke 7:13, Matt 9:36, Matt 14:14, Matt 15:32, Mark 6:34, Mark 8:2–3.
31. Luke 22:15.
32. Matt 26:36–46.
33. John 15:11, John 17:13.
34. John 14:27, Matt 5.
35. Matt 22:36–40.
36. Oswald and Jacobson, *The Emotional Intelligence of Jesus*, 12.
37. Matt 22:37–39.

are "under tremendous pressure to be super-human," they must embody authenticity and transparency in order to be at peace with who they are as God's children.[38] In a later section about "showing empathy," the authors write the following:

> As religious leaders, it can be difficult to refrain from judging others when they share their dark secrets, because part of our role includes preaching and teaching morality to others. As such, we sometimes think of ourselves as spiritual police officers or as guardians of truth. When people share things that violate our sensibilities, is it more important for us to set them straight, or to help them heal?[39]

While their intent here is admirable, this kind of religious presumption bears little witness to the EQ of Jesus. If leaders in the church must learn to "show empathy" rather than naturally embodying an empathy and compassion for others, should they be leaders in the church? If they must be told later in that same chapter to "suspend judgment" and "avoid the temptation to assume we know the intentions of others,"[40] should they really be guiding the church in the twenty-first century?

In the spring of 2018, I helped to design an experimental course for our university that includes attendance at the annual two-day Global Leadership Summit. The summit takes place at Willow Creek Community Church near Chicago each August and is simulcast to nearly half a million people in more than 135 countries. Produced by the nonprofit Willow Creek Association since the 1990s, the Global Leadership Summit began as an annual training event for ministry leaders and has grown into a widely publicized leadership event that boasts high-profile leaders such as Sheryl Sandberg, Simon Sinek, T. D. Jakes, and others. The course I designed began with three weeks of online work for students: TED Talks by many of the upcoming speakers, discussion forums about the videos they viewed, and a pre-summit paper to help students ask appropriate questions and focus their ideas. Students attended the summit at varying locations, and on the Saturday following the summit, we came together on campus for a four-hour debrief session before students were dismissed to complete a final summative paper.

What we did not anticipate as we designed the course was a summit tainted by the scandalous fall of its founder just weeks prior to the event itself. Bill Hybels founded Willow Creek Community Church in the 1970s,

38. West et al., *Emotional Intelligence for Religious Leaders*, 19.

39. West et al., *Emotional Intelligence for Religious Leaders*, 57.

40. West et al., *Emotional Intelligence for Religious Leaders*, 63.

and by the late 1990s it had grown into a prototypical megachurch with six services attended by more than 15,000 each weekend. Hybels founded the Willow Creek Association in the early 1990s, followed by the Global Leadership Summit in 1995.

In March and April 2018, the *Chicago Tribune* published allegations of sexual misconduct by Hybels that involved multiple women and spanned many decades. While Hybels initially denied the charges, he resigned his positions at Willow Creek Community Church, Willow Creek Association, and the Global Leadership Summit. The Willow Creek elder board initially published a response in support of Hybels, then later rescinded that support. Many associated with the church have expressed dismay about how the investigation was handled and have apologized to the women who filed complaints. Two lead pastors and many of the Willow Creek elder board subsequently resigned their posts because they believed the church investigation of Hybels was not handled appropriately. In response, several key speakers for the 2018 Global Leadership Summit stepped down, and more than 100 churches pulled out as host sites in the month before the event.

When the church site where many of my students and I planned to attend pulled out of the event, I pondered canceling the course. What inadvertent statement were we making by supporting an organization founded and run by a man who espoused Christian ethics but apparently lived a second unethical life of affairs and maltreatment of women? We chose to continue with the course and hold all of these developments as talking points in our exploration of leadership, Christianity, and Jesus' example.

While my students and I did not know whether the speakers at the summit would acknowledge the scandal or sidestep it, we were pleased to hear the new president of the Willow Creek Association, Tom DeViries, open the summit with an acknowledgement and apology for all that had transpired. The next speaker, author and pastor Craig Groeschel, offered an emotional apology in which he admitted shock and a sense of betrayal in hearing about the allegations against his friend. People would rather follow a leader who is real than always right, Groeschel said; a centered leader is one who is secure, stable, confident, fully engaged, boasts an internal alignment of values with external actions, is guided by values, is driven by purpose, and is obsessed by mission.

When my students and I gathered for our post-summit classroom session, what would have been a general discussion of the various speakers and their content instead opened with a consideration of how the scandal unfolded, why this kind of travesty happens among evangelical male leaders, and what checkpoints might have prevented the magnitude of what the story became. While it was a healthy discussion with thoughtful students, I am saddened by a larger church body that does not recognize the deep-set cultural harm incurred when we ignore accountability and training for such EQ competencies as self-awareness, self-management, and relationship management.

For the nonbelieving students in my class, the scandal was merely confirmation of what they have suspected all along: that Christianity itself is a simplistic, cult-like social structure that allows men to dominate, citing selective passages from Scripture to invoke "God" in support of their rules and obligations, and abusing those around them in the process. What kind of leaders would the church produce if we spent ample time considering IQ and EQ and the weight each carries when it is unexamined?

Chapter 6

Audience Quotient (AQ)

As Leonard Sweet writes in *From Tablet to Table,* true relationship demands far more than mere tolerance: "We don't love our neighbors merely by not bothering them or by doing nothing bad to them. We love our neighbors when we reach out to them, when we listen to them, when we 'give them something to eat' (Matthew 14:16)."[1] And when we enter fully into relationship, willingly and lovingly helping those around us, we are not called to defend or admonish, as both the secular and evangelical world might suggest. Instead, as Sweet suggests, we are to be humble, sometimes recognizing the need for silence as we seek truth together: "Disciples of Jesus who return from the mission field are like soldiers who return from the battlefield. The experience makes them not louder but quieter; they don't

1. Sweet, *From Tablet to Table*, 138.

pontificate, but stay humble, silent, considering when to leave things unsaid and when to simply listen to others."[2]

But the ability to sit comfortably with silence and in humility arises from a self-awareness and maturity that does not come easily for most. So what intentional changes do we need to be making? Behavioral scientists agree that IQ is measurable and somewhat immutable over the course of a lifetime. In other words, despite the self-help books that proclaim otherwise, IQ is a biological measure of intelligence that is difficult to change in any discernable way.[3] But EQ is another story. Once we agree on the assessment tools and competencies, it is possible for an individual to isolate EQ factors that he or she would like to improve, striving for a higher level of EQ. But is that enough?

Bar-On and Handley argue that self-assessment and improvement are key goals of any emotional audit. Bar-On defines emotional intelligence as "an array of emotional, personal, and social abilities and skills that influence one's overall ability to succeed in coping with environmental demands and pressures,"[4] and he lists the following emotional and social abilities as the factorial components of the "Bar-On Model"[5]:

- **Intrapersonal Components:**
  Self-Regard
  Emotional Self-Awareness
  Assertiveness
  Self-Actualization
- **Interpersonal Components:**
  Empathy
  Social Responsibility
  Interpersonal Relationship
- **Stress Management Components:**
  Stress Tolerance
  Impulse Control

2. Sweet, *From Tablet to Table*, 126–27.

3. While the IQ tool has been considered a reliable measure for more than a century, critics in recent years have questioned whether it carries inherent assumptions of white-Euro ethnocentricity. As the internet draws cultures more closely together, including our varying definitions of "intelligence," it will be interesting to see whether the presumed infallibility of this assessment comes into question.

4. Bar-On and Handley, *Optimizing People*, 2.

5. Bar-On and Handley, *Optimizing People*, 2.

Independence

- **Adaptability Components:**
  Reality Testing
  Flexibility
  Problem Solving
- **General Mood Components:**
  Optimism
  Happiness

Bar-On and Handley use the bulk of their 1999 book to elucidate these fifteen social and relational skills, defining them further and offering suggestions for improvement both for an individual and in a group setting. What is known as the "Bar-On Emotional Quotient Inventory" is only one of many tools for measuring Emotional Intelligence. Other assessment tools include the Emotional & Social Competence Inventory, the Genos Emotional Intelligence Inventory, the Group Emotional Competency Inventory, the Mayer-Salovey-Caruso EI Test (MSCEIT), the Schutte Self Report EI Test, the Trait Emotional Intelligence Questionnaire (TEIQue), the Work Group Emotional Intelligence Profile, and Wong's Emotional Intelligence Scale. Each of these emotional intelligence assessment measures is intended to inspire self-reflection and provide practical suggestions for self-improvement.

As universities nationwide bicker over the cross-purposes of administrators and faculty members, what effect might heightened Emotional Intelligence have on both sides of the equation? As students enter the classroom burdened by insecurities and anxieties, how might a professor with high Emotional Intelligence be more successful in creating a safe place for those students to unburden, listen well, and transform? As churches seek to share the gospel in new and inviting ways, how might it improve their effectiveness to have pastors, elders, and teachers who have high EQ ratings and are able to relate to one another and to the greater public in ways that are remarkably genuine, humble, consistent, and transparent? And while these considerations are all critical, at what point do we shift the lens from *self* to *the world?*

As Roxburgh and Boren write in *Introducing the Missional Church*, the evangelical effort to reach a broader population is both pervasive and admirable, particularly in light of changing social and political sensibilities. "The missional conversation has entered almost every stream of the church," Roxburgh and Boren argue. "The Spirit of God is moving in the church in creative, generative ways that call the people of God to engage their neighborhoods and display God's kingdom in everyday life. . . . Large churches are empowering people to listen to what God is doing outside the church buildings and blessing them to follow God's leading without having to call it a ministry of that church."[6] As churches are "empowering people to listen to what God is doing outside the church buildings," are they empowering people to both hear themselves well (IQ to EQ) and hear others well (EQ to AQ)? Sweet broaches this idea with his reference to "Peter the Ear" in *Nudge:*

> Peter didn't get his name changed to "the Rock" until after he proved he could be an ear-witness and he had listened to what the people were saying. *Simon* is a form of *Simeon*, which in Hebrew means "hearing." In Hebrew custom this meant Simon was "one who hears God" or even "one whom God has heard." Because he listened to what the people were saying, while at the same time was the first to confess Jesus as "the Son of the living God," Simon the Ear became Peter the Rock.[7]

God places enormous value on listening well, a skill that functions as a measure of both self-confidence (a clearly articulated sense of purpose) and EQ, and Jesus was our optimal example. Consider, for example, Jesus' exchange with the Samaritan woman at the well in Sychar. In a culturally explosive situation where most people would be so caught up in their own inner dialogue that effective listening would be an enormous struggle, Jesus listens, He questions, he suggests, he forgives, and he loves.[8] Someone mired by personal insecurities or the emotional backdrop of that moment would never have been able to both listen and affect that woman's life as Jesus did.

~

While I am suggesting the church and university leaders alike recognize the importance of Emotional Intelligence, I see a greater example in Jesus that must be our ultimate aspiration. Jesus did not ponder IQ or EQ. He knew His God-given purpose and his own emotional character so deeply that he was able to operate out of those foundations without pausing to ponder his alignment and next best step. Much as IQ has transcended to EQ in recent years, Jesus' example presses us to master EQ handily enough that we can step into a third quotient, a Jesus quotient, that is best referred to as AQ, or "Audience Quotient." As EQ calls us to name and consider the human

6. Roxburgh and Boren, *Introducing the Missional Church*, 52.

7. Sweet, *Nudge*, 158.

8. John 4:4–26.

emotions that influence our every move, AQ asks that we focus every ounce of who we are on the audience before us: measuring their emotional reactions, hearing their story, gauging their nonverbals, and considering what will help them to grow. In his book *What Good is God?*, Philip Yancey calls for a more Christ-like approach than mere culture-bashing and judgment: "We in twentieth-century America need not obsessively wring our hands over what offends us in the broader culture. Instead . . . we can refuse to believe the lies broadcast on the big screen. We can insist that a person's worth is not determined by his appearance or her income, or by ethnic background or even citizenship status, but rather is a sacred, inviolable gift from God."[9] But in order to insist on the inviolable God-given value of a person's worth, we must be able to see that person with Christ-like transparency, fully in control of our own EQ to a degree that we give it no more thought than the intake and outflow of our own breath.

AQ is our ability to focus fully on another: to love as we have been loved, to see as we are seen, and to teach and disciple as Jesus taught us to do. If we are mired in worldly worries or unable to articulate the truth of who we are and how we are called to live life well, we cannot expect to see our audience with the love and fierce purpose that Jesus did. But isn't this precisely what the Great Commission calls us to do? Shouldn't our personal mission statement align with Jesus' commission and example of how we are to live a missional life well? As Farley writes in *The Naked Gospel*, "You don't have to succumb to the paralysis of analysis. Christ is in you, and you are in Christ."[10] How, then, do we train university and church leaders to transcend from IQ to EQ to AQ, aspiring to a Jesus Quotient that aligns with the Great Commission in ways that will help us to (re)sign the church[11] as a safe place for renewal, energy, peace, and joy, rather than the hypocrisy and judgmentalism that has maligned its name for generations?

IQ (Intelligence Quotient)	**EQ (Emotional Quotient)**	**AQ (Audience Quotient)**
An individual's capacity to learn, reason, and think critically.	An individual's capacity to recognize, identify, and manage emotions appropriately.	An individual's capacity to focus consistently, completely, and effectively on others.

Here again, our twenty-first-century postmodern skepticism can hamper our ability to encounter the world more fully. Just as we are uneasy

9. Yancey, *What Good is God?*, 191.

10. Farley, *The Naked Gospel*, 213.

11. Downing, *Changing Signs of Truth*, 55–56.

about granting human emotions validity, a postmodern anxiety that previous generations did not hold, many of us find it difficult to conceptualize what it might mean to focus on another without losing ourselves in the process. Whether I am engaging with one person or a crowd of thousands, how do I focus completely on those before and around me without losing a sense of my own claim, argument, needs, and desires? If I truly listen to and enter into the reality of another, how do I simultaneously hold onto the pieces of myself that are important for me to remain standing and for the world to see? If I am holding one aloft alongside the other, am I truly focused on the other or am I distracted by my own ability to balance the two? How do I ensure that others are witnessing my intelligence, kindness, generosity, confidence, talent, or charm, while at the same time demonstrate that I am fully focused on the context that surrounds me?

If we acknowledge and accept our IQ, and if we embrace and commit to improve our EQ, we will be freed to pursue AQ in an effort to communicate more powerfully, empathize more fully, and ensure a more lasting impact on the world we encounter. We see this in Jesus' example as outlined in the four Gospels: the "Jesus Quotient" encompasses and embodies the trajectory of IQ to EQ to AQ.

When Jesus told his disciples in the Upper Room that he was leaving them, he did not remind them to live ethically or attend church regularly or finish their devotionals. "A new command I give you," he told them. "Love one another. As I have loved you, so you must love one another. By this everyone will know that you are my disciples."[12] The church has struggled for generations with how to share the Good News more widely, how to entice more people to join us, how to grow our numbers with better outreach and programming, but is it possible that we are complicating a rather simple commandment? Jesus did not ask us to do more or do better, as both would be antithetical to his death on the cross; he commanded us to love.

And while the command is simple enough, many of us do not love well. We extend what we think is love but what is really an effort at kindness that is laden with our own insecurities, hopes, ambitions, hurts, and desires. When Jesus called us to love, he called us to love selflessly and wholly, and we cannot accomplish that when we have not done the hard work to understand ourselves first so that we are able to more fully see the world around us. How would our twenty-first-century culture receive us differently if Christians were known as individuals who were comfortable in their own IQs, daily working to improve their EQs, and actively and effectively seeking to achieve high AQs?

12. John 13:34–35.

Much like IQ and EQ, it is helpful to consider AQ in its components, and Jesus offers us the markers of AQ throughout the New Testament. The beauty of his incarnate example, however, is that the markers of AQ stand outside of time, culture, socioeconomic class, gender, race, or even belief system. Jesus' example for us is eternal, as only God can accomplish. Below are ten markers of effective AQ:

Grounded	Functioning out of a firmly rooted ethics or worldview *(confident, centered, consistent)*
Authentic	True to one's character, intelligence, emotions, gifts, and flaws *(genuine, transparent, honest)*
Humble	Having a modest sense of one's own importance *(deferential, unpretentious, unassuming)*
Intentional	Demonstrating clear purpose and confidence *(decisive, focused, deliberate)*
Compassionate	Possessing a consciousness of others' pain and a desire to help assuage it *(sympathetic, empathetic, caring)*
Adaptable	Able to adjust quickly and smoothly to new conditions and situations *(flexible, versatile, adjustable)*
Resilient	Able to withstand difficult conditions and situations *(thick-skinned, tough, strong)*
Ardent	Demonstrating passion and drive *(enthusiastic, zealous, fervent)*
Present	Bringing full consciousness to the present moment *(engaged, aware, attentive)*
Prescient	Having exceptional foresight *(discerning, forward-thinking, visionary)*

When Jesus sat on the hillside in ancient Galilee, he called the people to a visionary and revisionary kind of truth—a message that carried the Jewish law into a new depth of honesty, humility, and genuine faith. "You must be poor in spirit," Jesus told them. "You must mourn for the world, and be meek, thirsty for righteousness, merciful towards others, pure in heart, and peacemakers. And you must be willing to be persecuted by the world for all of this."[13] What he calls the people to here—what he calls each of us to—is (1) the humility to know that what he lists here is more than our human hearts and minds can consistently accommodate, and (2) the faith to believe that he is our cornerstone.[14] "You are the light of the world," Jesus told them

13. Matt 5:3–10.
14. Psalm 118:22.

from his perch on the grassy hill. "Let your light shine before others, that they may see your good deeds and glorify your Father in heaven."[15]

AQ MARKER #1: GROUNDED

Grounded = Functioning out of a firmly rooted ethics or worldview (confident, centered, consistent)

From the moment that Jesus is baptized by his cousin John in the Jordan River, the essence of who he is and why he is on the earth is made clear:

> As soon as Jesus was baptized, he went up out of the water. At that moment heaven was opened, and he saw the Spirit of God descending like a dove and alighting on him. And a voice from heaven said, "This is my Son whom I love; with him I am well pleased."[16]

Jesus is thirty years old, he has lived a life of solitude, and he is ready to begin his tenure as an itinerant teacher and healer. His next three years are critical, and the blessing God the Father extends on his son here is beautiful and enduring. Jesus need not wonder who he is or where he came from or what his purpose should be. His heritage is clear, and his purpose is eternal.

On an internal door at Castle Church in Wittenberg, Germany, the cathedral where Martin Luther tacked his Ninety-Five Theses that spurred the Protestant Reformation in 1517, a tree of life stretches its branches toward the ceiling. Carved into a patina-green circle to commemorate the Reformation celebration of 2017, the tree boasts roots that spread wide beneath its trunk, tangling and stretching toward the floor. The ethical standards by which we live our lives must root as firmly and deeply as the Castle Church tree, rooting us in beliefs so solid that we will hold to them whether we are joyful or suffering, refreshed or exhausted, amorous or angry. For those who experienced a dramatic conversion, life may root out of a Jordan River-like moment, drawing us ever back to that first introduction to the Father. But for most people, the roots are more tenuous and sometimes difficult to find; yet the onus is on us to find them.

At the university where I teach, we press students to articulate their own worldviews, a process that is often arduous and somewhat painful. Most people live lives of reaction rather than action, responding to the slings and arrows of life without measuring their own responses. The danger, of course, is that we have little control over own behavior when we are not grounded

15. Matt 5:14, 16.
16. Matt 3:16–17.

in something that for us is tangible, definable, and real. The more intimately we understand our own roots, whether they are grounded in family heritage or a belief system that we have acquired in later years, the more consistently we will respond to varying situations.

An individual with high AQ will have a clear, consistent thread throughout his or her life, pointing ethical considerations back to the same subset of answers. High AQ individuals are the ones we seek out when we feel mired by a situation and are unsure which way to turn. They are not the "yes men" or "yes women" of our lives, but the individuals who answer truthfully, consistently, and calmly, their reasons always emerging from the same core truth. For Christians, our grounding is in Scripture, a personal relationship with Jesus, and the fellowship of other believers. The more soundly rooted we are in these tenets, the less surprised we will be by the unpredictable ebb and flow of life in a fallen world.

AQ MARKER #2: AUTHENTIC

Authentic = True to one's character, intelligence, emotions, gifts, and flaws (genuine, transparent, honest)

When Jesus is led into the wilderness shortly after his baptism, he does not pretend to be something that he is not. He is not tempted by Satan's lures; he is grounded in his Father's promises, and he neither inflates nor dilutes the truth of who he is. When Satan tempts him to display his power, Jesus answers with Deuteronomy 8:3: "Man shall not live on bread alone, but on every word that comes from the mouth of God."[17] When Satan challenges Jesus to leap from the highest point on the temple to prove God's authority, Jesus recites Deuteronomy 6:16: "Do not put the Lord your God to the test."[18] And when Satan offers Jesus all the earthly riches of the world, Jesus responds with Deuteronomy 6:13: "Worship the Lord your God, and serve him only."[19] After fasting for forty days and nights, Jesus surely was at his lowest point in terms of emotional responses, impulse control, and sheer survival instinct, and yet he holds to the truth of what he knows himself to be: the Son of God, yes, and also a human created to honor and glorify his Father. Jesus does not extrapolate fancy answers or compose his own poetic responses; he relies on the word of his Father and the truth of who he is.

When we attempt to paint ourselves as different than we really are in the eyes of others, we walk a dangerous path that invariably leads to alienation

17. Matt 4:4.
18. Matt 4:7.
19. Matt 4:10.

and disappointment. When I was in my twenties, one my best friends, Cora, had a mischievous sparkle in her eyes and masterful gift with the nuance of language. We laughed together often—over books we had read, stories we had lived, and the antics of people we knew. We were both living from meager minimum-wage paychecks in those days, but Cora sometimes surprised me with gifts: a bottle of Merlot and once a pair of sky-blue denim overalls that I wore until the knees tore away. I was thrilled when she and another best friend announced their engagement, and I looked forward to a wedding that would bely the strained formality of my own: something woodsy and barefoot, simple but profound.

Cora had worked part-time for a day care center in another town for more than two years, and she often came home with stories of the antics of her favorite kids or the frustration of working for a woman who was despotic but had fewer degrees than she. When her fiancé left his keys in her Wagoneer one day and found himself locked out of his apartment, workplace, and car, he called the main number for the day care to see when Cora would have time to return the keys. He called the day care twice just to be sure the woman who answered wasn't confused, and then he called another day care, and another, and another—his anxiety building as he wondered whether he had misheard the name of the day care. And then he called me at two in the afternoon and announced that he was headed to a nearby strip club.

I was confused at first, for obvious reasons, but it made sense as he explained. He remembered an awkward joke Cora had cracked about the bar when they drove by once, and suddenly the smell of cigarettes in her hair and the trays of make-up she never wore made sense to him. I prayed that afternoon that his hunch his wrong, but she was onstage when he walked in—every nightmare he had imagined reduced to that single spotlight on a fiancé who said she would be home at four, who wanted a raspberry torte instead of wedding cake, and who should have been fully clothed in that difficult moment.

While Cora's duplicity was extreme, many of us pass our days living by one standard and imagining another. How many of us have Facebook or Instagram or Snapchat accounts that reverberate with adventure and beauty? How well does our internet reality match the truth of who we are? How well does the person we are in the grocery store or the mall or church or at home match the truth of who we are? For an individual with high AQ, the self is singular, and honesty is a way of life.

AQ MARKER #3: HUMBLE

Humble = Having a modest sense of one's own importance (deferential, unpretentious, unassuming)

Despite his holy lineage, Jesus did not consider himself too esteemed to travel from town to town homeless and penniless, depending on others' generosity for survival. And he did not consider himself too esteemed to wash the feet of his dear friends. When he has finished, dried himself, and replaced his outer clothing, Jesus explains to his disciples the essence of what it means to be humble:

> "Do you understand what I have done for you?" he asked them. "You call me 'Teacher' and 'Lord,' and rightly so, for that is what I am. Now that I, your Lord and Teacher, have washed your feet, you also should wash one another's feet. I have set you an example that you should do as I have done for you. Very truly I tell you, no servant is greater than his master, nor is a messenger greater than the one who sent him.[20]

As counter-cultural as it sounds, humility can be empowering, shifting the focus from self to another in an emboldened, freeing manner. The more we focus inward, fussing about insufficiencies and pondering insecurities, the less we are able to engage with the world around us in healthy, invigorating ways. Humility renews our perspective, reminding us of the enormity of God's plan, God's love, and God's steadfast promises.

I had a friend many years ago who sat at my kitchen table one afternoon and told me he was one of the top three smartest minds in his industry. I was shocked by his presumption, and I questioned him, pressing gently but pressing nonetheless: "When have you spent time with the upper echelons?" I asked. "Until you have spent time there, how can you know?" He assured me that he knew, simply by reading and watching the news and considering. And I watched him frustrated again and again by missed opportunities, unoffered jobs, and windfalls never earned. The last time I saw him, he had lost his job, his home, his marriage and children, his mental health, and his hope. High AQ individuals recognize the emotional health of living life without pretention or a sense of self-aggrandization. Somehow my friend had never learned that happiness is fleeting when we receive, but our joy can be compounded in eternal ways when we give.

20. John 13:12–16.

AQ MARKER #4: INTENTIONAL

Intentional = Demonstrating clear purpose and confidence (decisive, focused, deliberate)

As we have concluded already, high-AQ individuals do not respond to life reflexively, blaming westerly winds for their misfortunes or shrugging their shoulders when others ask why they responded as they did. High-AQ individuals are intentional in all that they do, whether relational, professional, or at leisure. Intentionality does not suggest that one never binge-watches a television series or eats too much butter pecan ice cream, but even those choices are just that: choices rather than reactions.

Jesus demonstrates the intentionality of his mission on earth when he grants authority to his twelve disciples to heal those they encounter in the name of his Father:

> Do not get any gold or silver or copper to take with you in your belts—no bag for the journey or extra shirt or sandals or a staff, for the worker is worth his keep. Whatever town or village you enter, search there for some worthy person and stay at their house until you leave. As you enter the home, give it your greeting. If the home is deserving, let your peace rest on it; if it is not, let your peace return to you. If anyone will not welcome you or listen to your words, leave that home or town and shake the dust off your feet.[21]

Jesus' calm confidence here is infectious, demonstrating to his disciples that there will be no tiresome waffling between varying decisions, no drama as the group weighs and debates the most ethical next step. Instead he warns them of the hurt and betrayal they will face, drawing clear boundaries against the evil that will threaten them, and details the steps that will edify and the choices that will deter. How much of our lives do we spend questioning our convictions rather than stepping clearly and intentionally into them?

When I was a journalist, I worked for a time for a news editor who was indecisive and easily swayed from his purpose. He would call me into the office at varying times of the day, asking that I ponder with him the legality of including this source or that, of running one headline rather than another, of leading with one direct quote rather than another. While I enjoy mulling ethical considerations when the stakes are high and the lines are unclear, I soon realized that my editor was in the habit of responding rather than instigating. He did not have the confidence to make a clear choice and be

21. Matt 10:9–14.

deliberate with his actions, and so he needed me to help him process the options before him as he reacted to the news of each new day. My quandary lay in the hours that I spent with him pondering his job, while the responsibilities of mine stacked up on the side, waiting to fill my evening and weekend hours when I was not weighing each new ethical consideration anew with my low-AQ editor. With permission of the publisher, I stepped back from my job as his assistant as I was unable to ride on the wake of his meandering. He was disappointed in my choice to step away, but I knew I could not follow a leader who was unintentional and indecisive. We are naturally drawn to people whose actions are deliberate, even if we disagree, because at least we know they stand for something and can orient ourselves accordingly.

AQ MARKER #5: COMPASSIONATE

Compassionate = Possessing a consciousness of other's pain and a desire to help assuage it (sympathetic, empathetic, caring)

After I recovered from a childhood of assuming that Jesus was solemn-faced, rule-following, and unemotional, I was delighted to learn how often he proclaims his compassion for the people he encounters. Consider these:

- Jesus went through all the towns and villages, teaching in their synagogues, proclaiming the good news of the kingdom, and healing every disease and sickness. When he saw the crowds, he had *compassion* on them, because they were harassed and helpless, like sheep without a shepherd. Then he said to his disciples, "The harvest is plentiful but the workers are few. Ask the Lord of the harvest, therefore, to send out workers into his field."[22]
- When Jesus heard what had happened, he withdrew by boat privately to a solitary place. Hearing of this, the crowds followed him on foot from the towns. When Jesus landed and saw a large crowd, he had *compassion* on them and healed their sick.[23]
- When [the son] came to his senses, he said, "How many of my father's hired servants have food to spare, and here I am starving to death! I will set out and go back to my father and say to him: Father, I have sinned against heaven and against you. I am no longer worthy to be called your son; make me like one of your hired servants." So he got up and went to his father. But while he was still a long way off, his father

22. Matt 9:35–38.
23. Matt 14:13–14.

> saw him and was filled with *compassion* for him; he ran to his son, threw his arms around him, and kissed him.[24]

The beauty of these examples is that for Jesus, compassion is not measured or careful; his compassion is immediate, emotional, and real. How can we, too, learn to live in a way that allows us to experience the hurt others are experiencing, compelling us to seek a remedy in hopes of easing another's pain?

Individuals with high AQ do not exhibit mere sympathy or pity for others, both of which suggest a power-oriented distance. AQ-adept people experience true sorrow when they encounter injustice or trials that another is experiencing. Many of us feel compassion when we witness a child who is suffering, or a close friend or family member, or even a pet. But what about the coworker who has spoken ill of us behind our backs, or the homeless man who is shouting at something unseen and whose stench is evident from nearly a block away, or the population of people on the other side of the globe whose language, culture, ethics, and priorities have little to do with ours? How do we feel compassion for all of humanity, as Jesus did? How do we feel compassion when a thousand other obligations are pulling us this way and that, distracting us from the humanity before us? For high-AQ individuals, compassion is not just a response but a constant lens through which they view the world.

AQ MARKER #6: ADAPTABLE

Adaptable = Able to adjust quickly and smoothly to new conditions and situations (flexible, versatile, adjustable)

When the disciples wake Jesus from his slumber in the stern of the boat, what he opened his eyes to must have been startling and emotion-filled. Before he went to sleep, Jesus has been teaching by the lake to a crowd that grew so large that he taught from a boat, his voice amplified by the water. When he was done teaching for the evening, Jesus and his disciples separated from the crowd and sailed out into what appeared to be calm waters:

> A furious squall came up, and the waves broke over the boat, so that it was nearly swamped. Jesus was in the stern, sleeping on a cushion. The disciples woke him and said to him, "Teacher, don't you care if we drown?"

24. Luke 15:13–20.

> He got up, rebuked the wind, and said to the waves, "Quiet! Be still!" Then the wind died down and it was completely calm.
>
> He said to his disciples, "Why are you so afraid? Do you still have no faith?"
>
> They were terrified and asked each other, "Who is this? Even the wind and the waves obey him!"[25]

Jesus' response is swift, intentional, and 100 percent focused on his disciples. He adjusts quickly from sleep to storm and from storm to his disciples, never pausing to pity himself or try to slow things down.

An AQ-adept person is able to adapt quickly and easily, a capability that can be particularly challenging when one is speaking before a large audience. Some of the most painful sermons I have observed have come when a pastor is unable to recognize that the congregation is losing interest, taking offense, or simply not tracking with him or her. In one instance, I watched a young pastor whose seminary education was still fresh move from Scripture to life stories to an angry Jonathan Edwards-style hellfire-and-brimstone sermon that was hardly appropriate for the small gathering whose eyes widened as he became more impassioned with each new point. I appreciated his energy, but I was sorry that he was unable to read the faces of those who were listening: a mostly older group of kindhearted, giving servants who hardly needed to be threatened in order to open their Bibles. If anything, that group needed a word of encouragement and an encouragement to rest, and I was sorry that our young pastor was unable to see their shoulders sink and their eyes avert as his volume increased. When we are speaking to an audience and their walls begin to rise, is there really any reason to keep speaking? How can we hold our purpose in balance with the response of the audience, making adjustments as we go?

Another Sunday at this same church, a guest pastor with a wonderful sense of joy and humor told jokes throughout her sermon, laughing long and loud with each new joke. But beyond a few supportive smiles, the congregation was not laughing with her. So again, while I enjoyed her energy, I was sorry to see that she could not seem to gauge the mood in the room and recognize that her humor was sailing emptily across the pews rather than drawing everyone together with a joyful sense of camaraderie. A high-AQ individual is adaptable, observing keenly and adjusting his or her communication accordingly.

25. Mark 4:35–41.

AQ MARKER #7: RESILIENT

Resilient = Able to withstand difficult conditions and situations (thick-skinned, tough, strong)

Jesus' resiliency up until the moment of his death was astounding and a remarkable example for all of us. Even after he had been beaten horribly, mocked by Roman guards and the crowds, betrayed by his closest friends, and nailed bodily to planks of wood so he hung suffocating high above the ground, his emotional fortitude was profound: "Father, forgive them, for they do not know what they are doing."[26] While Jesus' example bears weight we will never be called to, those who are AQ-savvy have an ability to step past the insults of the world in ways that surpass the norm.

A missionary couple I admired immensely had dedicated their lives to the people of Ethiopia, working tirelessly to translate the Bible into a native language that had never known Scripture. For more than thirty years, they labored over the translation, traveling from continent to continent and facing challenges that no one could have anticipated. While I never pressed for details, I know that they lost an eight-year-old daughter while living in Ethiopia, a point of great grief for both of them. And as they aged and the need to finish the translation became more critical, health issues loomed and beckoned them back to medical care in the United States again and again. While in Ethiopia, they spent long hours huddled over transitory verbs and subject pronouns, and in the United States, they pressed doctors to slow the macular degeneration that threatened to stall the project. Yet through it all, they were two of the most humble, stable, and joyful people I have ever met. Clearly their resiliency was an example to the hundreds of people who watched their impressive life travels, inspiring the rest of us to persevere through our own trials that seemed far less devastating or exotic than what these two endured.

An AQ-adept leader often demonstrates resiliency simply in his or her ability to absorb and move past difficult conditions such as public accusations, personal affronts, or unnecessary conflict. As Jesus recognized in his days in Jerusalem, the human heart is tainted by self-centered ambitions, greed, and defensiveness, and we are sometimes daily called to endure the affronts of this world as we pronounce the joy of the next: "Now while he was in Jerusalem at the Passover Festival, many people saw the signs he was performing and believed in his name. But Jesus would not entrust himself to them, for he knew all people. He did not need any testimony about

26. Luke 23:34.

mankind, for he knew what was in each person."[27] Perhaps the lesson here is not the despair of human cruelty but the otherworldly hope of what we can bring to the world through the Holy Spirit that Jesus gifted to us two millennia ago. If we exude compassion and are resilient to the barbs that invariably will come our way, won't we learn to love in a way that is timeless and far superior to fleeting cultural swings and sociological entanglements?

AQ MARKER #8: ARDENT

Ardent = Demonstrating passion and drive (enthusiastic, zealous, fervent)

But while an AQ leader can demonstrate groundedness, intentionality, compassion, and a keen sense of purpose, little would be gained without true passion and fervency. A trial attorney who weaves her argument artfully and yet does not seem to favor her client's cause with any measure of enthusiasm will not convince a jury. A politician whose ethical standards are admirable but whose interest in his constituents is lukewarm at best will not engender votes. And a pastor who stands before a congregation speaking the words of Scripture but who does not demonstrate an enthusiasm for the peace and joy that Jesus promises will leave most congregation members dozing apathetically in the pews.

In his three short years of ministry, Jesus' passion for the people he encountered and the God he embodied was palpable. Consider the intensity of his disappointment in discovering yet another avenue where the religious leaders were counting coins rather than loving well:

> When it was almost time for the Jewish Passover, Jesus went up to Jerusalem. In the temple courts he found people selling cattle, sheep and doves, and others sitting at tables exchanging money. So he made a whip out of cords, and drove all from the temple courts, both sheep and cattle; he scattered the coins of the money changers and overturned their tables. To those who sold doves he said, "Get these out of here! Stop turning my Father's house into a market!" His disciples remembered that it is written: "Zeal for your house will consume me."[28]

The best professors at my university are not the ones who have published the most or planned the most creative classrooms or who have the most enticing content areas. The best professors, without exception, are those who are most passionate about the content they are sharing with students. It does

27. John 2:23–25.

28. John 2:13–17.

not matter whether a professor is discussing thermal dynamics, reaction formation, Civil War history, or the use of a hyphen: Students invariably will become excited and engaged or bored and disillusioned based on the level of passion coming from the one who is sharing the information.

If Jesus' passion was unchecked and empowering, what can we do to step outside of the cultural and social expectations that keep us locked inside an expected standard? Are we passionate about the messages we are called to share? And if we are, how evident is that passion to those who are actively listening and to those who may be watching when we don't even realize?

AQ MARKER #9: PRESENT

Present = Bringing full consciousness to the present moment (engaged, aware, attentive)

When Jesus encounters Zacchaeus the tax collector, his ability to spot the outlier amidst the chaos is something to admire:

> Jesus entered Jericho and was passing through. A man was there by the name of Zacchaeus; he was a chief tax collector and was wealthy. He wanted to see who Jesus was, but because he was short he could not see over the crowd. So he ran ahead and climbed a sycamore-fig tree to see him, since Jesus was coming that way.
>
> When Jesus reached the spot, he looked up and said to him, "Zacchaeus, come down immediately. I must stay at your house today." So he came down at once and welcomed him gladly.[29]

Time and again it is in the crowd, in the midst of the noise and dust and press and chaos, that Jesus spots an individual and calls upon them. Yes, his heightened awareness exemplifies God's desire to spot us amidst the busyness of our lives and the world, but isn't his example also something for us to emulate? What kind of leaders would we be if we had the capability of spotting the quiet soul who is hurting, despite the surrounding noise? And what if, instead of attempting to reason with or convince that quiet soul, we became the guest, stepping into his or her world so we can better understand and then better extend our love?

Our technology-rich, information-laden culture makes the marker of simply being present even more critical—both in terms of what we practice and in terms of what others observe in us. During Welcome Weekend each

29. Luke 19:1–6.

year, the university where I work sets up six- and eight-foot-tall white block letters in the grassy area around the clock tower: "Be Known," the letters read, and students snap photos posing by the letters as they unpack their dorm rooms and anticipate a new year. For the faculty and staff employed at our university, the letters are more than just a gimmicky photo op for each new year. The letters represent a promise we make that every student will be known personally, academically, and spiritually. This promise demands intentionality and it demands presence. All who are a part of our university family must set aside the deadlines and social media pressures and anxieties in order to simply be present before one another, asking questions as Jesus would and listening deeply as Jesus always did. As faculty, our prayer is twofold: (1) that students feel truly known in their time with us, and (2) that students learn what it means to be present for others, allowing them to experience the fullness of what it is to be known fully and well by someone else.

As one student said recently, "be known" is a three-dimensional concept, not just two-dimensional, which means we are each witnessing one another in the fullness of who we authentically are: "My professors have been able to empower me by knowing my weaknesses and my strengths, and discussing that with me in a really honest way." And in the words of another student, "The concept of 'being known' feels really Christ-like to me because it encourages us to love ourselves and to love others, and in order to truly love that we would truly see." Indeed it is freeing for others when we see them for who they truly are, not for who they imagine themselves to be or who we have decided they should be. Just as Jesus spotted Zacchaeus perched in the sycamore tree, can we be present enough to spot those who are hesitantly waiting in the shadows, unsure and not yet known?

AQ MARKER #10: PRESCIENT

Prescient = Having exceptional foresight (discerning, forward-thinking, visionary)

Jesus' ability to respond with peace and calm is grounded in that first moment when he emerged from the Jordan River, the heavens opened, and the Spirit of God descended on him like a dove. From that moment forward, his firm confidence in his origins and his purpose allowed him to be fully present as well as fully prescient. When we are fully prescient, we apprehend not only the context that surrounds us but also the precursors that came just before and the potential moments that lie just beyond. For Jesus, it often meant that he was defending one individual against the tyranny of others who struggled to see beyond the prison-house of their own culture, language, and limited expectations:

> While Jesus was in Bethany in the home of Simon the Leper, a woman came to him with an alabaster jar of very expensive perfume, which she poured on his head as he was reclining at the table.
>
> When the disciples saw this, they were indignant. "Why this waste?" they asked. "This perfume could have been sold at a high price and the money given to the poor."
>
> Aware of this, Jesus said to them, "Why are you bothering this woman? She has done a beautiful thing to me. The poor you will always have with you, but you will not always have me. When she poured this perfume on my body, she did it to prepare me for burial. Truly I tell you, wherever this gospel is preached throughout the world, what she has done will also be told, in memory of her."[30]

Despite the social indecency of a woman approaching Jesus in this way and appearing to be wasteful with wealth that could have been put to better use, Jesus is able to see beyond the confines of social assumptions to his own encroaching sacrifice and the profound symbolism of what she is offering. As leaders in the church, we frequently feel the eyes of the church body on us, much as Jesus was observed by his disciples and the crowds beyond, but does that limit us in ways that we have not realized? Is it possible that our efforts to provide an effective model for our congregation or the world beyond is as limiting as the repeated assumptions of the Pharisees in Jesus' time? What assumptions do we each hold about gender, race, age, education, class, status, career, physical ability, emotional stability, mental health, worldview, learning differences, or theology that may limit our ability to communicate effectively with those around us?

It is important that an AQ-adept individual have the ability to be fully present before the people in his or her life, but what about the ability to anticipate the future? We are in the midst of some of the most profound sociological shifts on a global level that the world has ever seen, and it amazes me that the church is still discussing whether we should build better buildings, better programs, or better mission field opportunities. Why are we bemoaning millennials, social media, false news, and a cultural climate that is shockingly hostile, rather than wrestling in and pointing toward the future? At what point do we stop shaming the cultural concepts that lurk in the trees above our heads, and instead invite ourselves over for a visit,

30. Matt 26:6–13.

asking questions, listening well, and pondering a future where an effective Audience Quotient allows us to reach people in ways we never have before?

Chapter 7

The Future Church

I PRESSED THE COOL brick with my fingertips and decided to let the others move on without me. I knew we would all be somewhere in the house together, but I was tired of listening for their footsteps as they moved from room to room, of trying to keep pace with their scurried race through Martin Luther's home. I would listen generally for their location, I decided, but I would allow myself to inhabit the rooms on my own, resting my hand on the table where Luther gathered for his famous Table Talks and lingering over the not-always-flattering sketches of Martin and his wife Katharina. I was 5,000 miles from home, standing in the stately brick house of Martin and Katharina Luther in Wittenberg, Germany, on Reformation Day 500 years after Luther tacked his Ninety-Five Theses to the outer door of Castle Church. I was there with hundreds of pastors from all over the world, a handful of whom were friends and colleagues of mine, and the pastor in charge carried anxiety on his face like a teenager's setting spray—his cheeks strained upwards and his lips pressed thin. I was sorry for his worry, but I was not interested in entering in.

Luther's house is now a museum, and it was difficult at times to tell what was new and what was original as hundreds of years of renovations blended together into one. Much had been renovated in order to allow for crowds to walk through, and it took a sharp eye to spot the original treasures tucked among the restorations. My favorite moments were those silent spaces when others in the museum had moved along and I found myself alone, listening to the walls and inhaling the air that surely was the same air exhaled in the beginnings of the protest movement 500 years prior. The brick wall where I pressed my fingers was a corner archway where Luther said he stood to feel the Holy Spirit's presence. I leaned my back to the bricks and turned my face to the room, as I imagined Luther would have in his moments of seeking a more profound encounter with God.

In that corner, in the yard, on the upper floors, and everywhere in that house I could feel a soul that pressed so deeply inward to God that he saw beyond the confines of culture, tradition, and ecclesiastical authority. What Jesus said in the New Testament was real to Luther, and he sought to live into it fully. Painted on one wall was the sweeping calligraphy of Luther's words from 1531: "Glaube an Christus und tue, was du schuldig bist zu tun in deinem Berufe." *"Believe in Christ and do whatever needs to be done in your profession."* And so he did, whether it was gathering the greatest thinkers of his time or writing hymns or preaching sermons or translating the Bible into German so the German people could read it for themselves rather than relying on a priest.

The first time I saw Luther's table where he and Katharina met regularly with university professors and other intellects to debate theology and the improprieties of the Catholic Church, the anxious pastor and his friends descended soon after. The famous table sits to one side in a narrow room, the light from the window tampered by the dark wood of the table and the walls that surround it. The table was smaller than I expected, a rectangle that would fit only six or eight adults comfortably, and its dappled, uneven surface was wonderfully metaphorical of a time when Luther and his friends labored to chip away at the legalisms of a hugely powerful religious bureaucracy.

When the anxious pastor breezed into the room, chattering with his assistant about why the leaders of his group were not all in that appointed place at once, the space suddenly felt narrower and the air thin. I stood near the table, my back to the wall, and I watched the group assemble and buzz about expectations, sending several members off to find missing pastors.

Once they had returned with the ones they could find, the group began to sing Luther's masterful hymn "A Might Fortress is Our God"; the title of Luther's prized composition is scripted around the exterior of the majestic tower that rises above Castle Church. They sang the first verse and then the second, a woman assistant photographing the group with her smart phone, and I wondered whether anyone had noticed the table.

When they had finished the second verse, the pastors hurried on and I remained, enjoying the image of Katharina bringing home-brewed beer to that table, bucking the gender expectations of her era by sitting down and joining the men in their debates about theology. A former nun, Katharina ran the family's hostel of forty-some students, managed the former monastery's brewery, raised the couple's six children, oversaw the many farm animals, and directed the family's finances. She respected her husband's position as a theology professor at the University of Wittenberg, but she knew the family's business decisions were better left in her capable hands.

Outside the Luther museum-house, pale yellow bricks pressed together to form the walls of Luther's original study. A dark opening that was roped off plunged deep beneath the earth besides Luther's tiny study, a tunnel to his private bathroom where he apparently spent many hours soothing bowels that did not handle well the foods that he was accustomed to eating. As I wandered the exterior brick area, marveling at how well preserved the outer buildings were five centuries later, I realized that I hadn't seen anyone from my group in quite some time. It was quiet in that courtyard except for the occasional breath of wind through the trees, blissfully quiet.

I walked back into the main-floor front rooms of the museum and soon realized that neither my friends nor the larger group of pastors were anywhere to be found. I texted two of my friends, thankful in that moment for the internet that I had paid to continue overseas. It turned out that they had left Luther's house en masse thirty minutes or more prior and walked together down the cobblestone street to Castle Church. Patrick, a Lutheran pastor for whom this trip was a culmination of many years of anticipation, offered to walk back for me, and I was thankful for his lead down the winding street that I would not have known how to find. The light began to dim into evening as we speed-walked the streets from Luther's house to Luther's church, passing his university on the way. Castle Church boasted an impressive spire above the wonderfully Bavarian-style streets, a castle-like beacon in the darkening distance.

Once we reached the church, the double doors where Luther tacked his theses looming large against the night sky, we were surprised to find the church doors locked from the inside where several hundred were waiting for the evening service to begin. A small crowd began gathering, and I recognized several of them as pastors from our larger group; all of us had been promised a worship service in Luther's Castle Church on October 31, 2017, the night commemorating the Reformation's five-hundredth anniversary, and it was both startling and amusingly symbolic to find ourselves locked out, banging on the formidable doors as we heard the pipe organ begin to play inside. After many minutes of determined knocking, and a telling observation of the pastors around me who were growing angry at the thought of missing the event they had paid so much to witness, someone unlocked a side door from the inside and ushered us through, admonishing us to be quiet as we slid to the front of the sanctuary to join our friends. I was excited to see the majestic interior of the old cathedral, but there was also something oddly magical about the moments just prior when we were locked outside of the church where the Reformation began.

The service that evening included a series of male pastors from various denominations in the United States. Some spoke passionately about new directions for the church, others were more subdued in their delivery, and all were Pentecostal on some level. I spent much of the time alternately craning to see past the heads to my left and gazing to my right at the intricacies of the neo-Gothic stained glass, statues, and careful woodwork that surrounded us. Luther's fateful doors were near the front of the church, replaced centuries earlier when a devastating fire burned much of the chapel. The heavy doors were carved on the exterior with the Latin words of Luther's Ninety-Five Theses, arguing against the authority of Catholic clergy and pronouncing the freedom that Jesus promised in commemorative bronze that weighed more than a ton.

When the service ended, we were whisked onto buses by the anxious pastor and driven in a scurry back to Berlin; but the wispy trees and quiet air of Wittenberg beckoned me to return. Several days later, my friend Patrick and I caught a ride back down to the quaint city with a family we knew, the two of us pressed into the back seat of their rental car with the couple's daughter. This time we wandered slowly, savoring the university, the calm streets, the shops and restaurants, and—of course—Castle Church. Martin Luther is buried in the front of the Castle Church sanctuary alongside his good friend and fellow academician Philipp Melanchthon, and it was astounding to stand alone with a hand on his grave, imagining all that had transpired there over the years.

A visiting Lutheran pastor from the Midwest invited us to stay for an English service while we were in Castle Church, and for a time we did, enjoying the tinny hymns sung by the fifteen or twenty people gathered in the enormity of that place. When the pastor began his sermon, though, we realized that if we stayed for the entirety of the service, we would miss the opportunity to visit the shops that would soon close along the cobblestone street that wound towards Luther's home. We tried to be discreet in our exit, tiptoeing back toward the giant patina tree of life in the back of the sanctuary and pressing gently on the door handle. But we had forgotten the German tradition of locking the church doors from the inside once a service began, allowing the pastor to focus on the service without concern of interruptions from outside. Castle Church had just one key for these doors, and it typically was held by the pastor.

I joked with my friend about the fire safety of sitting locked in a church originally constructed in the 1300s, a single key tucked in the pocket of a man who would have to run the sizeable length of the church, from pulpit to rear door, in order to free its inhabitants. Then again, what more remarkable way to meet Jesus than locked in the portal of the Protestant Reformation? Thankfully the kind pastor from the Midwest noticed our indiscreet exit and paused his sermon to unlock the rear doors, freeing us to wander the cobblestones in search of a Luther-approved Reformation beer.

Everywhere we went echoed with Luther's assumption-busting vision. Why do we continually bind ourselves in the rules that others write for us? I wondered. Jesus came two millennia ago to tell us to knock it off, and Luther echoed the plea with his protest at the youthful age of twenty-four. When Luther tacked his ideas to the door of Castle Church in 1517, he expected other professors or church leaders to call him to a meeting in a local pub to discuss the ideas, as was their custom in Wittenberg; university faculty regularly used the doors of Castle Church as a place to pin messages and notices, inspiring healthy discussion. But this time the request never came.

Luther was surprised and thought that because he was not hearing anything, perhaps the church leadership had decided that his suppositions were valid after all. But that was not the case at all. In the few days that passed before Luther heard a response, church leaders were seeking the proper legal grounding to have him tried as a heretic. In other circles, friends used the printing press in town to make copies of Luther's Ninety-Five Theses; soon the theses were distributed all over Germany, and then translated and distributed throughout Europe. Luther's chief complaint on the list was the practice of indulgences by the Catholic Church, which allowed the church to control its parishioners by claiming authority over each person's walk to salvation. Luther saw no biblical foundation for the requirement of indulgences in order to reduce one's punishment in the afterlife, and he called for a removal of all such ecclesial penalties.

~

When the businesses were mostly closed and it was time to say our farewells to the delightful town of Wittenberg, my friend and I dialed for an Uber car to deliver us back to Berlin. What a shock it was when the response on my phone told us that there would be no more Uber cars in our area that evening. Yes, it was nearly eleven at night, but it hadn't occurred to us that big-city transportation might not be an option in Luther's hometown.

We walked to the edge of town, following what we thought were signs to a transportation hub, and we soon found ourselves at a train station that looked promising. Although neither of us read German, the signs seemed to indicate that another high-speed train or two would be coming through that night, en route to Berlin and beyond. I tried to insert money in an automated ticket machine so we could buy our tickets right there, ensuring our safe travels back to the capital city, but the machine did not seem to be working. For twenty or thirty minutes we wandered to and fro between train portals connected by underground tunnels, wondering where a train would first appear and how we would convince someone to help us.

When we felt the grind of a train's engine rumbling up through the ground beneath our feet, we ran. And when the train's doors rolled open for just a moment, we ran to the train engineer shouting, "Berlin? Can you take us to Berlin?"

"Nein!" the man said sternly, his uniform creased and his eyes looking directly above our heads. "Nicht Englisch! Nur Deutsch!"

"Please," I begged him, hoping this train was pointing in a northeasterly direction. "We need to get to Berlin."

"Thirty euro," he said impatiently, looking me full in the eyes this time and extending a palm for the money. I tried not to think about the more than thirty dollars I was spending on a one-way, one-hour train ride to Berlin—more than I had spent in a single day since we arrived in Germany—and I handed him my American credit card, praying that he would charge only what was necessary to get us where we needed to go. After the doors rolled shut and we were speeding north towards our friends, our hotel rooms, and our return flights to the United States the next day, I sipped espresso from a tiny mug and marveled at the metaphors that marked my time in Wittenberg: left behind in Luther's home, nonplussed but decidedly left; locked outside of Luther's church, knocking on the formidable doors as the organ began to play; hurried by church leaders who wore anxiety like a stole, dashing from event to event without much notice of the places or people; mesmerized by the quiet of the winding streets, the majesty of Luther's university, and the remarkable beauty of Castle Church; locked inside Luther's church, dependent on a lone key in the robe of a single pastor; and, finally, begging our way onto the too-expensive last train to Berlin.

IN SEARCH OF PURPOSE

With the Great Commission in Jesus' final bodily moments on the earth, we get the ultimate fulfillment of the Abrahamic covenant as well as an eternal focal point for the daily purpose of life. What a gift, what a blessing, and what a superhuman calling by which we are to mindfully live our days: "Then Jesus came to them and said, 'All authority in heaven and on earth has been given to me. Therefore go and make disciples of all nations, baptizing them in the name of the Father and of the Son and of the Holy Spirit, and teaching them to obey everything I have commanded you. And surely I am with you always, to the very end of the age.'"[1] From the mountain where Jesus has asked his eleven remaining disciples to meet him, Jesus begins his Great Commission with a reminder that he is imbued with "all authority in heaven and on earth." Here we are drawn straight into C. S. Lewis's brilliant trilemma: "You must make a choice. Either this man was, and is, the Son of God, or else a madman or something worse. You can shut him up for a fool, you can spit at him and kill him as a demon, or you can fall at his feet and call him Lord and God, but let us not come with any patronizing nonsense about his being a great human teacher. He has not left that open to us. He did not intend to."[2] The Son of God has spoken, and He is not, as Lewis suggests, "a great human teacher"; instead, in his final words, he is calling his eleven disciples and all future disciples to be just that: great human teachers of all that he has taught them. Jesus begins by reminding his disciples that he stands before them with heaven's authority, and he closes with the assurance that hHe, the authority of heaven, will be with them always until the end of time. The pronouncements I hear in these few verses are humbling and profound: As disciples, we are called to be teachers, and as teachers, we carry within us the power, authority, and miracle of the Holy Spirit. Our purpose is clear, but how do we live into it fully and well as Christian leaders?

As Gordon Smith writes in *Courage and Calling,* our ability to live into who God has called us to be invariably comes down to a matter of courage: "Courage must be characterized by wisdom, moral integrity, gratitude, humility and patience. But the bottom line remains *courage*. . . . Do we have the courage to be—the courage to be who we are and do what we are called to do?"[3] I believe courage arises when two key components are articulated and assuaged: (1) our purpose and (2) our worthiness. As Linda Hill and others write in *Collective Genius,* a sense of purpose is what both brings people

1. Matt 28:17–20.
2. Lewis, *Mere Christianity,* 56.
3. Smith, *Courage and Calling,* 182.

together and moves them forward, a concept that echoes the intentionality of Jesus' Great Commission. "Purpose is often misunderstood," Hill writes. "It is not *what* a group does but *why* it does what it does. It's not a goal but a reason—the reason it exists, the need it fulfills, and the assistance it bestows. It is the answer to the question every group should ask itself: If we disappeared today, how would the world be different tomorrow?"[4] And yet, as Hill reminds us in a later chapter titled "Beyond Purpose," clarity of direction is not enough. In order to function with energy and creativity within our God-given purpose, we must first have a sense of awareness about ourselves and about those around us—an awareness, as Christian leaders, that mimics the supernatural awareness of Jesus Christ. As MaryKate Morse writes in *Making Room for Leadership*, when we are unaware, we are handicapped by our inability to see. "Awareness leads us to think about presence in a group. If you are aware of what you bring visually and viscerally into a group, and the amount of presence these markers generate, you can be more proactive in improving or moderating the use of influence and power. If the group as a whole is aware, the members can begin to discuss it. Awareness triggers a group's capacity to be Christlike."[5]

The concept of "missional church" is a mindful attempt to define our Great Commission-driven purpose in light of twenty-first-century western American secular assumptions. While the term *missional* has been obfuscated in the last decade into a general evangelical word whose purpose is vague and shifting, its original intent was a return to the essential call of the church. Here is AlanHirsch's definition in his 2007 book *The Forgotten Ways:*

> A missional church is a church that defines itself and organizes its life around its real purpose as an agent of God's mission to the world. In other words, the church's true and authentic organizing principle is mission. Therefore when the church is in mission, it is the true church. The church itself is not only a product of that mission but is obligated and destined to extend it by whatever means possible. The mission of God flows directly through every believer and every community of faith that adheres to Jesus.[6]

When the semantics slide, as has happened with the concept of "missional church," the sense of purpose tends to slide as well. Is it possible to regain the purpose of the missional movement and press it into a new realm that is

4. Hill et al., *Collective Genius*, 92.
5. Morse, *Making Room*, 123.
6. Hirsch, *The Forgotten Ways*, 285.

both meaningful and applied, rather than merely theoretical and too often misconstrued?

ARTICULATING PAIN

When Pastor Adam Phillips moved to Portland, Oregon, to start Christ Church in 2014 as an emerging leader in the Evangelical Covenant Church, the story that he likely anticipated was one of growth and good fruit. But when Phillips took a stance in favor of full inclusivity at his new church, including the LGBTQ community, his denomination kicked him out. "I've never gotten hate mail before—just terrible stuff, really toxic, saying that we had betrayed Jesus and that I was going to go to hell unless I repented and changed my beliefs," Phillips said in a documentary produced by *The Atlantic*.[7] While Phillips's Christ Church congregation has recovered from its split, Phillips' experience is familiar to far too many. "The Bible is very clear on what it means to love God and love our neighbor as ourself," Phillips said.[8] But how many people—Christians included—are aware of the reality of what Scripture teaches and what Jesus stood for? The hurt the church has incurred runs so deep that today's neo-postmodern culture simply assumes its presence. And the infractions occur not only church-to-culture but also church-within-church.

As Philip Yancey reminds us in *What Good Is God?*, the schisms within the church are ever-deepening, an example to the unchurched of how divisive Christians must be: "By last report there are 38,000 different Christian denominations in the world. There used to be 37,999 until one person decided he or she had a corner on truth that made his church more 'pure' than all the rest and formed a new denomination or cult."[9] For the authors of *Forgive Us: Confessions of a Compromised Faith*, the damage wrought is difficult to measure: "As Christians, we are guilty before God and before the world. God sees it. The world sees it—and because the world sees our sin and perceives that we have no removed the log from our own eye before calling out the specks in the eyes of others, our hypocrisy has been exposed. We have damaged our own witness to the world."[10]

Before we ask forgiveness and assure the world that we will change our ways, however, we need to articulate the hurt and measure the cost. When a child or spouse offers a blanket "I'm sorry" without acknowledging the

7. Blumberg, "Evangelical Pastor Shunned."
8. Blumberg, "Evangelical Pastor Shunned."
9. Yancey, *What Good is God?*, 274.
10. Cannon et al., *Forgive Us*, 21–22.

wrong that occurred, the recipient is often left feeling uneasy and distrustful. The best apology is one that fully defines the injustice, seeking reparation with humility, vulnerability, and an earnest desire to seek a new path. How, then, do we begin to repair?

We complicate things with our rules and dictates, our assumptions and self-imposed limitations. Luther longed for the freedom that Jesus promised not for himself but for the German people who were trapped beneath the unrighteous legislations of a too-powerful mother church. The reform he propelled was remarkable, a press through the heavy curtains of legalisms that had layered one upon the other for generations.

Curiously, we've done it again. While we use comfortably Christianese language like "missional" and "fellowship" and "hedge of protection" and "Proverbs 31 woman" and "quiet time," we have locked ourselves in linguistic legalisms that exclude rather than include, repel rather than attract. The secular culture of the twenty-first century does not see Christianity as a means of supernatural peace, love, and joy, as Jesus promises. So what can be done? How do we bring freedom to the people around us, just as Luther did 500 years ago? What reform is needed to open the doors of an era of social media, an increasingly global economy, and unprecedented demands of high efficiency? What role can IQ, EQ, and AQ play in the Christian church as we seek to enter more fully into a wounded, anti-church society? Let's consider where we've been as we consider the direction we should move next.

REFORMATION #1: JESUS ON EARTH

The greatest reformation the world has ever known came when God deigned to enter the earth in human form, humbling himself to be born as a helpless infant. He arrived in a world where religious leaders thought they knew best, following the dictates of God's Word with narrow precision. Their role as leaders was to uphold the laws of the temple, calling their people to a higher standard as they sought to honor God and step fully into their heritage as God's chosen people. They were waiting for a messiah, a king who would arrive in wealth, might, and glory, and save them from their oppressors. When word spread that the mMessiah was a baby wrapped in cloths and lying in a manger in the town of Bethlehem, the news was nonsensical to many who were trained to expect something far more grand—at least in the worldly way that made sense to them. What they could not conceptualize was that God's plan was better, and that their plan had never really been a plan at all. Hear God's emphasis on humility, on communicating through the unassuming:

> And there were shepherd living out in the fields nearby, keeping watch over their flocks at night. An angel of the Lord appeared to them, and the glory of the Lord shone around them, and they were terrified. But the angel said to them, "Do not be afraid. I bring you good news that will cause great joy for all the people. Today in the town of David, a Savior is born to you; he is the Messiah, the Lord."[11]

Our human hearts are remarkably fragile—easily bruised, scarred, and frightened. When we are cornered, some of us tremble with fear, and others of us build walls of protection, layering ourselves beneath armor that we imagine is secure and true. Imagine the challenge God has in trying to speak to us. Does he risk the booming voice that could send us scurrying into an eternal cower? Does he rely on the still, small voice, knowing full well that many of us will shout desperately above the whisper, never hearing him at all? Invariably he picks the unassuming among us to carry his word: shepherds in a field, a frightened teenaged mother, fishermen and tax collectors, women outside a tomb.

The reformation Jesus brought was not about new laws or new authority: "Do not think that I have come to abolish the Law or the Prophets; I have not come to abolish them but to fulfill them."[12] Jesus came to extend the promises of his Father with the simplicity of two commandments: Love the Lord your God with all your heart, soul, mind, and strength, and love your neighbor as yourself.[13] He came to eliminate the checklists and the legalisms, calling us all instead to the challenge of giving him everything that we are. For those of us who believe, we each experience the reformation individually in that remarkable moment when we choose to be freed.

I was alone in a tent when I started to wonder. I had heard the promises of Scripture for many years, but I wasn't sure why it would make a difference to pronounce the words for myself rather than simply listen to others. I had a headache that night, and I was angry with my body for failing me. I was thirteen years old, and I wanted to gather with my friends around the campfire, swapping stories and singing songs, but the steel bar that burned through the left side of my skull was debilitating. I crouched at the edge of the brush and threw up twice, succumbing to the pain, and then I crawled back into the tent to breathe slowly and will the pounding

11. Luke 2:8–11.

12. Matt 5:17.

13. Mark 12:30–31.

to subside. I listened to their joyful laughter, and I wondered if there was something more to the words that we spoke to one another.

The shadows tilted when the tent flap lifted and an older friend joined me inside the tent, stepping gently over the rows of sleeping bags to kneel by my head. She offered to massage my temples as I lay there, pressing into the pain, and I was thankful for her kindness. She told me that my friends had prayed for me, asking that the pain begin to dissipate, and I remember feeling overwhelmed by the idea that the raucous crowd gathered around the campfire had paused silliness to speak quiet words to God on my behalf. I had never been prayed for before. I told her that, and she offered to pray *with* me—there in that tent, with laughter outside and pain inside.

And so we prayed, and I asked God to forgive me and accept me and help me. It seemed simple enough, the words that we spoke, but it was a reformation into a freedom I never could have anticipated. I slept deeply that night, and the next morning it was as if a film had been wiped clear from my eyes. Everything seemed brighter, warmer, closer, and livelier. Something was inside me that wasn't there before, and it was all-consuming, ever-enduring, and solid—shockingly solid. I felt like even the birds were looking at me that next morning, acknowledging the transcendental Spirit that connected us all:

> Flesh gives birth to flesh, but the Spirit gives birth to spirit. . . . The wind blows wherever it pleases. You hear its sound, but you cannot tell where it comes from or where it is going. So it is with everyone born of the Spirit.[14]

Jesus' reformation is of the spirit, and it marked the first millennium after his death with awed confusion, desperate longing, and remarkable freedom.

REFORMATION #2: JESUS IN THE CHURCH

The second reformation came when Martin Luther tacked his folio on the door of Castle Church, urging the powers-that-be to reconsider the legalisms that kept the people locked in subservience. Luther's declarations reverberated worldwide, spurring debates about theology, church structure, and human authority. Because of the miracle of Gutenberg's printing press, Luther's words spread quickly throughout first Germany, then Europe, and then the world. In more ways than one, the authority necessary for widespread communication was dismantled under the mechanics of a machine that allowed conversation to spread beyond nationalities and the limitations

14. John 3:6–8.

of languages. Luther's life's work empowered the unassuming to assume: because of his translation of the Bible, the vernacular of his hymns, and his insistence on an individual relationship with Jesus, Luther ensured that the people around him could have direct access to the Father of creation. He successfully eliminated the middle-men, so to speak, and reestablished the direct line that Jesus had assured 1,500 years prior.

While the first reformation centered on the miracle of Jesus, the second reformation focused on a necessary deconstruction of the authorities that were keeping people at a distance from Jesus. The first reformation was all about the personhood of Jesus, and the second reformation was about the proper structure and role of the church. If we are called to be in Christian fellowship together, what should that look like? How can the theologically trained among us impart their wisdom but still allow each of us to experience God on our own? How will the leaders of the church ensure that the church remains on a righteous path, not deviating into the tides of culture or the whims of society? And when leaders are entrusted with responsibility, how do we ensure that they hold that responsibility reverentially, acknowledging that above it all, Jesus is Lord?

As an elder in the Presbyterian church for more than twelve years, I have walked two churches through the painful schism of a denominational change. I have seen adults spitting with anger about such details as liturgical order, clerical robes, and the authority of a subcommittee. I have watched people exit churches because they were uncomfortable, too comfortable, disillusioned, offended, unchallenged, lonely, unimpressed, too impressed, tired, overwhelmed, underwhelmed, and unheard. I have spent countless hours debating the order of a service, the style of worship music, the length of sermons, the frequency of communion, the logistics of baptism, the frequency level of bass guitars and drums, the precision of Google slides, and the size and style of communion cups, ballpoint pens, pew Bibles, church pews, sanctuary carpet, window coverings, ministry center banners, external signage, prayer gardens, fire pits, youth rooms, coffee bars, bathrooms, nurseries, Sunday school rooms, and parking lots. While God is in every detail, as our secular culture likes to remind us, I know Jesus is not mired in the inconsequentials; and sometimes I find myself fatigued by the emotional undercurrents and longing instead for the first fruits of the first reformation.

One of the more memorable meetings was an evening gathering of the denomination at a district level. Our church was on the agenda for dismissal that evening, and we were looking forward to exiting an increasingly acrimonious pairing in favor of a newer, younger Presbyterian denomination that promised individual church freedom and minimal bureaucracy. Our pastor encouraged as many of us as possible to attend, including our children, and we braved the three-hour drive through Friday afternoon traffic to honor his request. When we arrived, the church was already mostly full, and the only remaining seats were in a choir loft above the stage where the main speakers stood. We filed in as quietly as we could—my husband, me, and our five children who at the time were between the ages of five and thirteen. I had warned the kids that the meeting would be dull, so they had each brought something to occupy themselves. They were respectfully quiet throughout the evening, the older ones occasionally looking up to listen, particularly when the adults' voices below became strained with anger.

At one notably acerbic moment, my seven-year-old innocently asked whether she could change seats from one row to the next. I nodded my approval, my attention focused on the proceedings below as the speakers argued about whether our young church should be permitted to exit the denomination at all. As one male pastor sucked in his breath in measured anger, looking as if he might raise a hand to strike out, my daughter's orange knit cat-ear hat bobbed up and over, drawing the eyes of most of the adults on the floor below. My daughter didn't notice, but her presence was remarkable in that moment. The pastor who was about to spew angry words seemed to swallow his emotion, suddenly aware that there were children present and he was, after all, a pastor. Others in the room smiled and nodded in our direction. While the tension seemed to lift momentarily, we were relieved when those gathered voted in favor of our exit—by only a slight margin—and we were able to leave the meeting.

While Luther's reformation was remarkable in its impact and carries echoes of brilliance still today, we have somehow gotten ourselves entangled again in details that Jesus warned us to avoid. He commanded us to love God and love one another, not plan the perfect worship service or ordain the perfect pastors or announce the perfect programming. Church, in God's economy, is not the point. We are called to love, not to smugly mark off our checklist of prayer time, devotional, Sunday morning worship, community service, small group gathering, Bible study, and Wednesday evening church activity. Luther's reformation was about church and authority, but it was not intended to stay there; it was intended to lead us back to the heart of why any of this matters: Jesus. So where have we gone awry, and what needs to happen next?

REFORMATION #3: JESUS INSIDE

The ultimate reformation is not external. When I lay inside that tent in my early teens, I did not pray and then determine to cut my hair or wear a new outfit; I was remarkably changed from the inside. God promises us a dramatic spiritual transplant, and somehow we have gotten ourselves mired in the very stickiness that Jesus warned us about:

> For I will take you out of the nations; I will gather you from all the countries and bring you back into your own land. I will sprinkle clean water on you, and you will be clean; I will cleanse you from all your impurities and from all your idols. I will give you a new heart and put a new spirit in you; I will remove from you your heart of stone and give you a heart of flesh. And I will put my Spirit in you and move you to follow my decrees and be careful to keep my laws. Then you will live in the land I gave your ancestors; you will be my people, and I will be your God. I will save you from all your uncleanness.[15]

If we are called to Jesus in the first reformation, we have spent 500 years debating the structure of church in the second reformation, then perhaps the third revolution should take us to a place that we have not yet explored with the transparency that God requires: our hearts. If we are given a heart of flesh in place of a heart of stone, how do we ensure that we are living fully under God's promises? Do we have the language, tools, and understanding to embrace the gift we have been given?

I have known too many pastors who could memorize Scripture with the finesse of a Hollywood actor, but whose emotional and moral character was grossly unacknowledged and underdeveloped. I worked closely with a pastor for many years whose brusque hallway demeanor often offended congregation members, but whose sermons were revered for their delivery, depth, and application. As an elder and a friend of his, I was often approached by congregation members who felt bruised by his abrasiveness, and I soon became the go-to person for healing conversations and reassurance. "I'm just not good at that," he once told me, and I remember the fleeting thought that surely he could *become* good at interpersonal relationships, if he were to make it a priority. But I dismissed the thought as quickly as it entered my head, agreeing that he was a wise leader because he surrounded himself with people who filled the holes where he lacked. Many congregation members left that church in anger, shamed by his murmured threats and silenced by his admonitions. Looking back now with the perspective that time affords, I can see that he had an over-inflated sense of his own IQ, an underdeveloped understanding of his own EQ, and an only partially developed capacity for AQ. I wonder now how he might have benefited from time spent with each, bringing to fullness the character that God created him to be.

15. Ezek 36:24–29.

When I have attended large denominational gatherings in the past, I have been struck by the self-consciousness of the pastors gathered. While I expect ego and self-aggrandizement at academic conferences, I would hope that a Christian gathering would offer the opposite: a place of humility, seeking, and profound peace. But that has not been my experience, and it certainly has not been the experience of my nonbelieving students as they attempt to enter the Christian world to see what the fuss is all about. Invariably they exit again, shaking their heads with disdain or, worse yet, wounded by the unkind judgments of someone who had no cause to pass judgment. Remember Zacchaeus in the sycamore tree and Jesus' kind suggestion that Zacchaeus host him for the evening. Are we asking people to host us, or are we stepping into each new situation with an agenda, established programming, and lessons that we can't wait to impart?

Ordination does not grant us an authority to incriminate, shame, or alienate; Luther spoke to that half a millennium ago. As Christians, we are commanded to love with a completeness that the world has never known, and our leadership should set the standard:

- Why do you look at the speck of sawdust in your brother's eye and pay no attention to the plank in your own eye? How can you say to your brother, "Let me take the speck out of your eye," when all the time there is a plank in your own eye?[16]
- A new command I give you: Love one another. As I have loved you, so you must love one another. By this everyone will know that you are my disciples, if you love one another.[17]
- So in everything, do to others what you would have them do to you, for this sums up the Law and the Prophets.[18]
- But to you who are listening, I say: Love your enemies, do good to those who hate you, bless those who curse you, pray for those who mistreat you. . . . Do to others as you would have them do to you.[19]
- For if you forgive other people when they sin against you, your heavenly Father will also forgive you. But if you do not forgive others their sins, your Father will not forgive your sins.[20]

16. Matt 7:3–4.
17. John 13:34–35.
18. Matt 7:12.
19. Luke 6:27–28, 31.
20. Matt 6:14–15.

- Greater love has no one than this: to lay down one's life for one's friends.[21]

If we are called to this supernatural level of love, what can we do to ensure that our hearts are clear enough to step fully into it? How can we employ an acknowledgement of IQ, a dedication to EQ, and an effort to unpack AQ in our effort to be better leaders, better teachers, and better ambassadors for the truth, mercy, and love of the gospel?

THE JESUS QUOTIENT

The Jesus Quotient encompasses the fullness of all three: IQ, EQ, and AQ. IQ is a century-old, culturally entrenched measure of an individual's capacity to learn, reason, and think critically. EQ, a concept that has arisen in recent decades, is an individual's capacity to recognize, identify, and manage emotions appropriately. AQ, an idea that is a necessary extension of EQ into a complex twenty-first-century culture, is an individual's capacity to focus consistently, completely, and effectively on others. Jesus embodies all three concepts perfectly in the Gospels of the New Testament, and from his example we can find narratives to guide our own behavior and life choices. As the author of Hebrews writes, "Son though he was, he learned obedience from what he suffered and, once made perfect, he became the source of eternal salvation for all who obey him."[22] How can we, as leaders in the church, take deliberate steps to move ourselves away from the tired debates about church structure and instead focus on the perfect example that Jesus gave us and the imperfect ways that our new hearts attempt to emulate him?

The twenty-first century is defined by an interconnectedness and speed of information unlike the world has ever seen. While increased access to infinite ideas sounded exemplary back in the 1980s and 1990s, we are witnessing a scramble to manipulate and manage information that no one anticipated. Social media, for example, is an effective way to connect individuals across time, geography, and status, but what harm is caused by the gradual blending of fact and fiction as we post only the best posed photographs and wittiest euphemisms? While there is insincerity in the creation of ideals, we have seen even greater harm come from those who spend hours trolling through the careful creations, comparing themselves and sliding ever deeper into a sense of unrest, inadequacy, and even depression. We may joke with one another that what appears on the internet is rarely

21. John 15:13.
22. Heb 5:8–9.

truth, and yet on so many levels we believe that it is: from the news feeds we rely on to the Twitter feeds of celebrities to the boastings of our friends. If we truly believed that the information we encountered on the internet was mostly fiction, would we build our lives around the ideas and images that we see on our screens?

What we say and what we do have drifted further afield on a global scale than the world has ever seen before, and until we can call ourselves back to such primary tenets of good character as integrity, honesty, and authenticity, we will continue to spiral downward in a depressing swamp of doom-saying and false reality. If the culture cannot see the inherent duplicity of this information-frantic milieu, doesn't it behoove us as Christians to step in fully and offer to lead a way forward? If we are called to love completely and well, how can we not step in? But any time we step forward to lead, we must first ensure that we are equipped to lead effectively and not incur further hurt. And we are not ready.

The future church should not be about the components of church at all, but instead the individual souls within the church—pastors included. Now is the time to do the work necessary to understand ourselves fully: IQ, EQ, and AQ. The better we ground ourselves in the truth of who we each were created to be, the better able we will be to encounter those around us who are longing to be known. The better we understand ourselves, the better able we will be to ask others for the honor of sitting in their homes, listening to their stories and sharing a little of our own. The better we know our own purpose in Christ, the better we will be able to love God fully and love those around us as we love ourselves. That, after all, is what Jesus commanded us to do.

Church is not in the structure or the building or the lessons that we impart. Church is deep within our very souls; and it will only be when we do the difficult work of cleansing and renewing our souls that the church will experience the reformation necessary to bring peace to a culture whose self-protective walls are high and whose skepticism of Christianity runs understandably and painfully deep.

Chapter 8

AQ Assessment Tools

ANY TIME I TEACH a university-level course, I begin with a brief overview of a tool I call "Aristotle's Twenty-Firstt-Century Rhetorical Triangle." In the fourth century BC, Aristotle wrote a treatise on rhetoric that is often referenced in courses on argumentation, persuasion, and basic writing. The three rhetorical appeals Aristotle outlined are *logos* (an appeal to logic), *pathos* (an appeal to emotion), and *ethos* (an appeal to character or credibility). When we plant these concepts on the corners of a triangle, we acknowledge that the three are not hierarchical but instead are of equal importance. In order to make the triangle more relevant for today's students, I have revised it to the following:

Aristotle's 21st-Century Rhetorical Triangle

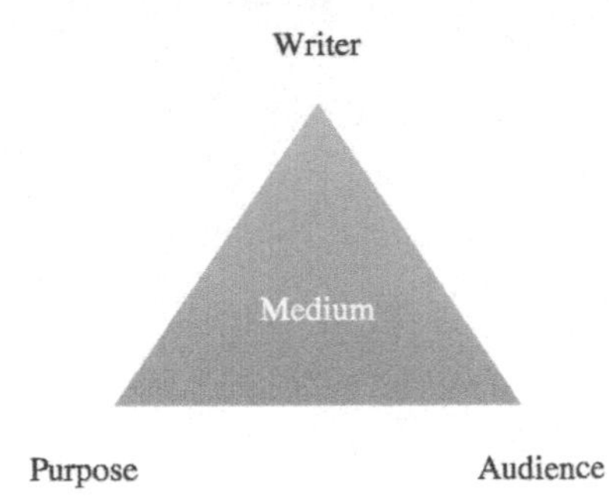

Any time we communicate—whether by writing a text, crafting an email, talking one-on-one, or preaching a sermon—the success of our communication is dependent on how well we consider and manage the elements of this triangle. While most of us approach these concepts subconsciously, filling in the details by habit depending on our education and life experiences, it is always beneficial when we take the time to consider the elements consciously, weighing whether our approach is the most effective for the situation at hand.

The *purpose* corner of the triangle refers to the speaker's intended purpose for the communication, a concept that most of us are taught from our early primary years in grade school. If our purpose for an essay is simply to complete the assignment adequately, or our purpose for a sermon is to fill the thirty minutes between the offering and communion, or our purpose for a conversation is to check a box that suggests we are engaging with friends or family appropriately, our purpose is not likely to be successful. The more intentional, important, and heartfelt our purpose is, the more memorable, persuasive, and successful our communication will be. When students write university-level essays in my courses, I encourage them to locate a purpose beyond the directions for the assignment. If, for example, a student writes a persuasive piece appealing for an increase in pay at work, and the student uses rhetorical tools that she believes will indeed appeal to the vice presidents at her firm, the essay itself will be far more likely to earn a high grade than an essay that argues for something bland and inconsequential.

The *audience* corner of the triangle asks that the speaker thoughtfully weigh the recipients of his or her communication before the communication actually occurs. If a student is preparing a speech, I encourage him to ponder the people who will be listening to the speech, including such details as the ratios of gender, age, class, education level, race, religion, upbringing, marital status, family background, health, interests, knowledge about the topic, issues of language or jargon, general mood, and so on. What is important to realize here is that in Aristotle's original model and in ours, the audience corner is of equal importance to the purpose corner. If we were to toss Aristotle's triangle across the floor, it would not matter which corner rose above another; all three are equivalent and deserve a speaker's full attention. Most of us were taught in school to consider purpose first, and then audience secondarily and only in terms of the presence of a teacher. Aristotle's Twenty-First-Century Rhetorical Triangle suggests that the audience is far more important than that, and no one who expects to communicate successfully should enter a room or writing space without researching an audience. Gone are the days of shrugging and accepting whatever comes; in this Google era, research is easily done and an unavoidable necessity for effective communication.

The *writer* corner of the triangle suggests more than just the writer's presence. This corner demands that a writer fully weigh his or her own role in the communication process. The same questions that are considered for the audience should be pondered regarding the writer or speaker as well: what is my gender, age, class, education level, race, religion, upbringing, marital status, family background, health, interests, knowledge about the topic, issues of language or jargon, and general mood? What effect do each of these issues have on my ability to communicate effectively with my listeners or readers, my inherent assumptions about the topic and my audience, and my ability to have a voice in the current cultural climate? If I anticipate barriers between my audience and me, or my topic and my ability to speak with authority, what can I do to assuage those potential hiccups? If I am a man speaking to a women's Bible study about Jesus' view of women, for example, what challenges do I face and what sensitivities should I have? Very few students or leaders are taught to weigh this third corner at all, much less with wisdom and acuity. How can we learn to consider all three corners equally and thoroughly each time we communicate?

The word *medium* in the center of the triangle is important in this twenty-first-century culture where communication occurs in a myriad of contexts and mediums: email, text, essay, report, article, book, letter, blog, web content, sermon, talk, speech, podcast, video, etc. The effectiveness of the words we choose vary greatly from one medium to the next, and it is critical that we intentionally weigh the variables.

As we consider how best to assess markers of Audience Quotient, it is helpful to ground ourselves in learning theories that move us beyond a twentieth-century conceptualization of learning as mere regurgitation of information. While memorization can be helpful in some contexts, most of us now have access to instant internet information that frequently renders mere fact retention unnecessary. What is instead critical as we learn to encounter an audience with grace and full presence is a cognitive flexibility that is capable of holding a variety of ideas uniquely in any given moment, all the while maintaining an awareness of the people with whom we are engaging. Aristotle's Twenty-First-Century Rhetorical Triangle is one such tool that can be practiced and tested, as are Bloom's Revised Taxonomy and David Kolb's Experiential Learning Theory (below).

BEYOND GOOGLE

American psychologist Benjamin Bloom (1913–1999) developed a classification of learning objectives in the 1950s that has become foundational in the field of educational psychology. Known as "Bloom's Taxonomy," the model organizes thinking skills in six levels, from the basic to the more complex. In the 1990s, a former student of Bloom's, Lorin Anderson, revisited the taxonomy and made a number of changes. Most notably, he revised the original nouns of the six major categories to more active process verbs (from "comprehension" to "understanding," for example). Many universities both teach and utilize a learning theory that relies on a revised version of Bloom's Taxonomy, and it is important to recognize in this era of instant information that learning is more than just receiving new information. Consider the components of Bloom's taxonomy below.

Bloom's Revised Taxonomy

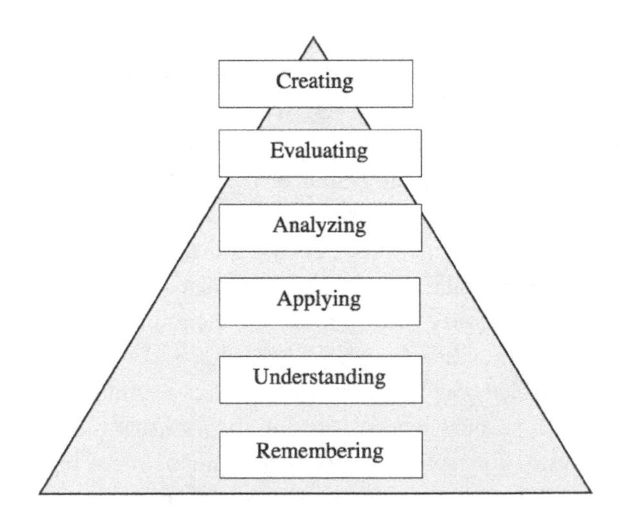

Here the triangle points upward to suggest higher levels of learning, from the base of "remembering" to the top tier of "creating." To receive a lesson about the Second World War, for example, a learner at the most basic level would hear that a war occurred on a global scale, key nations aligned with either the Axis powers or the Allies, and various countries were involved in varying time spans during the mid-twentieth century. *Remembering* is merely reciting back the information that was taught. *Understanding* means that a student can place the information in the context of history and discuss why the war occurred on the scale that it did. *Applying* means the student can ponder the First World War in light of the Second and draw some informed conclusions. *Analyzing* is when the student begins to compare and contrast the information learned with other historical or potential situations, categorizing the ideas appropriately. *Evaluating* suggests that a student is able to persuade others effectively regarding a unique understanding of the war. And *creating* might mean that the student is able to suggest a new and unique defense strategy for a current global conflict based on information learned in the initial lesson about the Second World War.

The AQ-adept individual will consider Bloom's Revised Taxonomy on two levels: (1) How do I receive information, and how can I ensure that I am assimilating new information in an engaged, creative, and innovative manner? And (2) how are the people with whom I communicate receiving the ideas I share, and how can I ensure that they are assimilating my words in an engaged, creative, and innovative manner? With the exception of learning someone's name or the time an event begins, any information-sharing in this era should regularly move into one of the top three levels of Bloom's Revised Taxonomy: analyzing, evaluating, and/or creating. If a sermon, essay, or blog does not rise to that level for the recipient, was the effort of communication really worthwhile in the first place?

FROM TEXTBOOK TO TEACHING

In the 1970s, American educational theorist David Kolb and his associate Roger Fry published an experiential learning theory that examines a learner's internal cognitive development. Kolb described learning as a process in which information is encountered and retained through direct experience. Effective learning occurs when a person progresses through a cycle of four sequential stages: (1) the initial concrete experience, (2) observation of and reflection on that experience, (3) the formation of abstract concepts and generalizations about the experience, and (4) the application of the new hypotheses in new experiences.

Kolb believed it is possible to enter the four-step cycle at any stage and follow it through its logical sequence, but that effective learning occurs only when a learner is able to execute all four stages of the model. Ideally, all four stages are experienced, and the effective learning process can be seen as an ongoing spiral that can be entered at any point.

(1) **Concrete Experience**—The learner describes an experience in an objective way, considering what occurred, where it occurred, and how it occurred, but reserving all emotions, hypotheses, and judgments for a later stage. While emotions and reflections are an important part of our human response to situations, it can be healthy and helpful to step back and reflect objectively before engaging fully with the emotions surrounding the event.

(2) **Reflective Observation**—The learner reflects on the experience subjectively, thoughtfully considering all emotions and reflections. The learner must be able to analyze his or her emotions and responses on a deeper level.

(3) **Abstract Conceptualization**—The individual next strives to articulate a general principle under which the particular instance falls. When we employ this learning model in a university course, we ask students to write three to five specific single-sentence learning outcomes in this stage, a difficult but fruitful task that requires a learner to name the specific concepts that he or she learned.

(4) **Active Experimentation**—The person then applies the general principle and/or learning outcomes from stage three to a new situation to see whether the hypotheses hold true. In a Kolb model essay, a learner is asked to apply the three to five learning outcomes from one employment or personal circumstance to an entirely new situation. An individual must engage effective analytical skills in this fourth stage.

Learners who are able to teach others new information based on experiences they have had are demonstrating a level of learning at the top of Bloom's Revised Taxonomy and desirable from any AQ-savvy individual.

AQ ASSESSMENT TOOLS

While the previous learning theories are an effective means of entering more fully into today's internet-driven, information-focused culture, what follows are experiential assessment tools that can be used to determine how well one is engaging with each of the ten markers of high Audience

Quotient (AQ). The assessment measure can be utilized as a self-assessment, completed in a collaborative group setting, or used in an interview or job performance evaluation. The core values on the measurement tool are from Kolb's experiential learning model:

Assessment for AQ Marker #1: Grounded

- **Tool**: Describe a time when you made a poor ethical decision. What happened, why did it happen, and what did you learn? Using a brief essay format or a short oral presentation, walk through the four points of the Kolb Experiential Learning Model.
- **Outcome**: Individual demonstrates that he or she is functioning out of a firmly rooted ethics or worldview (confident, centered, consistent).

Measure:

GROUNDED	**Exceeds (3–4 points)**	**Meets (1–2 points)**	**Fails to Meet (0 points)**	**Score**
The Experience	The learner identifies, describes, and discusses the experience. The voice is confident, centered, and consistent.	The learner identifies, describes, and discusses the experience. The involvement is clear.	The learner does not adequately describe the experience.	
Observations & Reflections	The learner demonstrates thoughtful reflections about the experience described in the experience. The voice is confident, centered, and consistent.	The learner demonstrates thoughtful reflections about the experience. The rationale for decisions is made clear.	The learner does not demonstrate thoughtful reflections about the experience.	
Articulated Learning Outcomes	The learner is able to put the analysis into a larger framework of learning so that specific learning outcomes can be articulated. The voice is confident, centered, and consistent.	The learner is able to put the analysis into a larger framework of learning so that learning outcomes can be applied to new experiences.	The learner is not able to effectively put the analysis into the larger framework of learning.	

Applying Concepts in New Situations	The learner tests the concepts in new situations and demonstrates changes in behavior/life, or the learner makes predictions based on new knowledge. The voice is confident, centered, and consistent.	The learner tests the concepts in new situations and demonstrates changes in behavior/life, or the learner makes predictions based on new knowledge.	The learner does not test the concepts in new situations or make predictions based on new knowledge.	
15–16 Exceeds **12–14 Meets** **6–11 Needs Improvement** **0–5 Deficient**	**Comments:**	**Comments:**	**Comments:**	**Total:**

Assessment for AQ Marker #2: Authentic

- Tool: Compare/contrast (1) a time when your greatest attribute was revealed and (2) a time when your most challenging character flaw arose. Using a brief essay format or a short oral presentation, walk through the four points of the Kolb Experiential Learning Model.
- Outcome: Individual demonstrates that he or she is true to his or her character, intelligence, emotions, gifts, and flaws (genuine, transparent, honest)

Measure:

AUTHENTIC	Exceeds (3–4 points)	Meets (1–2 points)	Fails to Meet (0 points)	Score

The Experience	The learner identifies, describes, and discusses the experience. The voice is genuine, transparent, and honest.	The learner identifies, describes, and discusses the experience. The involvement is clear.	The learner does not adequately describe the experience.	
Observations & Reflections	The learner demonstrates thoughtful reflections about the experience described in the experience. The voice is genuine, transparent, and honest.	The learner demonstrates thoughtful reflections about the experience. The rationale for decisions is made clear.	The learner does not demonstrate thoughtful reflections about the experience.	
Articulated Learning Outcomes	The learner is able to put the analysis into a larger framework of learning so that specific learning outcomes can be articulated. The voice is genuine, transparent, and honest.	The learner is able to put the analysis into a larger framework of learning so that learning outcomes can be applied to new experiences.	The learner is not able to effectively put the analysis into the larger framework of learning.	
Applying Concepts in New Situations	The learner tests the concepts in new situations and demonstrates changes in behavior/life, or the learner makes predictions based on new knowledge. The voice is genuine, transparent, and honest.	The learner tests the concepts in new situations and demonstrates changes in behavior/life, or the learner makes predictions based on new knowledge.	The learner does not test the concepts in new situations or make predictions based on new knowledge.	

15–16 Exceeds 12–14 Meets 6–11 Needs Improvement 0–5 Deficient	Comments:	Comments:	Comments:	Total:

Assessment for AQ Marker #3: Humble

- **Tool:** Discuss a time when you had an opportunity to empower someone else. What happened and why? Using a brief essay format or a short oral presentation, walk through the four points of the Kolb Experiential Learning Model.
- **Outcome:** Individual demonstrates that he or she has a modest sense of his or her own importance (deferential, unpretentious, unassuming)

Measure:

HUMBLE	Exceeds (3–4 points)	Meets (1–2 points)	Fails to Meet (0 points)	Score
The Experience	The learner identifies, describes, and discusses the experience. The voice is deferential, unpretentious, and unassuming.	The learner identifies, describes, and discusses the experience. The involvement is clear.	The learner does not adequately describe the experience.	

Observations & Reflections	The learner demonstrates thoughtful reflections about the experience described in the experience. The voice is deferential, unpretentious, and unassuming.	The learner demonstrates thoughtful reflections about the experience. The rationale for decisions is made clear.	The learner does not demonstrate thoughtful reflections about the experience.	
Articulated Learning Outcomes	The learner is able to put the analysis into a larger framework of learning so that specific learning outcomes can be articulated. The voice is deferential, unpretentious, and unassuming.	The learner is able to put the analysis into a larger framework of learning so that learning outcomes can be applied to new experiences.	The learner is not able to effectively put the analysis into the larger framework of learning.	
Applying Concepts in New Situations	The learner tests the concepts in new situations and demonstrates changes in behavior/life, or the learner makes predictions based on new knowledge. The voice is deferential, unpretentious, and unassuming.	The learner tests the concepts in new situations and demonstrates changes in behavior/life, or the learner makes predictions based on new knowledge.	The learner does not test the concepts in new situations or make predictions based on new knowledge.	

15–16 Exceeds 12–14 Meets 6–11 Needs Improvement 0–5 Deficient	**Comments:**	**Comments:**	**Comments:**	**Total:**

Assessment for AQ Marker #4: Intentional

- **Tool:** Discuss a time when things did not go the way that you intended. What happened and why? How did you respond? Using a brief essay format or a short oral presentation, walk through the four points of the Kolb Experiential Learning Model.
- **Outcome:** Individual demonstrates that he or she has a clear purpose and confidence (decisive, focused, deliberate)

Measure:

INTENTIONAL	**Exceeds (3–4 points)**	**Meets (1–2 points)**	**Fails to Meet (0 points)**	**Score**
The Experience	The learner identifies, describes, and discusses the experience. The voice is decisive, focused, and deliberate.	The learner identifies, describes, and discusses the experience. The involvement is clear.	The learner does not adequately describe the experience.	

Observations & Reflections	The learner demonstrates thoughtful reflections about the experience described in the experience. The voice is decisive, focused, and deliberate.	The learner demonstrates thoughtful reflections about the experience. The rationale for decisions is made clear.	The learner does not demonstrate thoughtful reflections about the experience.	
Articulated Learning Outcomes	The learner is able to put the analysis into a larger framework of learning so that specific learning outcomes can be articulated. The voice is decisive, focused, and deliberate.	The learner is able to put the analysis into a larger framework of learning so that learning outcomes can be applied to new experiences.	The learner is not able to effectively put the analysis into the larger framework of learning.	
Applying Concepts in New Situations	The learner tests the concepts in new situations and demonstrates changes in behavior/life, or the learner makes predictions based on new knowledge. The voice is decisive, focused, and deliberate.	The learner tests the concepts in new situations and demonstrates changes in behavior/life, or the learner makes predictions based on new knowledge.	The learner does not test the concepts in new situations or make predictions based on new knowledge.	

15–16 Exceeds 12–14 Meets 6–11 Needs Improvement 0–5 Deficient	Comments:	Comments:	Comments:	Total:

Assessment for AQ Marker #5: Compassionate

- **Tool:** Describe a time when you were challenged to reach out to or care for an individual you found distasteful. What were your concerns, and what did you learn about yourself? Using a brief essay format or a short oral presentation, walk through the four points of the Kolb Experiential Learning Model.
- **Outcome:** Individual demonstrates that he or she possesses a consciousness of others' pain and a desire to help assuage it (sympathetic, empathic, caring).

Measure:

COMPASSIONATE	Exceeds (3–4 points)	Meets (1–2 points)	Fails to Meet (0 points)	Score
The Experience	The learner identifies, describes, and discusses the experience. The voice is sympathetic, empathetic, and caring.	The learner identifies, describes, and discusses the experience. The involvement is clear.	The learner does not adequately describe the experience.	

Observations & Reflections	The learner demonstrates thoughtful reflections about the experience described in the experience. The voice is sympathetic, empathetic, and caring.	The learner demonstrates thoughtful reflections about the experience. The rationale for decisions is made clear.	The learner does not demonstrate thoughtful reflections about the experience.	
Articulated Learning Outcomes	The learner is able to put the analysis into a larger framework of learning so that specific learning outcomes can be articulated. The voice is sympathetic, empathetic, and caring.	The learner is able to put the analysis into a larger framework of learning so that learning outcomes can be applied to new experiences.	The learner is not able to effectively put the analysis into the larger framework of learning.	
Applying Concepts in New Situations	The learner tests the concepts in new situations and demonstrates changes in behavior/life, or the learner makes predictions based on new knowledge. The voice is sympathetic, empathetic, and caring.	The learner tests the concepts in new situations and demonstrates changes in behavior/life, or the learner makes predictions based on new knowledge.	The learner does not test the concepts in new situations or make predictions based on new knowledge.	

15–16 Exceeds 12–14 Meets 6–11 Needs Improvement 0–5 Deficient	Comments:	Comments:	Comments:	Total:

Assessment for AQ Marker #6: Adaptable

- **Tool:** Consider a time when you had to make a sudden change in social setting or cultural context. What happened, and how did you respond? What do you wish you had done differently, if anything? Using a brief essay format or a short oral presentation, walk through the four points of the Kolb Experiential Learning Model.
- **Outcome:** Individual demonstrates that he or she is able to adjust quickly and smoothly to new conditions and situations (flexible, versatile, adjustable).

Measure:

ADAPTABLE	Exceeds (3–4 points)	Meets (1–2 points)	Fails to Meet (0 points)	Score
The Experience	The learner identifies, describes, and discusses the experience. The voice demonstrates an ability to be flexible, versatile, and adjustable.	The learner identifies, describes, and discusses the experience. The involvement is clear.	The learner does not adequately describe the experience.	

Observations & Reflections	The learner demonstrates thoughtful reflections about the experience described. The voice demonstrates an ability to be flexible, versatile, and adjustable.	The learner demonstrates thoughtful reflections about the experience. The rationale for decisions is made clear.	The learner does not demonstrate thoughtful reflections about the experience.	
Articulated Learning Outcomes	The learner is able to put the analysis into a larger framework of learning so that specific learning outcomes can be articulated. The voice demonstrates an ability to be flexible, versatile, and adjustable.	The learner is able to put the analysis into a larger framework of learning so that learning outcomes can be applied to new experiences.	The learner is not able to effectively put the analysis into the larger framework of learning.	
Applying Concepts in New Situations	The learner tests the concepts in new situations and demonstrates changes in behavior/life, or the learner makes predictions based on new knowledge. The voice demonstrates an ability to be flexible, versatile, and adjustable.	The learner tests the concepts in new situations and demonstrates changes in behavior/life, or the learner makes predictions based on new knowledge.	The learner does not test the concepts in new situations or make predictions based on new knowledge.	

15–16 Exceeds 12–14 Meets 6–11 Needs Improvement 0–5 Deficient	Comments:	Comments:	Comments:	Total:

Assessment for AQ Marker #7: Resilient

- **Tool:** Describe a time when someone insulted, harmed, or threatened you. Why was the situation hurtful for you? What did you learn about yourself? Using a brief essay format or a short oral presentation, walk through the four points of the Kolb Experiential Learning Model.
- **Outcome:** Individual demonstrates that he or she is able to withstand difficult conditions and situations (thick-skinned, tough, strong).

Measure:

RESILIENT	Exceeds (3–4 points)	Meets (1–2 points)	Fails to Meet (0 points)	Score
The Experience	The learner identifies, describes, and discusses the experience. The voice is thick-skinned, tough, and strong.	The learner identifies, describes, and discusses the experience. The involvement is clear.	The learner does not adequately describe the experience.	

Observations & Reflections	The learner demonstrates thoughtful reflections about the experience described in the experience. The voice is thick-skinned, tough, and strong.	The learner demonstrates thoughtful reflections about the experience. The rationale for decisions is made clear.	The learner does not demonstrate thoughtful reflections about the experience.	
Articulated Learning Outcomes	The learner is able to put the analysis into a larger framework of learning so that specific learning outcomes can be articulated. The voice is thick-skinned, tough, and strong.	The learner is able to put the analysis into a larger framework of learning so that learning outcomes can be applied to new experiences.	The learner is not able to effectively put the analysis into the larger framework of learning.	
Applying Concepts in New Situations	The learner tests the concepts in new situations and demonstrates changes in behavior/life, or the learner makes predictions based on new knowledge. The voice is thick-skinned, tough, and strong.	The learner tests the concepts in new situations and demonstrates changes in behavior/life, or the learner makes predictions based on new knowledge.	The learner does not test the concepts in new situations or make predictions based on new knowledge.	

15–16 Exceeds 12–14 Meets 6–11 Needs Improvement 0–5 Deficient	Comments:	Comments:	Comments:	Total:

Assessment for AQ Marker #8: Ardent

- **Tool:** Consider a situation, task, or time in your life that you considered dull or uninspiring. What steps did you take to endure, and why? Using a brief essay format or a short oral presentation, walk through the four points of the Kolb Experiential Learning Model.
- **Outcome:** Individual demonstrates that he or she has a deep-set passion and drive (enthusiastic, zealous, fervent).

Measure:

ARDENT	Exceeds (3–4 points)	Meets (1–2 points)	Fails to Meet (0 points)	Score
The Experience	The learner identifies, describes, and discusses the experience. The voice is enthusiastic, zealous, and fervent.	The learner identifies, describes, and discusses the experience. The involvement is clear.	The learner does not adequately describe the experience.	

Observations & Reflections	The learner demonstrates thoughtful reflections about the experience described in the experience. The voice is enthusiastic, zealous, and fervent.	The learner demonstrates thoughtful reflections about the experience. The rationale for decisions is made clear.	The learner does not demonstrate thoughtful reflections about the experience.	
Articulated Learning Outcomes	The learner is able to put the analysis into a larger framework of learning so that specific learning outcomes can be articulated. The voice is enthusiastic, zealous, and fervent.	The learner is able to put the analysis into a larger framework of learning so that learning outcomes can be applied to new experiences.	The learner is not able to effectively put the analysis into the larger framework of learning.	
Applying Concepts in New Situations	The learner tests the concepts in new situations and demonstrates changes in behavior/life, or the learner makes predictions based on new knowledge. The voice is enthusiastic, zealous, and fervent.	The learner tests the concepts in new situations and demonstrates changes in behavior/life, or the learner makes predictions based on new knowledge.	The learner does not test the concepts in new situations or make predictions based on new knowledge.	

15–16 Exceeds 12–14 Meets 6–11 Needs Improvement 0–5 Deficient	Comments:	Comments:	Comments:	Total:

Assessment for AQ Marker #9: Present

- **Tool:** Describe a recent conversation, speech, or encounter with another individual. Who was involved, and what did you observe? How do you think someone else who was there would describe the same moment? Using a brief essay format or a short oral presentation, walk through the four points of the Kolb Experiential Learning Model.
- **Outcome:** Individual demonstrates that he or she is able to bring full consciousness to the present moment (engaged, aware, attentive).

Measure:

PRESENT	Exceeds (3–4 points)	Meets (1–2 points)	Fails to Meet (0 points)	Score
The Experience	The learner identifies, describes, and discusses the experience. The voice is engaged, aware, and attentive.	The learner identifies, describes, and discusses the experience. The involvement is clear.	The learner does not adequately describe the experience.	

Observations & Reflections	The learner demonstrates thoughtful reflections about the experience described in the experience. The voice is engaged, aware, and attentive.	The learner demonstrates thoughtful reflections about the experience. The rationale for decisions is made clear.	The learner does not demonstrate thoughtful reflections about the experience.	
Articulated Learning Outcomes	The learner is able to put the analysis into a larger framework of learning so that specific learning outcomes can be articulated. The voice is engaged, aware, and attentive.	The learner is able to put the analysis into a larger framework of learning so that learning outcomes can be applied to new experiences.	The learner is not able to effectively put the analysis into the larger framework of learning.	
Applying Concepts in New Situations	The learner tests the concepts in new situations and demonstrates changes in behavior/life, or the learner makes predictions based on new knowledge. The voice is engaged, aware, and attentive.	The learner tests the concepts in new situations and demonstrates changes in behavior/life, or the learner makes predictions based on new knowledge.	The learner does not test the concepts in new situations or make predictions based on new knowledge.	

15–16 Exceeds 12–14 Meets 6–11 Needs Improvement 0–5 Deficient	**Comments:**	**Comments:**	**Comments:**	**Total:**

Assessment for AQ Marker #10: Prescient

- **Tool:** Consider a presentation, speech, or talk you have given in recent months. Did you offer a broader context for the discussion? If so, how? If not, why not? How might you approach it differently today? Using a brief essay format or a short oral presentation, walk through the four points of the Kolb Experiential Learning Model.
- **Outcome:** Individual demonstrates that he or she has exceptional foresight (discerning, forward-thinking, visionary).

Measure:

PRESCIENT	Exceeds (3–4 points)	Meets (1–2 points)	Fails to Meet (0 points)	Score
The Experience	The learner identifies, describes, and discusses the experience. The voice is discerning, forward-thinking, and visionary.	The learner identifies, describes, and discusses the experience. The involvement is clear.	The learner does not adequately describe the experience.	

Observations & Reflections	The learner demonstrates thoughtful reflections about the experience described in the experience. The voice is discerning, forward-thinking, and visionary.	The learner demonstrates thoughtful reflections about the experience. The rationale for decisions is made clear.	The learner does not demonstrate thoughtful reflections about the experience.	
Articulated Learning Outcomes	The learner is able to put the analysis into a larger framework of learning so that specific learning outcomes can be articulated. The voice is discerning, forward-thinking, and visionary.	The learner is able to put the analysis into a larger framework of learning so that learning outcomes can be applied to new experiences.	The learner is not able to effectively put the analysis into the larger framework of learning.	
Applying Concepts in New Situations	The learner tests the concepts in new situations and demonstrates changes in behavior/life, or the learner makes predictions based on new knowledge. The voice is discerning, forward-thinking, and visionary.	The learner tests the concepts in new situations and demonstrates changes in behavior/life, or the learner makes predictions based on new knowledge.	The learner does not test the concepts in new situations or make predictions based on new knowledge.	

15–16 Exceeds 12–14 Meets 6–11 Needs Improvement 0–5 Deficient	Comments:	Comments:	Comments:	Total:

Conclusion

OUR VIEW WILL REMAIN myopic as long as we cling to a self-defensive ideology that is over-confident, agenda-driven, accusatory, and territorial. As Donald Miller reminds us in *Searching for God Knows What*, Paul did not turn on his aggressors after he switched from persecuting Christians to preaching the gospel. In fact, Paul so publicly appreciated the pagans who worshiped false idols that they sometimes invited him to join their gatherings to share about Jesus. Why are we not able to hold to such a loving, biblical approach? As Miller writes, Paul's empathy is a far cry from the top-down privileged stance of today's church in America: "We are in the margins of society and so we have to have our own radio stations and television stations and bookstores. Our formulaic, propositional, lifeboat-territorial methodology has crippled the kingdom of God."[1] The moral us-versus-them argument bears no resemblance to the gospel of grace, and it only serves to further the myopia that entraps and separates us from the culture that surrounds us.

1. Miller, *Searching for God Knows What*, 190.

As Peter reminds us in 1 Peter 2, we are called to live in the world in such a way that those around us witness the Holy Spirit: "Live such good lives among the pagans that, though they accuse you of doing wrong, they may see your good deeds and glorify God on the day he visits us."[2] When we don't, we become a part of the problem, which is directly antithetical to the gospel. And when we are the problem and we are espousing Jesus, those around us can't help but see Jesus as the problem. The battle we are waging is a spiritual battle against the principalities of darkness, Miller writes, not against the people who don't yet believe as we do: "In war you shoot the enemy, not the hostage."[3]

Jesus did not hesitate or equivocate; he entered in: when he reached out to heal the leper,[4] when he assured the Samaritan woman at the well,[5] when he healed the centurion's servant,[6] when he touched the hand of Peter's ill mother-in-law,[7] when he spoke to the two demon-possessed men,[8] when he told the paralytic man to take up his mat and walk,[9] when he ate dinner among sinners in Matthew's home,[10] when he went to the ruler's home and told the funeral crowds to leave,[11] when he touched the eyes of the blind men,[12] when he drove the demon out of the mute man,[13] when he went into the grainfields on the Sabbath,[14] when he healed the man's shriveled hand,[15] when he healed the blind and mute man,[16] when he sat in the boat and spoke to the crowds,[17] when he fed thousands with the five loaves and two fish,[18] when he walked across the lake to rejoin his disciples,[19] when

2. 1 Pet 2:12.
3. Miller, *Searching for God Knows What,* 191.
4. Matt 8:3.
5. John 4:7–26.
6. Matt 8:13.
7. Matt 8:15.
8. Matt 8:32.
9. Matt 9:6.
10. Matt 9:10.
11. Matt 9:24.
12. Matt 9:29.
13. Matt 9:33.
14. Matt 12:1.
15. Matt 12:13.
16. Matt 12:22.
17. Matt 13:2.
18. Matt 14:19.
19. Matt 14:25.

he defended the adulterous woman from the crowd,[20] when he reprimanded the Pharisees for their archaic traditions,[21] when he spoke kindly to the Canaanite woman,[22] when he fed the thousands with seven loaves and a few fish,[23] when he healed the boy with seizures,[24] when he commanded that the little children be brought to him,[25] when he touched the eyes of the two blind men,[26] when he calls Lazarus out of his tomb,[27] when he rode into Jerusalem on a donkey colt,[28] when he overturned the tables of the money changers in the temple area,[29] when he boldly entered the temple courts to teach,[30] when he corrected the theology of the Sadducees,[31] when he reprimanded his disciples and the gathered crowd,[32] when he defended Mary and her alabaster jar,[33] when he told Judas to "do what you came for" in the Gethsemane garden,[34] when he received the mockery and insults of the crucifixion.[35] Jesus' purpose and resolve came straight from his Father, and we are promised the same if we are humble and bold enough to receive. Are we ready to enter in?

(UN)COVERING THE CAMERA

When I had the stomach flu as a child and was permitted to stay home from school, the one pleasure amidst the fever and vomiting was the small black-and-white television my mother would prop next to my bed, close enough so I could reach the knob to click between the five broadcast stations. There were few daytime shows that held much appeal for kids in those days, but one that I always lingered over with guarded curiosity was *The*

20. John 8:7–11.
21. Matt 15:3–11.
22. Matt 15:28.
23. Matt 15:36.
24. Matt 17:18.
25. Matt 19:14.
26. Matt 20:34.
27. John 11:43.
28. Matt 21:7–9.
29. Matt 21:12.
30. Matt 21:23.
31. Matt 22:29–32.
32. Matt 23:2–39.
33. Matt 26:10–13.
34. Matt 26:50.
35. Matt 27:27–44.

People's Court. Joseph Wapner was a superior court judge in Los Angeles County, and each half-hour episode was an uncomfortable glimpse into the lives of people who were unable to resolve minor disputes. Judge Wapner arbitrated real small-claims matters in his court room, where California law in the early 1980s allowed litigants to sue for up to $1,500. Unlike regular television at the time, the people were not actors and their arguments were not scripted, which meant the show had a raw, unpredictable air that was new to network television. *The People's Court* has run for thirty-two seasons since its first pilot run in 1980, and it served in its earliest years as a somewhat awkward precursor to such globally popular shows as *Survivor, Big Brother, Duck Dynasty, American Idol, The Bachelor,* and *Dancing with the Stars*. Another early reality show precursor, *Candid Camera*, typified our fascination with peering into other people's lives, sometimes undetected, and secretly comparing whether we would or would not behave similarly.

I am always amused when I see coworkers with a strategic sticky note or square of tape over the camera that sits ready at the top of their laptop. What might others see that is worth taking the time to shield? As our Judge Wapner fascination has extended into shows like *Naked and Afraid* that would have shocked our sensibilities in the 1970s and 1980s, alongside an internet preoccupation with the images and thought-bursts of both friends and celebrities, the contradiction is curious. We are compelled to peer at others, but we are increasingly fearful that others may be peering at us. But why does it matter? If we are called as Christians to live with intentionality and authenticity, we should be living as if the cameras are on and the live shot is streaming worldwide, unabashed and unfiltered because of our grounding in who we are.

I have joked with our kids that a reality show based on our home would have low ratings indeed, because the lives we lead and the encounters we have smack of a normalcy that would not interest viewers for very long. Yes, we sometimes have disagreements or unresolvable conflict or emotional moments, but for the most part our interactions are undergirded with a consistency that would not lend itself to live streaming. When we watch shows like *Keeping Up with the Kardashians* or *The Real World*, we are looking for the discrepancies that lead to amusing and sometimes uncomfortable ethical rabbit trails. Of course we all commit moral failures as Christians—sometimes daily—but what should set us apart and dramatically lower the ratings is the consistent return to a deep-set grounding in our faith and our commitment to love well. While there is nothing wrong with a little sticky tape covering a camera lens so we feel less vulnerable, our lives should be genuine enough that we are the same people at home or at work, alone or in public, with a Jesus-inspired boldness that defies the scrutiny of others.

INVISIBLE ENVIRONMENTS

I sat on the floor in the mommy-and-me music class with a baby strapped across my chest in a sling and a toddler perched on each leg, my arms in the air as I shook the jingle bell sticks in time to the rhythms of "Risseldy, Rosseldy." I bounced my legs and jostled the toddlers to and fro, encouraging them to shake their bells, too. All three kids burbled and laughed, spurred by my goofiness as much as the curriculum. Twelve mothers sat in the circle that day, most with one child and some with two or three, and together we sang and drummed and stomped our feet as the children sat in our laps or danced around us. I signed up for these music classes each year while our children were in their pre-preschool years as I loved the interactions with others, the expectation that kids as young as eight and ten months old could follow simple directions, and the regular engagement with a variety of music. On this particular Tuesday morning, I noticed another mother across the circle watching my rather awkward juggling of multiple kids as her one preschooler sat patiently in her lap, waiting for the next song to begin. The mother smiled when she saw me looking and I returned the smile, grimacing at how strained I must appear as I struggled to keep all three kids engaged and appropriately focused. As the thirty-minute class ended and I pushed myself to my feet with one arm wrapped around the baby's body and the other trying to keep the two toddlers from cracking one another's skulls with their bright blue drumsticks, she walked over to greet us.

"It's so fun to see you," she said with a wide grin. "My daughter and I don't usually attend the Tuesday class, but I was so happy when I saw you were in it."

"Oh yes," I said, smiling back at her as I ushered kids toward the coat hooks. I looked from the woman to her daughter and back again, hoping for a clue that would jog my memory, but nothing came. I had no idea who this woman was. "It's great to see you, too," I said as I held one kid by the back of her t-shirt while I angled the other one's arms into her pink sweater.

"Every time I see you in Wal-Mart, I am so amazed," she said. "Here I am with only one child who can be a handful, but I see you getting groceries with *five*. How do you stay so calm?"

"Calm?" I laughed. Who was this woman? "Really? Oh, bribes and threats, I suppose. The secret to sane parenting, right? A careful balance of bribes and threats."

"Ah, that must be it!" the woman chuckled as she headed toward the door, her daughter's hand in hers. "I never want to bother you because you seem so focused. But I'm always amazed at how orderly you are."

"Orderly?" I said. I swore I had never seen this woman before.

"Yes! You must have everything planned out so perfectly each time you shop," she said. Her daughter pulled at her hand, and the woman smiled down at her. "We're off to ballet class now. It's great to see you again, and I'm sure we'll see you around town soon. Have a great day!"

"You as well," I said as the woman walked out into the bright sunshine. I was a little dizzy from a conversation I was having trouble tracking. I was sure I had never seen her before, and it was overwhelming to think that she was watching me as I slogged my way through a double-sided grocery list in Wal-Mart. How many times had I sweated through those aisles with crying children or fussy babies, speeding for the checkout line so I could escape into the safety of my own car? How many times had I barked at my kids or ordered them to grip the cart under threat of punishment or plied them with suckers to keep them quiet enough so I could think for just a moment? Wal-Mart was not the stage I wanted to stand on, and it unnerved me to think that she had been watching me for some time and I had had no idea.

But it was not my call to make. I realized in that moment how little control I had over the image I painted or the impression I made on others. If this woman was watching me from afar, how many others were as well? If I spent my life working to perfect an image for the office or Sunday mornings or social gatherings, how often was that image belied by me simply living out of who I was when I had no idea that others were watching? I didn't like the idea—I much preferred the control of preparing myself properly for each social interaction, from clothes to demeanor to proper amounts of coffee—but I realized when that woman looked at me with such genuine intimacy that the control was never really mine.

The mythologies that hold us to social expectations and proper responses to context cues are ultimately just that: mythologies of our own making that bear little fruit in God's economy of eternity, fullness of being, peace, joy, and love. When we lead duplicitous lives, we deplete our energy with careful fiction and fears of covering up the blemishes that embarrass us. How can we love others fully when we are busy covering, hiding, and preparing? What will it take for us to release the script and step fully into the live show, risking everything as we trust in the one who knows the pre-story, the subplots, and the twenty-eight sequels to come?

McLuhan, an English professor whose theories of media and culture were profoundly influential in the 1960s and 1970s, argued that a broader understanding of meaning should come from the medium itself rather than the content: "The 'message' of any medium or technology is the change of scale or pace or pattern that it introduces into human affairs."[36] When we are consumed by moral arguments about a twenty-first-century social media whose content we find offensive, in other words, we are missing the point of the larger cultural swing; we are succumbing to the us-versus-them that rarely allows for progressive thought or even adequate understanding.

In Quentin Fiore's image-laden reworking of McLuhan's text as *The Medium is the Massage*, we see echoes of cultural conflict that hold eerily true today: "Environments are invisible. Their ground rules, pervasive structure, and overall patterns elude easy perception," McLuhan writes on one code-free white double-truck page.[37] And later, on a page stamped with a black-and-white silhouette of figures prancing across a field in a Dance of Death, McLuhan writes, "Our official culture is striving to force the new media to do the work of the old."[38] Our responsibility here is unwavering: We are called to love God, love our neighbor, love our enemies, and go and make disciples of all nations. To begin to free ourselves from the myopic prison-house of our own postmodern cultural restraints, we must be humble, vulnerable, and Holy Spirit-reliant.

REDEFINING JESUS

The scriptural underpinnings of today's church rest primarily in the Great Commission: "Then Jesus came to [the disciples] and said, 'All authority in heaven and on earth has been given to me. Therefore go and make disciples of all nations, baptizing them in the name of the Father and of the Son and of the Holy Spirit, and teaching them to obey everything I have commanded you. And surely I am with you always, to the very end of the age.'"[39] But two problems are confronting us as we try to live into Jesus' commissioning: (1) We don't fully believe in our own authority and ability to do what Jesus is asking of us, and (2) We don't understand how to effectively speak to "all nations." In other words, while our godly purpose may make sense to us intellectually, we are not properly equipped to live into it. As Mark Galli argues in *Jesus Mean and Wild,* when we begin to rationalize Jesus, we render the Great Commission vacuous and ineffective:

36. McLuhan, *Understanding Media,* 20.

37. McLuhan and Fiore, *The Medium is the Massage,* 84–85.

38. McLuhan and Fiore, *The Medium is the Massage,* 94.

39 Matt 28:18–20.

> We avoid the reality of Christ's power in a number of ways. For instance, we're tempted to spiritualize his power, to reduce the elemental potency and energy to a moment of personal religious inspiration. The stilling of the storm is about psychological storms in our lives. The healing of the lame is about solving emotional problems that cripple us. Jesus bringing sight to the blind is about God's ability to help us see our lives clearly. And so on and so forth. If we do that enough, we begin to think the Gospel stories are nothing but metaphors, and metaphors primarily about us.[40]

How do we rescue Jesus' meaning "from the barnacles that have attached themselves to it over the centuries"?[41]

As Michael Frost and Alan Hirsch argue in *ReJesus,* we need a recalibration—a reboot back to Jesus: "Christology is the key to the renewal of the church in every age and in every possible situation it might find itself."[42] In our effort to recalibrate, what if we ground ourselves in the Scripture that begins Jesus' ministry before we turn with confidence to the commission that ends it? When Jesus returns to Galilee after his time in the desert, we witness his first public act and a remarkable demonstration of his life's purpose:

> He went to Nazareth, where he had been brought up, and on the Sabbath day he went into the synagogue, as was his custom. He stood up to read, and the scroll of the prophet Isaiah was handed to him. Unrolling it, he found the place where it is written:
>
> "The Spirit of the Lord is on me,
> because he has anointed me
> to proclaim good news to the poor.
> He has sent me to proclaim freedom for the prisoners
> and recovery of sight for the blind,
> to set the oppressed free,
> to proclaim the year of the Lord's favor."
>
> Then he rolled up the scroll, gave it back to the attendant and sat down. The eyes of everyone in the synagogue were fastened on him. He began by saying to them, "Today this scripture is fulfilled in your hearing."[43]

40. Galli, *Jesus Mean and Wild,* 113.
41. Bailey, *Jesus Through Middle Eastern Eyes,* 343.
42. Frost and Hirsch, *ReJesus,* 42.
43. Luke 4:16–21.

While some theologians argue that this Sabbath message may not have been Jesus' inaugural sermon,[44] the content is more important than the chronology. First, Jesus grounds his words in Isaiah, Scripture that his audience already knew, trusted, and believed. Rather than appealing to his audience with what they might consider his own wisdom, emotion, or story, Jesus relies on the truth of God's word to introduce himself to those in attendance. Second, Jesus announces with confidence, using the prophet's poetry, that the Spirit of the Lord has anointed him. Jesus does not waver, question, or wonder; he knows who he is, and he steps forward boldly. Third, Jesus states that his God-given purpose is singular and simple: to proclaim the gospel. Again, he does not waver, question, or wonder; God gave him a purpose, and he announces to the gathered listeners that his purpose is to proclaim to the poor the good news that he has come to offer. Fourth, Jesus articulates clearly the content of his purpose: to free the imprisoned and oppressed, to offer sight to the blind, and to usher in an ongoing Year of Jubilee. Jesus does not equivocate or justify; he boldly proclaims. Finally, Jesus announces that the Messianic prophecy he has just read aloud is his to fulfill in this very moment, an announcement that arouses anger and suspicion among his listeners.

In books such as Jeff Vanderstelt's *Saturate* and Kara Powell's *Sticky Faith*, I see an earnest searching that should be fostered and affirmed—a searching not unlike that of the nonbeliever who pours his money into finite satisfactions or flits from relationship to relationship. If we are searching for *what*, our answer is Jesus; and if we are searching for *how*, our answer is the same: Jesus.

In his book *Happy Church*, Tim McConnell calls for joy: "God intends to make his promises come true, to create pockets of happy people in this world—people whose joy serves his purposes for his glory."[45] Yes, but how?

In *It's Not What You Think*, Jefferson Bethke reminds us of the importance of a shared meal: "The reason table and intimacy and story and temple and Sabbath are so important is that they are relational. You can't tell a story unless you have relationship with your listeners. You can't have intimacy without another person. You can't enjoy the power of the table unless other people are there."[46] Yes, but how?

Philip Yancey asks in *What Good is God?* what role faith can play in a world where tragedies confront us daily. In a chapter titled "I Wish I'd Known," Yancey admits that he once had it all wrong: "I came to this school

44. Porter, "Luke," 1151.

45. McConnell, *Happy Church*, 16.

46. Bethke, *It's Not What You Think*, 195.

with a distorted image of God, as a frowning Supercop looking to squash anyone who might be having a good time. How wrong I was."[47] Yes, but then what?

When our view is muddied by the complexity of being human, we typically have taken our eyes off of the *what* and the *how* of Jesus. When Jesus stood up to read in the Nazareth synagogue at the onset of his ministry, he turned to his Old Testament foundation, he pronounced his anointment by the Spirit of the Lord, and he proclaimed his purpose. He did not equivocate because both his sense of self and his awareness of audience were exquisite. As John Ortberg writes in his foreword to Mark Labberton's *The Dangerous Act of Worship*, the answer need not be complicated:

> The prophet Micah said a long time ago that the divine requirements for human life are not rocket science: Do justice, love mercy and walk humbly before your God. Worship is the humble walk. It is the knee-buckling, jaw-dropping acknowledgement of the gap between the creature and the Creator, the finite and the Infinite, the sinful and the Holy. It is the heart-rending, spirit-mending gratitude and joy of those who have tasted the wonder that words like *redemption* can only hint at.[48]

The church needs a recalibration back to the simplest answer: a Jesus Quotient. If the life metaphor is a game of tag, as Sweet suggests in *Nudge*, a clear sense of self (IQ, EQ) and an empathetic understanding of audience (AQ) will free us to race around tagging others rather than standing frozen, waiting for something we cannot articulate. "Every Jesus tag offered freedom."[49]

To the church, leaders of the church, and all who call themselves Christians: Are you ready to stop reciting the rules and play? And if you know you aren't playing an honest game, are you able to do the hard work of stepping aside, recalibrating, and entering back in when your heart is clear and your joy is genuine?

Jesus is waiting, and the world around you is longing for peace.

Tag, you're it.

47. Yancey, *What Good is God?*, 136.
48. Labberton, *The Dangerous Act of Worship*, 9.
49. Sweet, *Nudge*, 242.

Bibliography

Aniol, Scott. "A Brief History of the Missional Church Movement." *Religious Affections Ministries.* http://religiousaffections.org/articles/articles-on-church/a-brief-history-of-the-missional-church-movement/

Bailey, Kenneth E. *Jesus Through Middle Eastern Eyes: Cultural Studies in the Gospels.* Downers Grove, IL: InterVarsity, 2008.

Bar-On, Reuven, and Rich Handley. *Optimizing People.* New Braunfels, TX: Pro-Philes, 1999.

Benjamin, Ludy T., Jr. "The Birth of American Intelligence Testing." *American Psychological Association* 40 (2009) 20. http://www.apa.org/monitor/2009/01/assessment.aspx.

Bethke, Jefferson. *It's Not What You Think: Why Christianity Is About So Much More Than Going to Heaven When You Die.* Nashville: Nelson, 2015.

Billings, J. Todd. "The Problem with 'Incarnational Ministry.'" *Christianity Today* 56 (2012) 58. http://jtoddbillings.com/2012/12/the-problem-with-incarnational-ministry/.

———. "What Makes a Church Missional?" *Christianity Today* 52 (2008) 56. http://www.christianitytoday.com/ct/2008/march/16.56.html.

Blumberg, Antonia. "Evangelical Pastor Shunned for Welcoming LGBT People Has a New, Thriving Congregation." *The Huffington Post.* http://www.huffingtonpost.com/entry/evangelical-pastor-shunned-for-welcoming-lgbt-people-has-a-new-thriving-congregation_us_5848a876e4b0d0aa037f31ad.

Bradberry, Travis. "Are You Emotionally Intelligent? Here's How To Know For Sure." *Forbes*, June 2, 2015. https://www.forbes.com/sites/travisbradberry/2014/01/09/emotional-intelligence/#662a3d271ac0.

Breen, Mike. "Why the Missional Movement Will Fail." *Verge*, September 14, 2011. www:vergenetwork.org/2011/09/14/mike-breen-why-the-missional-movement-will-fail/.

Brooks, David. *The Social Animal: The Hidden Sources of Love, Character, and Achievement.* New York: Random House, 2012.

Cannon, Mae Elise, Lisa Sharon Harper, Troy Jackson, and Soong-Chan Rah. *Forgive Us: Confessions of a Compromised Faith.* Grand Rapids: Zondervan, 2014.

Carey, Benedict. *How We Learn: The Surprising Truth About When, Where, and Why It Happens.* New York: Random House, 2014.

Chasmar, Jessica. "Texas pastor films himself telling children in line at mall that Santa isn't real." *The Washington Times*. http://www.washingtontimes.com/news/2016/dec/12/david-grisham-texas-pastor-tells-kids-in-line-at-m/.

Coates, Ta-Nehisi. *Between the World and Me*. New York: Spiegel and Grau, 2015.

Covey, Sean. *The 7 Habits of Highly Effective Teens*. New York: Simon & Schuster, 1998.

De Choudhury, Munmun, Scott Counts, and Eric Horvitz. "Social Media as a Measurement Tool of Depression in Populations." Redmond, WA: Microsoft Research, 2013. www.munmund.net/pubs/websci_13.pdf.

Downing, Crystal. *Changing Signs of Truth: A Christian Introduction to the Semiotics of Communication*. Downers Grove, IL: IVP Academic, 2012.

Farley, Andrew. *The Naked Gospel*. Grand Rapids: Zondervan, 2005.

Frost, Michael, and Alan Hirsch. *ReJesus: A Wild Messiah for a Missional Church*. Peabody, MA: Hendrickson, 2009.

Furnham, Adrian. "Self Awareness: How Self Aware Are You? Do You Know How You Come Across?" *Psychology Today*, November 27, 2015. https://www.psychologytoday.com/blog/sideways-view/201511/self-awareness.

Galli, Mark. *Jesus Mean and Wild: The Unexpected Love of an Untamable God*. Grand Rapids: Baker, 2006.

Goleman, Daniel. "Emotional Intelligence." http://www.danielgoleman, info/topics/emotional-intelligence/.

———. *Emotional Intelligence: Why It Can Matter More Than IQ*. New York: Bantam, 1995.

Goleman, Daniel, Richard Boyatzis, and Annie McKee. *Primal Leadership: Unleashing the Power of Emotional Intelligence*. Boston: Harvard Business Review, 2013.

Gordon, Bruce. "Late Medieval Christianity." In *The Oxford Illustrated History of the Reformation*, edited by Peter Marshall, 1–41. Oxford: Oxford University Press, 2015.

Guder, Darrell L., ed. *Missional Church: A Vision for the Sending of the Church in North America*. Grand Rapids: Eerdmans, 1998.

Hanh, Thich Nhat. *Anger: Wisdom for Cooling the Flames*. New York: Penguin, 2001.

Haught, John F. *Resting on the Future: Catholic Theology for an Unfinished Universe*. New York: Bloomsbury, 2015.

Heye, Bob. "Police: Teen Dies After Playing Russian Roulette in Sherwood Home." *KATU*. http://katu.com/news/local/police-teen-dies-after-playing-russian-roulette-in-sherwood-home.

Hill, Linda H., Greg Brandeau, Emily Truelove, and Kent Lineback. *Collective Genius: The Art and Practice of Leading Innovation*. Cambridge, MA: Harvard Business Review Press, 2014.

Hirsch, Alan. *The Forgotten Ways: Reactivating the Missional Church*. Grand Rapids: Brazos, 2006.

Hirsch, Alan, and Tim Catchim. *The Permanent Revolution: Apostolic Imagination and Practice for the 21st Century Church*. San Francisco: Jossey-Bass, 2012.

Irons, Kendra Weddle, and Melanie Springer Mock. *If Eve Only Knew: Freeing Yourself From Biblical Womanhood and Becoming All God Means for You to be*. St. Louis: Chalice, 2015.

Irving, Debby. *Waking Up White: And Finding Myself in the Story of Race*. Cambridge, MA: Elephant Room, 2014.

Jameson, Fredric. *The Prison-House of Language: A Critical Account of Structuralism and Russian Formalism*. Princeton, NJ: Princeton University Press, 1972.

———. *The Political Unconscious*. In *The Critical Tradition: Classic Texts and Contemporary Trends*, 2d ed., edited by David H. Richter, 1172–88. Boston: Bedford, 1998.

Joe Versus the Volcano. Directed by John Patrick Shanley, featuring Tom Hanks and Meg Ryan. Warner Bros., 1990.

Joseph, Stephen. "What is Self-Actualization?" *Psychology Today*, September 13, 2016. https://www.psychologytoday.com/blog/what-doesn't-kill-us/201609/what-is-self-actualization.

Kachka, Boris. "The Power of Positive Publishing: How Self-Help Ate America." *New York Magazine*, January 2013. http://nymag.com/health/self-help/2013/self-help-book-publishing/.

Kimball, Dan. *They Like Jesus but Not the Church: Insights from Emerging Generations*. Grand Rapids: Zondervan, 2007.

Knorr, Caroline. "How Girls Use Social Media to Build Up, Break Down Self-Image." *CNN*, January 12, 2017. www.cnn.com/2017/01/12/health/girls-social-media-self-image-partner/index.html.

Labberton, Mark. *The Dangerous Act of Worship: Living God's Call to Justice*. Downers Grove, IL: InterVarsity, 2007.

Lewis, C. S. *Mere Christianity*. Rev. ed. New York: HarperOne, 2015.

Matsakis, Louis. "The Logan Paul Video Should Be a Reckoning for YouTube." *Wired*, January 3, 2018. https://www.wired.com/story/logan-paul-video-youtube-reckoning/.

McConnell, Tim. *Happy Church: Pursuing Radical Joy as the People of God*. Downers Grove, IL: InterVarsity, 2006.

McLuhan, Marshall. *Understanding Media: The Extensions of Man*. Reprint, originally published in 1964. Berkeley, CA: Gingko, 2015.

McLuhan, Marshall, and Quentin Fiore. *The Medium is the Massage: An Inventory of Effects*. Rev. ed. Berkeley, CA: Gingko, 1996.

Mears, Daniel P., and Joshua C. Cochran. "What is the Effect of IQ on Offending?" *Criminal Justice and Behavior* 40 (2013) 1280–1300.

Merchant, Dan. *Lord Save Us from Your Followers: Why is the Gospel of Love Dividing America?* Nashville: Thomas Nelson, 2008.

Meyer, Erin. *The Culture Map: Breaking through the Invisible Boundaries of Global Business*. New York: Perseus, 2014.

Migliore, Daniel L. *Faith Seeking Understanding: An Introduction to Christian Theology*. 3rd ed. Grand Rapids: Eerdmans, 2013.

Miller, Donald. *Searching for God Knows What*. Nashville: Thomas Nelson, 2004.

———. *A Million Miles in a Thousand Years: How I Learned to Live a Better Story*. Nashville: Thomas Nelson, 2009.

Molina, Maribel. "If You've Ever Taken a College Final, You Can Relate to This UT Student's Struggle." *Statesman*, December 18, 2017. www.statesman.com/news/state—regional-education/you-ever-taken-college-final-you-can-relate-this-student-struggle/od3SKz529srgIsXoLbgyDM/.

Moos, Jeanne. "Pastor to kids: Santa is a man in a suit." *CNN*. http://www.cnn.com/videos/us/2016/12/13/santa-yells-kids-texas-mall-moos-pkg-erin.cnn/video/playlists/wacky-world-of-jeanne-moos/

Morse, MaryKate. *Making Room for Leadership: Power, Space and Influence.* Downers Grove, IL: InterVarsity, 2008.

Myers, Joseph R. *The Search to Belong: Rethinking Intimacy, Community, and Small Groups.* Grand Rapids: Zondervan, 2003.

Oswald, Roy M., and Arland Jacobson. *The Emotional Intelligence of Jesus: Religious Smarts for Religious Leaders.* New York: Rowman & Littlefield, 2015.

Patterson, Kerry, Joseph Grenny, Ron McMillan, and Al Switzler. *Crucial Conversations: Tools for Talking When the Stakes Are High.* New York: McGraw Hill, 2012.

Payne, Roberta. *Speaking to My Madness: How I Searched for Myself in Schizophrenia.* North Charleston, SC: CreateSpace, 2013.

Piper, John. *Desiring God: Meditations of a Christian Hedonist.* Rev. ed. Colorado Springs: Multnomah, 2011.

Porter, Laurence E. "Luke." In *Zondervan Bible Commentary,* edited by F. F. Bruce, 1137–1193. Grand Rapids: Zondervan, 2008.

Postman, Neil. *Amusing Ourselves to Death: Public Discourse in the Age of Show Business.* New York: Penguin, 1985.

Roche, Bryan. "Your IQ May Not Have Changed, But Are You Any Smarter?" *Psychology Today,* July 15, 2014. https://www.psychologytoday.com/us/blog/iq-boot-camp/201407//your-iq-may-not-have-changed-are-you-any-smarter.

Roid, Gale H., and R. Andrew Barram. *Essentials of Stanford-Binet Intelligence Scales (SB5) Assessment.* Hoboken, NJ: John Wiley, 2004.

Roper, Lyndal. "Martin Luther." In *The Oxford Illustrated History of the Reformation,* edited by Peter Marshall, 42–75. Oxford: Oxford University Press, 2015.

Roxburgh, Alan J., and M. Scott Boren. *Introducing the Missional Church: What It Is, Why It Matters, How to Become One.* Grand Rapids: Baker, 2009.

Roxburgh, Alan J. *Missional: Joining God in the Neighborhood.* Grand Rapids: Baker, 2011.

Russell, Bertrand. *Why I Am Not a Christian.* New York: Simon & Schuster, 1957.

Scazzero, Peter. *Emotionally Healthy Spirituality: It's Impossible to be Spiritually Mature While Remaining Emotionally Immature.* Grand Rapids: Zondervan, 2006.

Smith, Gordon T. *Courage and Calling: Embracing Your God-Given Potential.* Downers Grove, IL: InterVarsity, 1999.

Stone, Madeline. "Inside Facebook's Futuristic New Campus." *Business Insider,* March 30, 2015. https://www.businessinsider.com/facebook-new-campu-pictures-2015-3

Sweet, Leonard. *Aqua Church 2.0: Piloting Your Church in Today's Fluid Culture.* Colorado Springs: David C. Cook, 1999.

———. *The Bad Habits of Jesus: Showing Us the Way to Live Right in a World Gone Wrong.* Carol Stream, IL: Tyndale, 2016.

———. *From Tablet to Table: Where Community Is Found and Identity Is Formed.* Colorado Springs: NavPress, 2014.

———. *Me and We: God's New Social Gospel.* Nashville: Abingdon, 2014.

———. *Nudge: Awakening Each Other to the God Who's Already There.* Colorado Springs: David C. Cook, 2010.

Syed, Matthew. *Bounce: Mozart, Federer, Picasso, Beckham, and the Science of Success.* New York: HarperCollins, 2010.

Taylor, Kathleen, and Catherine Marienau. *Facilitating Learning with the Adult Brain in Mind: A Conceptual and Practical Guide.* San Francisco: Jossey-Bass, 2016.

Tett, Gillian. *The Silo Effect: The Peril of Expertise and the Promise of Breaking Down Barriers.* New York: Simon & Schuster, 2015.

Tjan, Anthony K. "5 Ways to Become More Self-Aware." *Harvard Business Review,* February 15, 2015. https://hbr.org/2015/02/5-ways-to-become-more-self-aware.

Van Gelder, Craig, and Dwight J. Zscheile. *The Missional Church in Perspective: Mapping Trends and Shaping the Conversation.* Grand Rapids: Baker Academic, 2011.

Walsham, Alexandra. "Reformation Legacies." In *The Oxford Illustrated History of the Reformation,* edited by Peter Marshall, 227–68. Oxford: Oxford University Press, 2015.

West, John Lee, Roy M. Oswald, and Nadyne Guzman. *Emotional Intelligence for Religious Leaders.* Lanham, MD: Rowman & Littlefield, 2018.

Wiley Fernando, Joy. *Pondering Privilege: Toward a Deeper Understanding of Whiteness, Race, and Faith.* Minneapolis: NextStep, 2014.

Willard, Dallas. *The Divine Conspiracy: Rediscovering Our Hidden Life in God.* San Francisco: HarperCollins, 1997.

Wright, N. T. *The Day the Revolution Began: Reconsidering the Meaning of Jesus's Crucifixion.* New York: HarperOne, 2016.

———. *Simply Christian: Why Christianity Makes Sense.* New York: HarperOne, 2006.

Yancey, Philip. *What Good is God? In Search of a Faith That Matters.* New York: FaithWords, 2010.

Zauzmer, Julie. "Pope Francis Suggests It's Better to be an Atheist than a Hypocritical Catholic." *The Washington Post,* February 23, 2017. https://www.washingtonpost.com/news/acts-of-faith/wp/2017/02/23/pope-francis-praises-the-torah-and-suggests-its-better-to-be-an-atheist-than-a-bad-catholic/?utm_term=.38913072ce11.

Made in the USA
Las Vegas, NV
27 January 2022